EMPIRE OF ILLUSION

Empire of Illusion

The End of Literacy
and the Triumph of Spectacle

CHRIS HEDGES

NATION
BOOKS

Published by Nation Books, A Member of the Perseus Books Group

116 East 16th Street, 8th Floor

New York, NY 10003

Nation Books is a co-publishing venture of the Nation Institute
and the Perseus Books Group

Books published by Nation Books are available at special discounts for
bulk purchases in the United States by corporations, institutions, and other
organizations. For more information, please contact the Special Markets
Department at the Perseus Books Group, 2300 Chestnut Street, Suite 200,
Philadelphia, PA 19103, or call (800) 810-4145, extension 5000,
or e-mail special.markets@perseusbooks.com.

Design and composition by Cynthia Young.

Library of Congress Cataloging-in-Publication Data
Hedges, Chris.
Empire of illusion :
the end of literacy and the triumph of spectacle / Chris Hedges.
p. cm.
Includes bibliographical references and index.
ISBN 978-1-56858-437-9
1. Mass media—United States.   2. Popular culture—United States.
1. Title.
P92.U5H365 2009
302.23—dc22

2009013585

10 9 8 7 6 5 4 3 2 1

For Eunice,

soles occidere et redire possvnt: nobis cvm semel occidit brevis

lvx, nox est perpetva vna dormienda. da mi basia mille.

People who shut their eyes to reality simply invite their own destruction, and anyone who insists on remaining in a state of innocence long after that innocence is dead turns himself into a monster.

—JAMES BALDWIN

Contents

I / The Illusion
of Literacy

Now the death of God combined with the perfection of the image has brought us to a whole new state of expectation. We are the image. We are the viewer and the viewed. There is no other distracting presence. And that image has all the Godly powers. It kills at will. Kills effortlessly. Kills beautifully. It dispenses morality. Judges endlessly. The electronic image is man as God and the ritual involved leads us not to a mysterious Holy Trinity but back to ourselves. In the absence of a clear understanding that we are now the only source, these images cannot help but return to the expression of magic and fear proper to idolatrous societies. This in turn facilitates the use of the electronic image as propaganda by whoever can control some part of it.

—JOHN RALSTON SAUL, *Voltaire's Bastards*[1]

We had fed the heart on fantasy,
The heart's grown brutal from the fare.

—WILLIAM BUTLER YEATS,
The Stare's Nest By My Window

JOHN BRADSHAW LAYFIELD, tall, clean-cut, in a collared shirt and white Stetson hat, stands in the center of the ring holding a heavy black microphone. Layfield plays wrestling tycoon JBL on the World Wrestling Entertainment tour.[2] The arena is filled with hooting and jeering fans, including families with children. The crowd yells and boos at JBL, who has had a long career as a professional wrestler. Many chant, "You suck! You suck! You suck!"

"Last week I made Shawn Michaels an offer, and I have yet to hear back from the Heartbreak Kid," drawls Layfield. Michaels, another WWE wrestler, is a crowd favorite. He is a self-professed born-again Christian with a working-man persona. "So earlier today I made Shawn Michaels an offer that was a lot easier to understand," Layfield continues. "I challenge Shawn Michaels to a street fight tonight! So Shawn, I know you're back there. Now what's your answer?"

"HBK, HBK, HBK!!!" the crowd intones. A pulsing rock beat suddenly shakes the arena as action shots of the Heartbreak Kid flash across the Titantron, the massive screen suspended over the ring. The crowd cheers, leaping up as Shawn Michaels, in jeans and an army-green shirt, whirls onstage, his long, blond hair flying. Pyrotechnics explode. The deafening sound system growls, "I know I'm sexy . . . I got the looks . . . that drive the girls wild. . . ."

Michaels bursts into the ring, fists pumping, stalking back and forth. The ref steps in to begin the match.

"HBK! HBK! HBK!" chants the crowd.

"Hold on, hold on, referee," Layfield says, putting his hand on the referee's shoulder. People in the crowd begin to heckle.

"Shawn," he says, "you got a choice to make. You can either fight me right now in this street fight, or you can do the right thing for you, your family, and your extended family, and take care of them in a financial crisis you never dreamed would happen a year ago today."

Michaels stands silently.

"You see, I know some things, Shawn," continues Layfield. "Rich people always do. Before this stock market crashed, nobody saw it coming, except, of course, my wife, but that didn't help you, did it? See, I was hoarding cash. I was putting money in gold. While most Americans followed the leader—blindly, stupidly followed the leader—I was making money. In fact, Shawn, I was prospering while you were following the herd, losing almost everything, right, Shawn?"

"Fight!! Fight!! Fight!! Fight!!" urges the crowd. Michaels looks hesitantly back and forth between the heaving crowd and Layfield.

"You lost your 401(k). You lost your retirement. You lost your nest egg. You lost *your children's education fund*," Layfield bellows into the mic, his face inches from Michaels's. "You got to support your extended family, Shawn, and now you look around with all this responsibility, and you look at your beautiful wife, she's a beautiful lady, you look at your two little wonderful kids, and you wonder: 'How in the world . . . am I going to send them . . . to college?' "

Layfield pauses heavily. Michaels' face is slack, pained. Small, individual voices shout out from the crowd.

"Well, I've got an answer," Layfield goes on. "I'm offering you a job. I want you to come work—for *me*."

"No! No! No!" yells the crowd. Michaels blinks slowly, dazed, and lowers his eyes to the mat.

"See, there's always alternatives, Shawn. There's alternatives to everything. You can always wrestle until you're fifty. You might even wrestle till you're sixty. In fact, you could be a lot like these has-beens who are disgracing themselves in high school gyms all over the country, bragging about their war stories of selling the place out while they're hawking their eight-by-tens and selling Polaroids. Shawn, you could be that guy, or you could take my offer, because I promise you this: All the revenue that you're goin' to make off your DX T-shirts will not compare to the offer that I . . . made . . . to you."

He tells the Heartbreak Kid to look in the mirror, adding, "The years haven't been kind to you, have they, Shawn?" He reminds him that one more bad fall, one more injury, and "you're done, you're done."

The crowd begins to rally their stunned hero, growing louder and louder. "HBK! HBK! HBK!"

"What else can you really do besides this?" Layfield asks. "You get a second chance in life."

Layfield sweeps off his white Stetson. "Go ahead," he screams into Michaels's face. "Ever since you walked out here . . . people have been wantin' you to kick me in the face. So why don't you do it? I'm gonna give you a free shot, Shawn, right here."

The crowd erupts, roaring for the Heartbreak Kid to strike.

"HBK!! DO IT!! DO IT!! HBK!! HBK!!!"

"Listen to 'em. Everybody wants it. Shawn, it's what you want. You're twitching. You're begging to pull the trigger, so I'm telling you right now, take a shot! Take it!"

The Heartbreak Kid takes one step back, his stubbled face trembling, breathing rapidly like a rabbit. The crowd is leaping out of their seats, thrusting their arms in the air, holding up handmade banners.

"HBK!!! HBK!!! HBK!!!"

"Do it, Shawn," Layfield hollers, "before it's too late. This is your second chance, but understand this, understand this—"

"HBK!!! HBK!!! HBK!!!"

"—Listen to me and not them! If you take this shot . . . then this offer is off the table . . . *forever.*"

The crowd stops chanting. Different cries are heard: boos, shouts to attack, shouts to stop. There is no longer unity in the auditorium.

Layfield holds his head outstretched until the Heartbreak Kid slowly turns his back. Layfield leers. Shawn Michaels climbs through the ropes out of the ring and walks heavily back to the dressing room, his dull gaze on the ground.

"Lookin' forward to doin' business with ya, Shawn," Layfield shouts after him.

The crowd screams.

Layfield, like most of the wrestlers, has a long, complicated fictional backstory that includes a host of highly publicized intrigues, fights, betrayals, infidelities, abuse, and outrageous behavior—including goose-stepping around the ring and giving the Nazi salute during a wrestling bout in Germany. But tonight he has come in his newest incarnation as the "self-made millionaire," the capitalist, the CEO who walked away with a pot of gold while workers across the country lost their jobs, saw their savings and retirement funds evaporate, and fought off foreclosure.

As often happens in a celebrity culture, the line between public and fictional personas blurs. Layfield actually claims to have made a fortune as a stock market investor and says he is married to the "richest woman on Wall Street." He is a regular panelist on Fox News Channel's *The Cost of Freedom* and previously appeared on CNBC, not only as a celebrity wrestler but as a savvy investor whose conservative political views are worth airing. He also has written a best-selling book on financial planning called *Have More Money Now*. He hosts a weekend talk-radio program syndicated nationally by Talk Radio Network, in which he discusses politics.

The interaction between the crowd and Layfield is vintage professional wrestling. The twenty-minute bouts employ the same tired gimmicks, the same choreographed moves, the endless counts to two by the referee that never seem to get to three without the pinned wrestler leaping up from the mat to continue the fight. There is the desperate struggle of a prostrate wrestler trying to reach the hand of his or her partner to be relieved in the ring. This pantomime, with his opponent on his back and his arm outstretched, can go on for a couple of minutes. There are a lot of dirty shots when the referee is distracted—which is often.

The bouts are stylized rituals. They are public expressions of pain and a fervent longing for revenge. The lurid and detailed sagas behind each bout, rather than the wrestling matches themselves, are what drive crowds to a frenzy. These ritualized battles give those packed in the arenas a temporary, heady release from mundane lives. The burden of real problems is transformed into fodder for a high-energy pantomime. And the most potent story tonight, the most potent story across North America, is one of financial ruin, desperation, and enslavement of a frightened and abused working class to a heartless, tyrannical, corporate employer. For most, it is only in the illusion of the ring that they are able to rise above their small stations in life and engage in a heroic battle to fight back.

As the wrestlers appear and strut down the aisle, the crowd, mostly young, working-class males, knows by heart the long list of vendettas and betrayals being carried into the ring. The matches are always acts of retribution for a host of elaborate and fictional wrongs. The narratives of emotional wreckage reflected in the wrestlers' stage biographies mirror the emotional wreckage of the fans. This is the deep appeal of professional wrestling. It is the appeal of much of popular culture, from Jerry Springer to "reality" television to Oprah Winfrey. The narratives expose the anxiety that we will die and never be recognized or acclaimed, that we will never be wealthy, that we are not among the chosen but remain part of the vast, anonymous masses. The ringside sagas are designed to reassure us. They hold out the hope that we, humble and unsung as these celebrities once were, will eventually be blessed with grace and fortune.

The success of professional wrestling, like most of the entertainment that envelops our culture, lies not in fooling us that these stories are real. Rather, it succeeds because we ask to be fooled. We happily pay for the chance to suspend reality. The wrestlers, like all celebrities, become our vicarious selves. They do what we cannot. They rise up from humble origins into a supernatural world of tyrants, divas, and fierce opponents who are huge and rippling with muscles—mythic in their size and power. They face momentous battles and epic struggles. They win great victories. They garner fame and vanquish their anonymity. And they return to befriend and confer some of their supernatural power on us. It is the stuff of classical myths, including the narrative of Jesus Christ. It is the yearning that life conform to a recognizable pattern and provide ultimate fulfillment before death.

"For the truth is," wrote José Ortega y Gasset, "that life on the face of it is a chaos in which one finds oneself lost. The individual suspects as much but is terrified to encounter this frightening reality face to face, and so attempts to conceal it by drawing a curtain of fantasy over it, behind which he can make believe that everything is clear."[3]

Clashes in the professional wrestling ring from the 1950s to the 1980s hinged on a different narrative. The battle against the evil of communism and crude, racial stereotypes stoked the crowd. The bouts, which my grandfather religiously watched on Saturday afternoons, were raw, unvarnished expressions of the prejudices of the white working class from which he came. They appealed to nationalism and a dislike and distrust of all who were racially, ethnically, or religiously different. During these matches, some of which I watched as a boy, there was usually some huge hulk of a man, known invariably as "The Russian Bear," who would say things like "Ve vill bury you." Nikolai Volkoff, who wrestled during these years under the name Boris Breznikoff, used to sing the Soviet National Anthem and wave the Soviet flag before matches to bait the crowd. He eventually teamed up with an Iranian-born wrestler, Hossein Khosrow Ali Vaziri, known as The Iron Sheik. In the midst of the Iranian hostage crisis, the Iron Sheik bragged in the ring about his devotion and friendship with Ayatollah Khomeini. The Iron Sheik was regularly pitted against a wrestler known as Sergeant Slaughter, All-American G. I. During the first Gulf War; the Iron Sheik reinvented himself, as often happens with wrestlers who shed one persona and name for another, as Colonel Mustafa, an Iraqi who was a close confidant of Saddam Hussein. In wrestling, villains were nearly always foreigners. They were people who wanted to destroy "our way of life." They hated America. They spoke in strange accents and had swarthy skin.

But that hatred, once directed outward, has turned inward. Wrestling fans, whose numbers have been swelled by new immigrants and are no longer limited to the white working class, began to come in too many colors. The steady loss of manufacturing jobs and decline in social services meant that blue-collar workers—people like my grand-parents—could no longer find jobs that provided a living wage, jobs with benefits, jobs that could support a family. The hulks of empty manufacturing centers began to dot the landscape, including the abandoned mills in Maine, where my family lived. The disparity between the elite, the rich, and the rest of the country grew obscenely. The growing class division and hopelessness triggered a mounting rage toward the elite, as well as a sense of powerlessness. Communities began to crumble. Downtown stores went out of business and were boarded up. Domestic abuse and drug and alcohol addiction began to plague working-class neighborhoods and towns.

The story line in professional wrestling evolved to fit the new era. It began to focus on the petty, cruel, psychological dramas and family dysfunction that come with social breakdown. The enemy became figures like Layfield, those who had everything and lorded it over those who did not. The anger unleashed by the crowd became the anger of people who, like the Heartbreak Kid, felt used, shamed, and trapped. It became the anger of class warfare. Figures such as Layfield—who arrives at professional matches in a giant white limousine with Texan "hook 'em" horns on the hood—are created by wrestling promoters to shove these social disparities in the faces of the audience, just as the Iron Sheik mocked the crowd with his hatred of America.

Wrestlers work in "stables," or groups. These groups, all of which have managers, are at war with the other groups. This motif, too, is new. It represents a society that has less and less national cohesion, a society that has broken down into warlike and antagonistic tribes. The stables cheat, lie, steal one another's women, and ignore all rules in the desperate scramble to win. Winning is all that matters. Morality is irrelevant. These wrestling clans have their own logos, uniforms, slogans, theme songs, cheerleaders, and other badges of communal identity.

They do not, however, stay consistent in their "good guy" or "bad guy" status. A clan, like an individual wrestler, can be good one week and evil the next. All that matters is their own advancement. Week after week, they act out scenarios that are psychological windows into what has happened to our culture.

Ray Traylor was a prison guard in Georgia before debuting as a professional wrestler in 1985. Known on the wrestling circuit as Big Boss Man, he was portrayed as a brutal, sadistic wrestler devoid of human compassion. Traylor showed up at the ring with a nightstick, a flak jacket, handcuffs, and a ball and chain. During a match in 1992 a digitized voice came over the loudspeaker. It warned the Boss Man that someone from his past was coming to exact revenge. Sure enough, the Boss Man was ambushed in the ring by Nailz, a wrestler who claimed to be a former inmate brutalized by the Boss Man during his time as a correctional officer. Nailz, a six-foot, eight-inch brute with severe post-traumatic stress disorder, appeared in the arena wearing an orange prison jumpsuit. The two began a bitter, long feud. It was a feud many in the crowd knew too well. It was the feud between prisoners and guards. It was the feud between those who had once been incarcerated and who wanted to do to their keepers what had been done to them. Traylor later adopted a new persona in the ring, also known as the Boss Man, but now a hated security guard, dressed in a SWAT-like outfit, for Vince McMahon's Corporation, which owns the wrestling franchise. McMahon, in tune with the passions of his audience, is always trying to exploit, threaten, and cheat the wrestlers who work for him.

The Boss Man's most infamous stunt was publicly taunting a wrestler named Big Show when it was announced that Big Show's father had cancer. The Boss Man, at least in the scripted melodrama, hired a police impersonator to go into Big Show's locker room moments before a match and tell him his father had died. Big Show, shown weeping, withdrew from the match, and the Boss Man won by forfeit. A grainy black-and-white video, purportedly lifted from a surveillance camera in the Boss Man's locker room, showed Traylor asking the impersonator for a detailed report on how Big Show reacted.

"What he do, what he do?" the Boss Man asked, eagerly shifting from side to side.

The police impersonator pinched the bridge of his nose and bowed his head. "My daddy! My daddy!"

"My daddy! My daddy!" the Boss Man squealed. "Waaaa! My daddy gone!"

In the ring he imitated Big Show and wailed to the crowd, "My daddy! My daddy! Waaaa! Waaa!" Stalking the ring in mirrored sunglasses, he read a ditty to the booing, enraged crowd:

With the deepest regrets and tears that are soaked
I'm sorry to hear your dad finally croaked.
He lived a full life on his own terms,
Soon he'll be buried and eaten by worms.
But if I could have a son as stupid as you
I'd wish for cancer so I could die too.

Boss Man then supposedly smashed Big Show's family heirloom, his grandfather's gold pocket watch, with a hammer and anvil. A video of the Boss Man was played to the crowd, showing him at the graveside service of Big Show's father, in a Blues Brothers–inspired police car with a huge loudspeaker on the roof. The Boss Man blared through the speaker as he drove up the cemetery path, "He's dead as a doornail, and no matter how much you cry and cry, nobody but nobody gonna bring him back. . . . You're nothin' but a momma, and speakin' of yo' momma, hey, Ms. Wight [Big Show's mother], now that you're a single woman, how'd you like to go out with a man like me?"

He then drove the car into Big Show, who weighed close to 500 pounds. As the mourners huddled around the fallen Big Show, the Boss Man hooked the coffin up to the police car with a chain and dragged it away. Big Show got up and ran after the casket, clinging to it until he fell off.

Boss Man then "secretly" taped a meeting with Big Show's weeping mother in her kitchen. He held up a manila envelope and shook it in her face.

"If you don't tell him what's in this envelope, I will," he threatened.

"Let me tell him, it should come from me," she sobbed. She confessed that she had had an affair during her marriage and that Big Show was the illegitimate result. Big Show's father was not his biological father.

"So what you're saying is, your son is a bastard?" the Boss Man asked the bawling widow.

"Yee-ess," she whimpered between sobs.

"Hey, Paul Wight," the Boss Man turned and yelled into the hidden camera, using Big Show's real name. "You're a nasty bastard and yo' mama said so!"

"You know, I thought it was real funny when Big Freak Show's fake daddy died and went to hell," the Boss Man told the crowd afterward from the ring. "But you know what's ten times funnier than his fake daddy's dying? That's Big Show walking around, 'Waaa, waaa, where's my daddy? Who's my daddy?' Well, that's the million-dollar question. Your daddy could be any one of these stinkin' morons sittin' in this arena tonight. But the fact remains: After I get through kicking your ass, I will be the World Wrestling Federation champion, and I guess that makes *me* your daddy."

City after city, night after night, packed arena after packed arena, the wrestlers play out a new, broken social narrative. No one has a fixed identify, not the way a Russian communist or an evil Iranian or an American patriot once had an intractable identity. Identities and morality shift with the wind. Established truths, mores, rules, and authenticity mean nothing. Good and evil mean nothing. The idea of permanent personalities and permanent values, as in the culture at large, has evaporated. It is all about winning. It is all about personal pain, vendettas, hedonism, and fantasies of revenge, while inflicting pain on others. It is the cult of victimhood.

The wrestler known as the Undertaker frequently battles a wrestler known as Kane. Kane is the supposed result of an affair between the Undertaker's mother and the Undertaker's manager, whose stage name is, appropriately, Paul Bearer. Paul Bearer, fans were told, was at the time of the affair an employee at the funeral home in Death Valley owned by the Undertaker's parents. Kane, in the story line, "accidentally" burned down the funeral home as a child. The parents died in the fire. Kane was hideously scarred. The Undertaker and Kane each thought the other had been lost in the conflagration.

Paul Bearer had, it turned out, hidden young Kane in a mental asylum. It was when Paul Bearer had a falling out with the Undertaker that he had Kane released and signed Kane on as his agent of revenge. Kane and Paul Bearer, during one event in Long Island, ostensibly exhumed the parents' bodies for the crowd. They carried the purported remains into the arena. The younger brother had a series of bouts against the older. Paul Bearer was finally kidnapped and trapped in a concrete crypt. The Undertaker refused to rescue his manager. He buried him alive. As Paul A. Cantor notes in his essay on professional wrestling, "All the elements are there: sibling rivalry, disputed parentage, child neglect and abuse, domestic violence, family revenge."[4]

Those who were once born with the virus of inherent evil, the Russian communist or the Iranian, now become evil for a reason. It is not their fault. They are victims. Self-pity is the driving motive in life. They were abused as children or in prison or by friends or lovers or spouses or employers. The new mantra says we all have a right to seek emotional gratification if we have been abused, even if it harms others. I am bad, the narratives say, because I was neglected and poorly treated. I was forced to be bad. It is not my fault. Pity me. If you do not pity me, screw you. I pity myself. It is the undiluted narcissism of a society in precipitous decline.

The referee, the only authority figure in the bouts, is easily distracted and unable to administer justice. As soon as the referee turns his back, which happens in nearly every match, the second member of the opposing tag team, who is not supposed to be in the ring at the same time as his or her partner, leaps through the ropes. The two wrestlers pummel an opponent lying helpless on the mat behind the referee's back. They often kick, or pretend to kick, the downed wrestler in the gut. The referee, preoccupied, never notices. The failure to enforce the rules, which usually hurts the wrestler who needs the rules the most, is vital to the story line. It reflects, in the eyes of the fans, the greed, manipulation, and abuse wreaked by the powerful and the rich. The world, as professional wrestling knows, is always stacked against the little guy. Cheating becomes a way to even the score. The system of justice in the world of wrestling is always rigged. It reflects, for many who watch, the tainted justice system outside the ring. It promotes the morality of cheat or die.

I watch Irish-born wrestler Dave Finley, with a shamrock on his costume and brandishing his signature shillelagh, enter the ring in Madison Square Garden with a four-foot, five-inch midget known as

Hornswoggle, who is dressed as a leprechaun. The two are battling a massive African American wrestler known as Mark Henry. Henry is bearded and grimacing and weighs 380 pounds. He shouts insults at the crowd. When Hornswoggle enters the ring in the middle of the match to assist a beleaguered Finley, the referee tries to get Hornswoggle out. Finley, now unobserved by the referee, grabs his shillelagh and hits Mark Henry on the head. The referee, preoccupied with Hornswoggle, sees nothing. Mark Henry holds his head, spins around the ring, and collapses. Finley leaps on Mark Henry's bulk. He attracts the attention of the referee, and with the count of three wins the match. The crowd cheers in delight.

Wrestling operates from the popular (and often inarguable) assumption that those in authority are sleazy. Finley is a favorite with the crowd, although tonight he cheats to win. If the world is rigged against you, if those in power stifle your voice, outsource your job, and foreclose your house, then cheat back. Corruption is part of life. The most popular wrestlers always defy and taunt their employers and promoters.

Women, although they enter the ring to fight other women wrestlers, are almost always cast as temptresses. They steal each other's boyfriends. They are often prizes to be won by competing wrestlers. These vixens, supposedly in relationships with one wrestler, are often caught on surveillance videos flirting with rival wrestlers. This provokes matches between the jealous boyfriend and the new love interest.

The plotlines around the women, or "divas," are lurid, bordering on soft porn. Torrie Wilson is a female wrestler engaged in a long and popular feud with another female wrestler named Dawn Marie. Dawn Marie, who was originally called Dawn Marie Bytch, announced, on one occasion, that she wanted to marry Torrie Wilson's father, Al Wilson. Torrie was appalled. Dawn, however, also supposedly found Torrie attractive. Dawn told Torrie she would cancel the wedding with Al if Torrie would spend the night with her in a hotel. In a taped segment, the two women met in a hotel room. They kissed and fondled in their underwear. As they began to undress, screens in the arena went black, leaving the rest to the imagination of the fans. Dawn, despite the tryst, married Al anyway. The two held their ceremony in the ring in their underwear. Al, fans were told afterward, collapsed and died of a heart attack after marathon sex sessions on their honeymoon. Torrie Wilson then had numerous grudge matches with Dawn, whom she blamed for killing her father. Sordid domestic scenarios, which resonate in a world of broken and troubled homes, are also staples of television talk and reality shows.

The divas in the ring are there to fuel sexual fantasy. They have no intrinsic worth beyond being objects of sexual desire. It is all about their bodies. They engage in sexually provocative "strap matches," in which two women are tied together with a long strap. During the bout, combatants use the strap to whip each other, including smacking exposed buttocks. They grab a short length of the strap between their two hands and wrap it around the neck of the opponent to simulate choking. In "evening gown matches," women wrestle in long evening gowns ripped to expose lacy bras and thongs. Evening gown matches, involving two and sometimes three women, have also been filmed in swimming pools. Such matches frequently result in "accidental" exposure of breasts, which sets crowds roaring in lewd gratification.

Female wrestlers often try to sabotage matches or seduce male wrestlers who oppose allies or members of their clan. In one episode broadcast on the big screens in the arena, a female wrestler named Melina enters the locker room of a wrestler named Batista. The scene has the brevity and stilted dialogue of a porn film. Melina, in a sequined red tank top and micro-miniskirt, stands awkwardly behind the brawny and tattooed Batista, who is seated on the bench, dressed in a tiny bikini brief. Melina self-consciously rubs her palms up and down his expansive pecs. "My boys, Mercury and Nitro, have a match against the Mexicools, and they could really use this time to prepare. So if you could . . . withdraw yourself from the match tonight?"

"Naw, I don't think so," rumbles Batista.

"I could really make it worth your while," whines Melina, straddling one of Batista's massive thighs.

"How you gonna do that?" Batista mutters.

"Let me show you," Melina pouts. She kisses him, wriggling her shoulders in a caricature of passion. Batista finally figures it out and yanks her down as they kiss, spreading her legs open over his lap. The crowd is heard whooping.

The video cuts to a close-up of Melina's black bra strap. She turns around, pulling her tank top down over her bra.

"So we have a deal, right?" she simpers, blowing her hair out of her face.

"A deal? No, no deal," Batista chuckles. "Thanks for the warm-up, though. I feel great." He flexes his chest muscles, making them jump. "I'm going to kill those guys." He cuffs her on the shoulder. "See you out there."

"Oh, my God," sniggers the announcer. "Did he say, 'Thanks for the warm-up'? What a backfire!"

The camera zooms in on Melina's humiliation. "No, no, nooooo!" she shrieks, clapping her hands to her face, squinting malevolently after Batista.

Fans chant, "Slut! Slut! Slut!" when Melina appears in the arena. Melina, although the temptress in the story, later announces she has filed a lawsuit for sexual harassment against Batista.

⌒

In *The Republic*, Plato imagines human beings chained for the duration of their lives in an underground cave, knowing nothing but darkness. Their gaze is confined to the cave wall, upon which shadows of the world above are thrown. They believe these flickering shadows are reality. If, Plato writes, one of these prisoners is freed and brought into the sunlight, he will suffer great pain. Blinded by the glare, he is unable to see anything and longs for the familiar darkness. But eventually his eyes adjust to the light. The illusion of the tiny shadows is obliterated. He confronts the immensity, chaos, and confusion of reality. The world is no longer drawn in simple silhouettes. But he is despised when he returns to the cave. He is unable to see in the dark as he used to. Those who never left the cave ridicule him and swear never to go into the light lest they be blinded as well.

Plato feared the power of entertainment, the power of the senses to overthrow the mind, the power of emotion to obliterate reason. No admirer of popular democracy, Plato said that the enlightened or elite had a duty to educate those bewitched by the shadows on the cave wall, a position that led Socrates to quip: "As for the man who tried to free them and lead them upward, if they could somehow lay their hands on him and kill him, they would do so."

We are chained to the flickering shadows of celebrity culture, the spectacle of the arena and the airwaves, the lies of advertising, the endless personal dramas, many of them completely fictional, that have become the staple of news, celebrity gossip, New Age mysticism, and pop psychology. In *The Image: A Guide to Pseudo-Events in America*, Daniel Boorstin writes that in contemporary culture the fabricated, the inauthentic, and the theatrical have displaced the natural, the genuine, and the spontaneous, until reality itself has been converted into stagecraft. Americans, he writes, increasingly live in a "world where fantasy is more real than reality." He warns:

> We risk being the first people in history to have been able to make their illusions so vivid, so persuasive, so "realistic" that they can live in them. We are the most illusioned people on earth. Yet we dare not become disillusioned, because our illusions are the very house in which we live; they are our news, our heroes, our adventure, our forms of art, our very experience.[5]

Boorstin goes on to caution that

> an image is something *we* have a claim on. It must serve our purposes. Images are means. If a corporation's image of itself or a man's image of himself is not useful, it is discarded. Another may fit better. The image is made to order, tailored to us. An ideal, on the other hand, has a claim on us. It does not serve us; we serve it. If we have trouble striving towards it, we assume the matter is with us, and not with the ideal.[6]

Those who manipulate the shadows that dominate our lives are the agents, publicists, marketing departments, promoters, script writers, television and movie producers, advertisers, video technicians, photographers, bodyguards, wardrobe consultants, fitness trainers, pollsters, public announcers, and television news personalities who create the vast stage for illusion. They are the puppet masters. No one achieves celebrity status, no cultural illusion is swallowed as reality, without these armies of cultural enablers and intermediaries. The sole object is to hold attention and satisfy an audience. These techniques of theater, as Boorstin notes, have leeched into politics, religion, education, literature, news, commerce, warfare, and crime. The squalid dramas played out for fans in the wrestling ring mesh with the ongoing dramas on television, in movies, and in the news, where "real-life" stories, especially those involving celebrities, allow news reports to become mini-dramas complete with a star, a villain, a supporting cast, a good-looking host, and a neat, if often unexpected, conclusion.

The nation can sit rapt at one of these real-life stories, as happened when O. J. Simpson went on trial for the murder of his estranged wife and her purported lover. A carefully manipulated image of real life, which can be based either on utter fiction or, as in Simpson's case, real tragedy, can serve as a myth on which millions can hang their fears and hopes. The problems of existence are domesticated and controlled. We measure our lives by those we admire on the screen or in the ring. We seek to be like them. We emulate their look and behavior. We escape the chaos of real life through fantasy. We see ourselves as stars of our own movies. And we are, as Neal Gabler writes in *Life: The Movie: How Entertainment Conquered Reality,* "all becoming performance artists in and audiences for a grand, ongoing show."[7]

We try to see ourselves moving through our life as a camera would see us, mindful of how we hold ourselves, how we dress, what we say. We invent movies that play inside our heads. We imagine ourselves the main characters. We imagine how an audience would react to each event in the movie of our life. This, writes Gabler, is the power and invasiveness of celebrity culture. Celebrity culture has taught us to generate, almost unconsciously, interior personal screenplays in the mold of Hollywood, television, and even commercials. We have learned ways of speaking and thinking that disfigure the way we relate to the world. Gabler argues that celebrity culture is not a convergence of consumer culture and religion, but rather a hostile takeover of religion by consumer culture. Commodities and celebrity culture define what it means to belong, how we recognize our place in society, and how we conduct our lives.

I visited the Hollywood Forever Cemetery in Los Angeles. It is advertised as "the final resting place to more of Hollywood's founders and stars than anywhere else on earth." The sixty-acre cemetery holds the remains of 135 Hollywood luminaries, including Rudolph Valentino, Tyrone Power, Cecil B. DeMille, Douglas Fairbanks, Nelson Eddy, Bugsy Siegel, Peter Lorre, Mel Blanc, and John Huston, as well as many wealthy non-celebrities. Celebrity culture is, at its core, the denial of death. It is the illusion of immortality. The portal to Valhalla is through the perfect, eternally beautiful celebrity. "There's nothing tragic about being fifty," Joe Gillis says in the 1950 film *Sunset Boulevard*, speaking of the faded movie star Norma Desmond, who dreams of making a triumphant return to the screen. "Not unless you're trying to be twenty-five."

We all have gods, Martin Luther said, it is just a question of which ones. And in American society our gods are celebrities. Religious belief and practice are commonly transferred to the adoration of celebrities. Our culture builds temples to celebrities the way Romans did for divine emperors, ancestors, and household gods. We are a de facto polytheistic society. We engage in the same kind of primitive beliefs as older polytheistic cultures. In celebrity culture, the object is to get as close as possible to the celebrity. Relics of celebrities are coveted as magical talismans. Those who can touch the celebrity or own a relic of the celebrity hope for a transference of celebrity power. They hope for magic. The personal possessions of celebrities, from John F. Kennedy's gold golf clubs to dresses worn by Princess Diana, to forty-dollar Swatch watches once owned by Andy Warhol, are cherished like relics of the dead among ancestor cults in Africa, Asia, or the medieval Catholic Church. They hold, somehow, faint traces of the celebrities themselves. And they are auctioned off for hundreds of thousands of dollars. Pilgrims travel to celebrity shrines. Graceland receives 750,000 visitors a year. Hard Rock Cafe has built its business around the yearning for intimacy with the famous. It ships relics of stars from one restaurant to another the way the medieval Church used to ship the bones and remains of saints to its various cathedrals.

Charlie Chaplin's corpse, like that of Eva Perón, was stolen and held for ransom. John Wayne's family, fearing grave robbers, did not mark his burial spot until twenty years after his death. The headstones of James Dean, Dylan Thomas, Sylvia Plath, Buddy Holly, and Jim Morrison have all been uprooted and carted away. Those who become obsessed with celebrities often profess a personal relationship with them, not unlike the relationship a born-again Christian professes to have with Jesus. The hysteria thousands of mourners in London displayed for Princess Diana in 1997 was real, even if the public persona they were mourning was largely a creation of publicists and the mass media.

Hollywood Forever is next to Paramount Studios. The massive white HOLLYWOOD letters tower on the hillside above the tombs and faux Italian Renaissance marble buildings that contain rows of crypts. Maps with the locations of stars' graves, along with a glossy booklet of brief star biographies, are handed out at the gate. Tourists are promised "visits" with dead stars, who are referred to as "residents." The cemetery, which has huge marble monuments to the wealthy and the powerful, many of them non-celebrities, is divided into sections with names like Garden of Eternal Love and Garden of Legends. It has two massive marble mausoleums, including the Cathedral Mausoleum, with six thousand crypts—the largest mausoleum in the world when it was built in the 1930s. Most of the celebrities, however, have plain bronze plaques that seem to indicate a yearning for the simplicity and anonymity denied to them in life.

The cemetery, established in 1899 and originally called Hollywood Memorial Park, fell into disrepair and neglect some eight or nine decades after it was opened. By the 1990s, families, including relatives of the makeup artist Max Factor, paid to have their loved ones removed from the grounds. By April 1996, the property was bankrupt. The cemetery was only months away from being condemned. It was bought by Tyler Cassidy and his brother Brent, who renamed the cemetery Hollywood Forever Cemetery and began a marketing campaign around its celebrity residents. The brothers established the Forever Network, where the non-celebrity departed could, at least in death, be the stars of their own customized video tributes. The cemetery Web site archives the tributes. "Families, young and old, are starting their LifeStories now, and adding to them as the years pass," the cemetery's brochure states. "What this means—having our images, voices, and videos available for future generations—has deep importance, both sociologically and for fully celebrating life." At funerals, these carefully produced movies, which often include highlights from home videos, are shown on a screen next to the caskets of the deceased. The cemetery's business is booming.

It costs a lot to be buried near a celebrity. Hugh Hefner reportedly paid $85,000 to reserve the crypt next to Marilyn Monroe at Westwood Cemetery in Los Angeles. The "prestige service" offered by Hollywood Forever runs $5,400. Jay Boileau, the executive vice president of the cemetery, conceded that a plot near Valentino would cost even more, although he did not have the price list with him. "We have sold most of them," he said of those spaces. "Visits to his crypt are unique. Every year we hold a memorial service for him on the day he passed away. He was the first true sex symbol. Ten thousand people came to his funeral. He was the first Brad Pitt. He was the first true superstar in film and the greatest screen lover."

The most moving memorial in the cemetery is a small glass case containing the cremated remains of the actor David White and his son Jonathan White. White played Larry Tate, the Machiavellian advertising executive, on the television show *Bewitched*, and he had a long stage career. He was married to the actress Mary Welch, who died during a second childbirth in 1958. David was left to raise Jonathan, his only child. Next to the urns are pictures of the father and boy. There is one of Jonathan as a tall young man in a graduation gown, the father's eyes directed up toward his son's face. Jonathan died at the age of thirty-three, a victim of the 1988 bombing of Pan Am Flight 103 over Lockerbie, Scotland. His father was devastated. He entered into a long period of mourning and seclusion. He died of a heart attack shortly before the two-year anniversary of his son's death. The modest memorial is a simple and poignant veneration of the powerful bond between a father and a son. It defies the celebrity culture around it. It speaks to other values, to loss, to grief, to mortality, and to the awful fragility of life. It is a reminder, in a sea of kitsch, of the beauty of love.

Buses wind their way through the Hollywood hills so tourists can gawk at the walls that barricade the homes of the famous. The celebrity interview or profile, pioneered on television by Barbara Walters and now a ubiquitous part of the news and entertainment industry, gives us the illusion that we have intimate relations with celebrities as well as the characters they portray. Real life, our own life, is viewed next to the lives of celebrities as inadequate and inauthentic. Celebrities are portrayed as idealized forms of ourselves. It is we, in perverse irony, who are never fully actualized, never fully real in a celebrity culture.

Soldiers and marines speak of first entering combat as if they are entering a movie, although if they try to engage in Hollywood-inspired heroics they often are killed. The chasm between movie exploits and the reality of war, which takes less than a minute in a firefight to grasp, is immense. The shock of reality brings with it the terrible realization that we are not who we thought we were. Fear controls us. We do not control it. The movie-inspired images played out in our heads, the fantasies of racing under a hail of bullets toward the enemy or of rescuing a wounded comrade, vanish. Life, the movie, comes to an abrupt halt. The houselights go on. The harsh glare of our limitations, fear and frailty blinds and disorients us.

Wounded marines booed and hissed John Wayne when he visited them in a hospital ward in Hawaii during the Second World War. Wayne, who never served in the military and for the visit wore a fancy cowboy outfit that included spurs and pistols, would later star in the 1949 gung-ho war movie *The Sands of Iwo Jima*. The marines, some of whom had fought at Iwo Jima, grasped the manipulation and deceit of celebrity culture. They understood that mass culture contributes to self-delusion and social control and elicits behavior that is often self-destructive.

Illusion, especially as presented in movies, can replace reality. When Wayne made *The Sands of Iwo Jima,* director Allan Dwan recreated the iconic image taken by photographer Joe Rosenthal of five marines and a navy corpsman raising the American flag on top of Mount Suribachi during the battle at the end of the film. Dwan coaxed Rene Gagnon, Ira Hayes, and John Bradley, the three surviving soldiers from the flag-raising, to appear briefly in the film to reenact the scene with Wayne, who handed them the original flag, loaned to the moviemakers by the Marine Corps.

The photo, later used by Felix de Weldon to sculpt the massive United States Marine Corps War Memorial near Arlington National Cemetery, had already made the three veterans celebrities. It was widely reprinted. President Franklin D. Roosevelt used the photo as the logo for the Seventh War Loan Drive in 1945. The Pentagon brought the three men back to the United States, where they toured as part of the fund-raising effort. The veterans helped raised $26.3 billion, twice the original goal. But the publicity, along with the transformation from traumatized veterans to poster children for the war, left the three soldiers alienated, bitter, and depressed. They were prisoners to the image and the patriotic myth built around it. Hayes and Gagnon became alcoholics and died early—Hayes at thirty-two and Gagnon at fifty-four. Bradley rarely took part in ceremonies celebrating the flag-raising and by the 1960s had stopped attending them. He was plagued by nightmares. He discussed the war with his wife Betty only once during his forty-seven-year marriage, and that was on their first date. He gave one interview, in 1985, at the urging of his wife, who told him to do it for the sake of their grandchildren. He was haunted by the death of his friend Iggy—Ralph Ignatowski, who had been captured, tortured, and killed by Japanese soldiers. When he found Iggy's body a few days after he had disappeared, he saw that the Japanese had ripped out Iggy's toenails and fingernails, fractured his arms, and bayonetted him repeatedly. The back of his friend's head had been smashed in, and his penis had been cut off and stuffed in his mouth.

"And then I visited his parents after the war and just lied to them," John Bradley told his son James, in one of the very rare comments he made to his children about the war. "'He didn't suffer at all,' I told them. 'He didn't feel a thing, didn't know what hit him,' I said. I just lied to them."[8]

Bradley's family went to Suribachi in 1997 after his death and placed a plaque on the spot where the flag-raising took place. James Bradley investigated this buried part of his father's past and interviewed the families of all the flag raisers. He published his account of the men's lives in his book *Flags of Our Fathers*.

The veterans saw their wartime experience transformed into an illusion. It became part of the mythic narrative of heroism and patriotic glory sold to the public by the Pentagon's public relations machine and Hollywood. The reality of war could not compete against the power of the illusion. The truth did not feed the fantasy of war as a ticket to glory, honor, and manhood. The truth did not promote collective self-exaltation. The illusion of war peddled in *The Sands of Iwo Jima*, like hundreds of other Hollywood war films, worked because it was what the public wanted to believe about themselves. It was what the government and the military wanted to promote. It worked because it had the power to simulate experience for most viewers who were never at Iwo Jima or in a war. But as Hayes and the others knew, this illusion was a lie. Hayes, arrested dozens of times for drunkenness, was discovered dead, face-down in his own vomit and blood, near an abandoned hut close to his home on the Gila River Indian Reservation. The coroner ruled that Hayes died of exposure and alcohol. It was left to the songwriter Peter LaFarge and Johnny Cash to memorialize the tragic saga of Hayes' brief life. "The Ballad of Ira Hayes" told a tale about war the producers of *The Sands of Iwo Jima*, who made the movie not to tell a truth but to feed the public's appetite and make a profit, studiously ignored.[9]

Celebrity worship banishes reality. And this adulation is pervasive. It is dressed up in the language of the Christian Right, which builds around its leaders, people like Pat Robertson or Joel Osteen, the aura of stardom, fame, and celebrity power. These Christian celebrities travel in private jets and limousines. They are surrounded by retinues of bodyguards, have television programs where they cultivate the same false intimacy with the audience, and, like all successful celebrities, amass personal fortunes. The frenzy around political messiahs, or the devotion of millions of women to Oprah Winfrey, is all part of the yearning to see ourselves in those we worship. We seek to be like them. We seek to make them like us. If Jesus and *The Purpose Driven Life* won't make us a celebrity, then Tony Robbins or positive psychologists or reality television will. We are waiting for our cue to walk onstage and be admired and envied, to become known and celebrated.

"What does the contemporary self want?" asked critic William Deresiewicz:

> The camera has created a culture of celebrity; the computer is creating a culture of connectivity. As the two technologies converge— broadband tipping the Web from text to image; social-networking sites spreading the mesh of interconnection ever wider—the two cultures betray a common impulse. Celebrity and connectivity are both ways of becoming known. This is what the contemporary self wants. It wants to be recognized, wants to be connected: It wants to be visible. If not to the millions, on *Survivor* or *Oprah,* then to the

hundreds, on Twitter or Facebook. This is the quality that validates us, this is how we become real to ourselves—by being seen by others. The great contemporary terror is anonymity. If Lionel Trilling was right, if the property that grounded the self in Romanticism was sincerity, and in modernism was authenticity, then in postmodernism it is visibility.[10]

We pay a variety of lifestyle advisers—Gabler calls them "essentially drama coaches"—to help us look and feel like celebrities, to build around us the set for the movie of our own life. Martha Stewart built her financial empire, when she wasn't insider trading, telling women how to create and decorate a set design for the perfect home. The realities within the home, the actual family relationships, are never addressed. Appearances make everything whole. Plastic surgeons, fitness gurus, diet doctors, therapists, life coaches, interior designers, and fashion consultants all, in essence, promise to make us happy, to make us celebrities. And happiness comes, we are assured, with how we look and how we present ourselves to others. Glossy magazines like *Town & Country* cater to the absurd pretensions of the very rich to be celebrities. They are photographed in expensive designer clothing inside the lavishly decorated set-pieces that are their homes. The route to happiness is bound up in how skillfully we show ourselves to the world. We not only have to conform to the dictates of this manufactured vision, but we also have to project an unrelenting optimism and happiness.

The Swan was a Fox reality makeover show. The title of the series referred to Hans Christian Andersen's fairy tale "The Ugly Duckling," in which a bird thought to be homely grew up and became a swan. "Unattractive" women were chosen to undergo three months of extensive plastic surgery, physical training, and therapy for a "complete life transformation." Each episode featured two "ugly ducklings" who compete with each other to go on to the beauty pageant. "I am going to be a new person," said one contestant in the opening credits.

In one episode, Cristina, twenty-seven, an Ecuador-born office administrator from Rancho Cordova, California, was chosen to be on the program.

"It's not just the outside I want to change, but it's the inside, too," Cristina told the camera mournfully. She had long, black hair and light brown skin. She wore baggy, gray sweatshirts and no makeup. Her hair was pulled back. We discovered that she was devastatingly insecure about being intimate with her husband because of her post-pregnancy stretch marks. The couple considered divorce.

"I just want to be, not a completely different person, but I want to be a better Cristina," she said.

As a "dream team" of plastic surgeons discussed the necessary corrections, viewers saw a still image of Cristina, in a gray cotton bra and underwear, superimposed on a glowing blue grid. Her small, drooping breasts, wrinkled stomach, and fleshy thighs were apparent. A schematic figure of an idealized female form revolved at the left of the screen. Crosshairs targeted and zoomed in on each flawed area of Cristina's face and body. The surgical procedures she would undergo were typed out beside each body part. Brow lift, eye lift, nose job, liposuction of chin and cheeks, dermatologist visits, collagen injections, LASIK eye surgery, tummy tuck, breast augmentation, liposuction of thighs, dental bleaching, full dental veneers, gum tissue recontouring, a 1,200-calorie daily diet, 120 hours in the gym, weekly therapy, and coaching. The effect was suggestive of a military operation. The image of a blueprint and crosshairs was used repeatedly through the program.

Cristina was shown writing in her diary: "I want a divorce because I think that my husband can do better without me. And it would be best for us to go in different directions. I am not happy with myself at all, so I think, why make this guy unhappy for the rest of his life?"

At the end of the three months, Cristina and her opponent, Kristy, were finally allowed to look in a mirror for "the final reveal." They were brought separately to what looked like a marble hotel foyer. Curving twin staircases with ornate iron banisters framed the action. A crystal chandelier glittered at the top of the stairs. Sconces and oil paintings in gold frames hung on the cream-colored walls.

The "dream team" was assembled in the marble lobby. Massive peach curtains obscured one wall.

"I think Cristina has really grown into herself as a woman, and she's ready to go back home and start her marriage all over again," said the team therapist.

Two men in tuxedos opened a set of tall double doors. Cristina entered in a tight, black evening gown and long black gloves. She was meticulously made up, and her hair had been carefully styled with extensions. The "dream team" burst into applause and whoops.

"I've been waiting twenty-seven years for this day," Cristina tearfully told host Amanda Byram. "I came for a dream, the American dream, like all the Latinas do, and I got it!"

"You got it!" cheered Byram. "Yes, you did!"

Reverberating drumbeats were heard. "Behind that curtain," says Byram, "is a mirror. We will draw back the curtain, the mirror will be revealed, and you will see yourself for the first time in three months. Cristina, step up to the curtain."

Short, suspenseful cello strokes were heard. There was a tumbling drumroll.

"I'm ready," quavered Cristina.

The curtain parted slowly in the middle. An elaborate full-length mirror reflected Cristina. The cello strokes billowed into the *Swan* theme song.

"Oh, my God!" she gasped, covering her face. She doubled over. Her knees buckled. She almost hit the floor. "I am so beautiful!!!" she sobbed. "Thank you, oh, thank you so much!! Thank you, God!! Thank you, thank you, thank you so much for this!! Look at my arms, my figure . . . I love the dress! Thank you, oh!! I'm in love with myself!"

The "dream team" burst into applause again. "Well, you owe this to yourself," said Byram. "But you also owe it to these fantastic experts. Guys, come on in."

The crowd of smiling experts closed in on their creation, clapping as they approached.

At the end of each episode, the two contestants were called before Byram to hear who would advance to the pageant. The winner often wept and was hugged by the loser. Byram then pulled the loser aside for "one final surprise." The double doors opened once more, and her family was invited onto the set for a joyful reunion. In celebrity culture, family is the consolation prize for not making it to the pageant.

The Swan's transparent message is that once these women have been surgically "corrected" to resemble mainstream celebrity beauty as closely as possible, their problems will be solved. "This is a positive show where we want to see how these women can make their dreams come true once they have what they want," said Cecile Frot-Coutaz,

CEO of FremantleMedia North America, producers of *The Swan*. Troubled marriages, abusive relationships, unemployment, crushing self-esteem problems—all will vanish along with the excess fat off their thighs. They will be new. They will be flawless. They will be celebrities.

In the Middle Ages, writes Alain de Botton in his book *Status Anxiety*, stained glass windows and vivid paintings of religious torment and salvation controlled and influenced social behavior. Today we are ruled by icons of gross riches and physical beauty that blare and flash from television, cinema, and computer screens. People knelt before God and the church in the Middle Ages. We flock hungrily to the glamorous crumbs that fall to us from glossy magazines, talk and entertainment shows, and reality television. We fashion our lives as closely to these lives of gratuitous consumption as we can. Only a life with status, physical attributes, and affluence is worth pursuing.

Hedonism and wealth are openly worshipped on shows such as *The Hills, Gossip Girl, Sex and the City, My Super Sweet 16*, and *The Real Housewives of*. . . . The American oligarchy, 1 percent of whom control more wealth than the bottom 90 percent combined, are the characters we envy and watch on television. They live and play in multimillion-dollar beach houses and expansive modern lofts. They marry professional athletes and are chauffeured in stretch limos to spa appointments. They rush from fashion shows to movie premieres, flaunting their surgically enhanced, perfect bodies in haute couture. Their teenagers throw $200,000 parties and have $1 million dollar weddings. This life is held before us like a beacon. This life, we are told, is the most desirable, the most gratifying.

The working classes, comprising tens of millions of struggling Americans, are shut out of television's gated community. They have become largely invisible. They are mocked, even as they are tantalized, by the lives of excess they watch on the screen in their living rooms. Almost none of us will ever attain these lives of wealth and power. Yet we are told that if we want it badly enough, if we believe sufficiently in ourselves, we too can have everything. We are left, when we cannot adopt these impossible lifestyles as our own, with feelings of inferiority and worthlessness. We have failed where others have succeeded.

We consume countless lies daily, false promises that if we spend more money, if we buy this brand or that product, if we vote for this candidate, we will be respected, envied, powerful, loved, and protected. The flamboyant lives of celebrities and the outrageous characters on television, movies, professional wrestling, and sensational talk shows are peddled to us, promising to fill up the emptiness in our own lives. Celebrity culture encourages everyone to think of themselves as potential celebrities, as possessing unique if unacknowledged gifts. It is, as Christopher Lasch diagnosed, a culture of narcissism. Faith in ourselves, in a world of make-believe, is more important than reality. Reality, in fact, is dismissed and shunned as an impediment to success, a form of negativity. The New Age mysticism and pop psychology of television personalities, evangelical pastors, along with the array of self-help best-sellers penned by motivational speakers, psychiatrists, and business tycoons, all peddle a fantasy. Reality is condemned in these popular belief systems as the work of Satan, as defeatist, as negativity, or as inhibiting our inner essence and power. Those who question, those who doubt, those who are critical, those who are able to confront reality and who grasp the hollowness of celebrity culture are shunned and condemned for their pessimism. The illusionists who shape our culture and who profit from our incredulity hold up the gilded cult of Us. Popular expressions of religious belief, personal empowerment, corporatism, political participation, and self-definition argue that all of us are special, entitled, and unique. All of us, by tapping into our inner reserves of personal will and undiscovered talent, by visualizing what we want, can achieve, and deserve to achieve, happiness, fame, and success. This relentless message cuts across ideological lines. This mantra has seeped into every aspect of our lives. We are all entitled to everything.

American Idol, a talent-search reality show that airs on Fox, is one of the most popular shows on American television. The show travels to different American cities in a "countrywide search" for the contestants who will continue to the final competition in Hollywood. The producers of the show introduced a new focus in the 2008–2009 season on the personal stories of the contestants.

During the Utah auditions, we met Megan Corkrey, twenty-three, the single mother of a toddler. She has long dirty-blonde hair, and a wholesome, pretty face. A tattoo sleeve covers her right arm from the shoulder to below the elbow. She wears a black, grey, and white dress reminiscent of the 1950s, and ballet flats. She is a font designer.

In an interview, Corkrey says, "I am a mother. He will be two in December." We see Corkrey with a little blond boy, reading a book together on a beanbag chair. Breezy guitar music plays. "His name is Ryder." We see Corkrey kissing Ryder and putting him to bed. "I recently decided to get a divorce, which is new." The guitar music turns pensive. "The life I had planned for us, the life I'd pictured, wasn't going to happen. I cried a lot for a while. I don't think I stopped crying. And Ryder, of course, you can be crying, and then he walks by, and does something ridiculous, and you can't help but smile and laugh." We see Corkrey laughing with her son on the floor. "And a little piece kind of heals up a little bit."

The montage of Corkrey's life fills the screen as the rock ballad swells. "I can laugh at myself, while the tears roll down . . . ," sings the band. We see Corkrey and her son looking out a window. She holds her son up to a basketball hoop as he clutches a blue ball.

"It was kind of crazy, I found out *Idol* was coming to Salt Lake, and I'd just decided on the divorce, and for the first time in my life it was a crossroads where *anything* can happen!! So why not go for what I love to do?"

Corkrey enters the audition room. The judges—Simon Cowell, Paula Abdul, Randy Jackson, and Kara DioGuardi—are seated behind a long table in front of a window. They each have large, red tumblers with "Coca-Cola" printed on them. They seem charmed by her exuberant presence. She sings "Can't Help Lovin' Dat Man" from *Show Boat*. Her performance is charismatic and quirky. She improvises freely and assuredly with the rhythms and notes of the song, beaming the whole time.

"I really like you," says Abdul. "I'm bordering on loving you. I think I'm loving you. Yeah, I do. Simon?"

"One of my favorite auditions," says Cowell in a monotone.

"Yess!!" grins Corkrey.

"Because you're different," continues Cowell sternly. "You are one of the few I'm going to remember. I like you, I like your voice, I mean seriously good voice. I loved it."

"You're an interesting girl. You have a glow about you, you have an *incredible* face," says DioGuardi.

The judges vote.

"Absolutely yes," says Cowell.

"Love you," says Abdul.

"Yes!" says DioGuardi.

"One hundred percent maybe," smiles Jackson.

"You're goin' to Hollywood!" cheers DioGuardi as the inspirational rock music swells.

"YESS!!! Thank you, guys!" Corkrey screams with delight. She runs out of the audition room into a crowd of her cheering friends. The music plays as she dances down the street, waving her large yellow ticket, the symbol of her success.

Celebrities, who often come from humble backgrounds, are held up as proof that anyone, even we, can be adored by the world. These celebrities, like saints, are living proof that the impossible is always possible. Our fantasies of belonging, of fame, of success, and of fulfillment, are projected onto celebrities. These fantasies are stoked by the legions of those who amplify the culture of illusion, who persuade us that the shadows are real. The juxtaposition of the impossible illusions inspired by celebrity culture and our "insignificant" individual achievements, however, eventually leads to frustration, anger, insecurity, and invalidation. It results, ironically, in a self-perpetuating cycle that drives the frustrated, alienated individual with even greater desperation and hunger away from reality, back toward the empty promises of those who seduce us, who tell us what we want to hear. We beg for more. We ingest these lies until our money runs out. And when we fall into despair, we medicate ourselves, as if the happiness we have failed to find in the hollow game is our deficiency. And, of course, we are told it is.

Human beings become a commodity in a celebrity culture. They are objects, like consumer products. They have no intrinsic value. They must look fabulous and live on fabulous sets. Those who fail to meet the ideal are belittled and mocked. Friends and allies are to be used and betrayed during the climb to fame, power, and wealth. And when they are no longer useful, they are to be discarded. In *Fahrenheit 451*, Ray Bradbury's novel about a future dystopia, people spend most of the day watching giant television screens that show endless scenes of police chases and criminal apprehensions. Life, Bradbury understood, once it was packaged and filmed, became the most compelling form of entertainment.

The moral nihilism of celebrity culture is played out on reality television shows, most of which encourage a dark voyeurism into other people's humiliation, pain, weakness, and betrayal. Education, building community, honesty, transparency, and sharing are qualities that will see you, in a gross perversion of democracy and morality, voted off a reality show. Fellow competitors for prize money and a chance for fleeting fame elect to "disappear" the unwanted. In the final credits of the reality show *America's Next Top Model*, a picture of the woman expelled during the episode vanishes from the group portrait on the screen. Those cast aside become, at least to the television audience, non-persons. Life, these shows teach, is a brutal world of unadulterated competition. Life is about the personal humiliation of those who oppose us. Those who win are the best. Those who lose deserve to be erased. Compassion, competence, intelligence, and solidarity with others are forms of weakness. And those who do not achieve celebrity status, who do not win the prize money or make millions in Wall Street firms, deserve to lose. Those who are denigrated and ridiculed on reality television, often as they sob in front of the camera, are branded as failures. They are responsible for their rejection. They are deficient.

In an episode from the second season of the CBS reality game show *Survivor*, cast members talk about exceptional friendships they have made within their "tribe," or team. Maralyn, also known as Mad Dog, is a fifty-two-year-old retired police officer with a silver crew cut and a tall, mannish build. She is sunning herself in a shallow stream, singing "On the Street Where You Live." Tina, a personal nurse and mother, walks up the stream toward her.

"Sing it, girl! I just followed your voice."

"Is it that loud?"

"Maralyn, she's kind of like our little songbird, and our little cheerleader in our camp," Tina says in an interview. "Maralyn and I have bonded, more so than I have with any of the other people. It might be our ages, it might just be that we kind of took up for one another."

We see Tina and Maralyn swimming and laughing together in the river.

"Tina is a fabulous woman," says Maralyn in an interview. "She is a star. I trust Tina the most."

Maralyn and Tina's tribe, Ogakor, loses an obstacle course challenge, in which all the tribe members are tethered together. If one person falls, the entire team is slowed. Mad Dog Maralyn falls several times and is hauled back to her feet by Colby, the "cowboy" from Texas.

Because they lost, the members of Ogakor must vote off one of their tribe members. The camera shows small groups of twos and threes in huddled, intense discussion.

"The mood in the camp is a very sad mood, but it's also a very strategic mood," says Tina. "Everyone's thinking, 'Who's thinking what?'"

The vote is taken at dusk, in the "tribal council" area. It resembles a set from Disney World's Adventureland. A ring of tall stone monoliths is stenciled with petroglyphs. It is lit by torches. A campfire blazes in the center of the ring. Primitive drums and flutes are heard.

The Ogakor team arrives at dusk, each holding a torch. They sit before *Survivor*'s host, Jeff Probst.

"So I just want to talk about a couple of big topics," says Probst, who wears a safari outfit. "*Trust.* Colby, is there anyone here that you don't trust, wouldn't trust?"

"Sure," says Colby.

"Tell me about that."

"Well, I think that's part of the game," says Colby. "It's way too early to tell exactly who you can trust, I think."

"What about you, Mitchell? Would you trust everyone here for forty-two days?" asks Probst. "I think the motto is, 'Trust no one,'" answers Mitchell. "I have a lot of faith in a good number of these people, but I couldn't give 100 percent of my trust."

"What about you, Mad Dog?" asks Probst. "These all your buddies?"

Maralyn looks around at her team members. "Yes," she says unequivocally. "Yes. And, Jeff, I trust with my heart."

"I think friendship does enter into it at some point," says Jerri. "But I think it's very important to keep that separate from the game. It's two totally different things. And that's where it gets tricky." Jerri will say later, as she casts her vote, "This is probably one of the most difficult things for me to do right now. It's purely strategic, it's nothing personal. I am going to miss you dearly."

"Jeff," Maralyn breaks in. "I'm *conjoined* with Tina. She is a constellation. And, the cowboy [Colby]! The poor cowboy has dragged me around so many times [during the obstacle course challenge]. I appreciate it."

"I'd do it again," laughs Colby broadly.

"Hey, you hear that? He'd do it again!" says Maralyn.

It is time to vote. Each team member walks up a narrow bridge lit by flaring torches, again looking like something out of Disney's Enchanted Tiki Room, made of twisted logs lashed with vines, to a stone table. They write the name of the person they want to eliminate and put it in a cask with aboriginal carvings. Most of the votes are kept anonymous, the camera panning away as each person writes. But as Tina, Mad Dog Maralyn's best friend and "constellation," casts her vote, she shows us her ballot: Mad Dog. "Mad Dog, I love you," she says to the camera, "I value your friendship more than anything. This vote has everything to do with a promise I made, it has nothing to do with you. I hope you'll understand." She folds her vote and puts it in the cask.

"Once the vote is tallied, the decision is final, and the person will be asked to leave the tribal council area immediately," says Probst.

Five people of the seven voted to eliminate Maralyn.

"You need to bring me a torch, Mad Dog," says Probst. She does so, first taking off her green baseball cap and putting it affectionately on Amber, who sits next to her and gives her a hug. The camera shows Tina looking impassive.

"Mad Dog," says Probst, holding the flaming torch Maralyn has brought him, "the tribe has spoken." He takes a large stone snuffer and extinguishes the torch. The camera shows Marilynn's rueful face behind the smoking, blackened torch. "It's time for you to go," says Probst. She leaves without speaking or looking at anyone, although there are a few weak "bye" 's from the tribe.

Before the final credits, we are shown who, besides her friend Tina, voted to eliminate Maralyn. They are Amber, who gave Maralyn a farewell hug, along with Mitchell, Jerri, and Colby, Maralyn's "cowboy."

Celebrity culture plunges us into a moral void. No one has any worth beyond his or her appearance, usefulness, or ability to "succeed." The highest achievements in a celebrity culture are wealth, sexual conquest, and fame. It does not matter how these are obtained. These values, as Sigmund Freud understood, are illusory. They are hollow. They leave us chasing vapors. They urge us toward a life of narcissistic self-absorption. They tell us that existence is to be centered on the practices and desires of the self rather than the common good. The ability to lie and manipulate others, the very ethic of capitalism, is held up as the highest good. "I simply agreed to go along with [Jerri and Amber] because I thought it would get me down the road a little better," says young, good-looking Colby in another episode of *Survivor*. "I wanna win. And I don't want to talk to anybody else about loyalties—don't give me that crap. I haven't trusted anyone since day one, and anyone playing smart should have been the same way."

The cult of self dominates our cultural landscape. This cult has within it the classic traits of psychopaths: superficial charm, grandiosity, and self-importance; a need for constant stimulation, a penchant for lying, deception, and manipulation, and the inability to feel remorse or guilt. This is, of course, the ethic promoted by corporations. It is the ethic of unfettered capitalism. It is the misguided belief that personal style and personal advancement, mistaken for individualism, are the same as democratic equality. In fact, personal style, defined by the commodities we buy or consume, has become a compensation for our loss of democratic equality. We have a right, in the cult of the self, to get whatever we desire. We can do anything, even belittle and destroy those around us, including our friends, to make money, to be happy, and to become famous. Once fame and wealth are achieved, they become their own justification, their own morality. How one gets there is irrelevant. Once you get there, those questions are no longer asked.

It is this perverted ethic that gave us Wall Street bankers and investment houses that willfully trashed the nation's economy, stole money from tens of millions of small shareholders who had bought stock in these corporations for retirement or college. The heads of these corporations, like the winners on a reality television program who lied and manipulated others to succeed, walked away with hundreds of millions of dollars in bonuses and compensation. In his masterful essay "The Work of Art in the Age of Mechanical Reproduction," Walter Benjamin wrote: "The cult of the movie star, fostered by the money of the film industry, preserves not the unique aura of the person but the 'spell of the personality,' the phony spell of a commodity."[11]

"The professional celebrity, male and female, is the crowning result of the star system of a society that makes a fetish of competition," wrote C. Wright Mills:

> In America, this system is carried to the point where a man who can knock a small, white ball into a series of holes in the ground with more efficiency and skill than anyone else thereby gains access to the President of the United States. It is carried to the point where a chattering radio and television entertainer becomes the hunting chum of leading industrial executives, cabinet members, and the higher military. It does not seem to matter what the man is the very best at; so long as he has won out in competition over all others, he is celebrated. Then, a second feature of the star system begins to work: all the stars of any other sphere of endeavor or position are drawn toward the new star and he toward them. The success, the champion, accordingly, is one who mingles freely with other champions to populate the world of the celebrity.[12]

Degradation as entertainment is the squalid underside to the glamour of celebrity culture. "If only that were me," we sigh as we gaze at the wealthy, glimmering stars on the red carpet. But we are as transfixed by the inverse of celebrity culture, by the spectacle of humiliation and debasement that comprise tabloid television shows such as *The Jerry Springer Show* and *The Howard Stern Show*. We secretly exult: "At least that's not me." It is the glee of cruelty with impunity, the same impulse that drove crowds to the Roman Colosseum, to the pillory and the stocks, to public hangings, and to traveling freak shows.

In one segment from *Jerry Springer: Wild & Outrageous, Volume 1*, a man and his wife sit on the Springer stage. They are obese, soft, and pale, with mounds of fluffy, brown hair. Their bodies look like uncooked dough. The man wears a blue polo shirt and brown pants. The woman wears a dark pink shirt with long sleeves and a long black skirt.

"I have a sex fantasy," the man tells his wife solemnly. His voice is quiet and nasal. She recoils with raised eyebrows. "Do you remember that bachelor party I went to three weeks ago? There was a stripper there. She was dressed up as a cheerleader, and she just turned me on. I mean, I got—I have this thing—I don't know if it's her or the outfit, I think it's the outfit. But, I'd really love for you to dress up as a cheerleader. For me. And do a cheer that's especially for me, and. . . . You could be my cheerleader . . . of my heart."

The woman, still sitting in her chair, has her hands on her hips and looks affronted. There are close-ups of the Springer audience bursting into raucous laughter, hoots, and applause.

"I brought her here to show you—" continues the man. He is cut off by the whoops of the audience.

"Let's bring her out!" says Jerry. The audience cheers.

Shaking yellow pom-poms, a skinny blonde girl in a purple-and-yellow cheerleader outfit runs out onstage. Her body is like a stick. She turns a cartwheel and moons the audience, smacking her own bottom several times. Behind her, the obese man is shown grinning. The obese woman is waving in disgust at the cheerleader.

"Is everybody ready to do a cheer just for Jerry?!" squeaks the cheerleader.

"YEAAAHHH!!!" hollers the audience.

"I can't hear yoooouuuuuuu . . ." pipes the cheerleader, lifting her skirt up to her waist.

The audience goes crazy. She leads a cheer, spelling out Jerry's name.

"Now that you've seen these pom-poms, how'd you like to see *these* pom-poms?" she squeaks, shaking her flat chest. A rapid electronic beat fills the studio, and the lights dim. She takes off her top, her bra, and, gyrating her hips, slides off her skirt and underwear. Her bottom is about three feet from the whooping men in the front row. The obese man's arms and legs are waving around in excitement, as his grimacing wife shakes her head repeatedly. The naked cheerleader leans back on the floor and does the splits in the air. She then jumps into the fat man's lap and smothers his face in her tiny chest. She runs into the audience and does the same to another man and a gray-haired woman in a cardigan who looks like a grandmother. The cameramen follow the cheerleader closely, zooming in on her breasts and ass.

While the naked, ponytailed girl runs around leaping into the laps of members of the audience, the crowd begins chanting, under the deafening electronic music, "JER-RY! JER-RY! JER-RY! JER-RY!"

The girl finally runs back onstage. The music stops. She collects her pom-poms and sits down naked, dressed only in a pair of white tennis shoes and bobby socks.

"JER-RY! JER-RY! JER-RY!" chants the crowd.

In a later portion of the episode, Jerry says to the man, "So this is really what you want your wife to be doing?" The naked cheerleader is seated beside him, and his wife is no longer onstage.

"Oh, yes!" he exclaims. The audience laughs at his fervor. "It *really* excites me, Jerry. It *really* does."

"All right," says Jerry. "Well, are we ready to bring her out?"

"YEESSSSS!!!" bellows the audience.

"Here she is!" announces Jerry. "Cheerleading Kristen!"

The wife runs out onto the stage. She is in an identical purple-and-yellow cheerleading outfit, with yellow pom-poms. Her fluffy brown hair is tied into two bunches on the sides of her head. She resembles a poodle. Her exposed midriff is a thick, white roll of fat that hangs over her short, purple skirt and shakes with every step.

She turns a clumsy somersault. She prances heavily back and forth on the stage. She does cancan kicks. She yells "WHOOOOOO!!!" Her husband is seen behind her, yelling with the rest of the audience. She leads a cheer of Jerry's name, but forgets the Y. The audience laughs. She finishes the cheer. There is a shot of Jerry watching quietly at the back of the studio, leaning against the soundman's booth, his hand covering his mouth.

The wife continues to high-step back and forth. The clapping and cheers subside. The audience has fallen silent. "WHOOO!!" she yells again. She does, in complete silence, a few more lumbering kicks. A few individuals snicker in the crowd. Jerry is shown at the soundman's booth, doubled over in soundless laughter. The woman is confused. She looks to the side of the stage, as though she is being prompted. "Oh—OK," she says.

She takes center stage again. "All right," she says. "You've seen these pom-poms." Individual giggles are heard from the audience. "Now what about THESE?" Her husband watches eagerly. The naked stripper, sitting behind her, laughs.

The stripping music comes on. The lights dim. The wife does more cancan kicks. She trots back and forth. She takes off all her clothes except her underpants. The audience is clapping to the beat, whooping, and laughing. Some of them are covering their eyes. Others are covering their mouths. She continues prancing onstage, doing the occasional kick, until the music stops.

"JER-RY!! JER-RY!! JER-RY!!" chants the crowd. Her husband wraps his arms around her naked torso and kisses her.

"You made my wildest dreams come true," he tells her.

Individuals laugh in the audience.

"Aww," says Jerry, shaking his head. "That is true love." The woman collects her scattered clothes. "That is—that is—that is—true love."

Celebrities are skillfully used by their handlers and the media to compensate for the increasingly degraded and regimented existences that most of us endure in a commodity culture. Celebrities tell us we can have our revenge. We can triumph. We can, one day, get back at the world that has belittled and abused us. It happens in the ring. It happens on television. It happens in the movies. It happens in the narrative of the Christian Right. It happens in pornography. It happens in the self-help manuals and on reality television. But it almost never happens in reality.

Celebrity is the vehicle used by a corporate society to sell us these branded commodities, most of which we do not need. Celebrities humanize commercial commodities. They present the familiar and comforting face of the corporate state. Supermodel Paulina Porizkova, on an episode of *America's Next Top Model*, gushes to a group of aspiring young models, "Our job as models is to *sell*." But they peddle a fake intimacy and a fantasy. The commercial "personalizing" of the world involves oversimplification, distraction, and gross distortion. "We sink further into a dream of an unconsciously intimate world in which not only may a cat look at a king but a king is really a cat underneath, and all the great power-figures Honest Joes at heart,"[13] Richard Hoggart warned in *The Uses of Literacy*. We do not learn more about Barack Obama by knowing what dog he has brought home for his daughters or if he still smokes. Such personalized trivia, passed off as news, divert us from reality.

In his book *Celebrity*, Chris Rojek calls celebrity culture "the cult of distraction that valorizes the superficial, the gaudy, the domination of commodity culture." He goes further:

Capitalism originally sought to police play and pleasure, because any attempt to replace work as the central life interest threatened the economic survival of the system. The family, the state, and religion engendered a variety of patterns of moral regulation to control desire and ensure compliance with the system of production. However, as capitalism developed, consumer culture and leisure time expanded. The principles that operated to repress the individual in the workplace and the home were extended to the shopping mall and recreational activity. The entertainment industry and consumer culture produced what Herbert Marcuse called "repressive desublimation." Through this process individuals unwittingly subscribed to the degraded version of humanity.[14]

This cult of distraction, as Rojek points out, masks the real disintegration of culture. It conceals the meaninglessness and emptiness of our own lives. It seduces us to engage in imitative consumption. It deflects the moral questions arising from mounting social injustice, growing inequalities, costly imperial wars, economic collapse, and political corruption. The wild pursuit of status and wealth has destroyed our souls and our economy. Families live in sprawling mansions financed with mortgages they can no longer repay. Consumers recklessly rang up Coach handbags and Manolo Blahnik shoes on credit cards because they seemed to confer a sense of identity and merit. Our favorite hobby, besides television, used to be, until reality hit us like a tsunami, shopping. Shopping used to be the compensation for spending five days a week in tiny cubicles. American workers are ground down by corporations that have disempowered them, used them, and have now discarded them.

Celebrities have fame free of responsibility. The fame of celebrities, wrote Mills, disguises those who possess true power: corporations and the oligarchic elite. Magical thinking is the currency not only of celebrity culture, but also of totalitarian culture. And as we sink into an economic and political morass, we are still controlled, manipulated and distracted by the celluloid shadows on the dark wall of Plato's cave. The fantasy of celebrity culture is not designed simply to entertain. It is designed to keep us from fighting back.

"What Orwell feared were those who would ban books," Neil Postman wrote:

> What Huxley feared was that there would be no reason to ban a book, for there would be no one who wanted to read one. Orwell feared those who would deprive us of information. Huxley feared those who would give us so much that we would be reduced to passivity and egoism. Orwell feared that the truth would be concealed from us. Huxley feared the truth would be drowned in a sea of irrelevance. Orwell feared we would become a captive culture. Huxley feared we would become a trivial culture, preoccupied with some equivalent of the feelies, the orgy porgy, and the centrifugal bumblepuppy. As Huxley remarked in *Brave New World Revisited*, the civil libertarians and rationalists who are ever on the alert to oppose tyranny "failed to take into account man's almost infinite appetite for distractions." In *1984*, Huxley added, people are controlled by inflicting pain. In *Brave New World*, they are controlled by inflicting pleasure. In short, Orwell feared that what we hate will ruin us. Huxley feared that what we love will ruin us.[15]

Mark Andrejevic, a professor of communication studies at the University of Iowa at Iowa City, writes that reality shows like *Big Brother* and *Survivor* glamorize the intrusiveness of the surveillance state, presenting it as "one of the hip attributes of the contemporary world," "an entrée into the world of wealth and celebrity," and even a moral good. In his book *Reality TV: The Work of Being Watched,* he quotes veterans of *The Real World*, *Road Rules*, and *Temptation Island* who speak about their on-air personal growth and the therapeutic value of being constantly watched. As Josh on *Big Brother* explains, "Everyone should have an audience." *Big Brother*, in which ten cohabiting strangers willingly submit to round-the-clock video monitoring, is a celebration of the surveillance state. More than twice as many young people apply to MTV's *Real World* show than to Harvard, for a chance to live under constant surveillance. But the use of hidden cameras—part of professional wrestling's attraction as well as a staple on reality television—reinforces celebrity culture's frightening assumption that it is normal, indeed enviable, to be constantly watched. For corporations and a government that seeks to make surveillance routine, whether to study our buying habits or read our e-mails or make sure we do not organize social protest, these shows normalize what was once considered a flagrant violation of our Constitutional right to privacy.[16]

There is a rapacious appetite for new, "real-life" drama and a desperate thirst for validation by the celebrity culture. This yearning to be anointed worthy of celebrity was captured in Dave Eggers's book *A Heartbreaking Work of Staggering Genius*. He writes a satirical transcript of an interview/audition tape he purportedly made for *The Real World*.

Eggers eagerly discloses to the interviewer the most sensational episodes of his life, including his daily habit of masturbating in the shower. His parents both died of cancer thirty-two days apart, leaving him at twenty-two to raise his eight-year-old brother Toph. Mr. T from the A-Team moved into the town he grew up in. His childhood friend's father doused himself in gasoline and set himself on fire. He drew a picture of his mother on her deathbed. His father was a devious alcoholic who drank vodka out of tall soda glasses.

Eggers muses on the hunger for celebrity:

> Because, see, I think what my town, and your show, reflect so wonderfully is that the main by-product of the comfort and prosperity that I'm describing is a sort of pure, insinuating solipsism . . . we've grown up thinking of ourselves in relation to the political-media-entertainment ephemera, in our safe and comfortable homes, given the time to think about how we would fit into this or that band or TV show or movie, and how we would look doing it. These are people for whom the idea of anonymity is existentially irrational, indefensible.[17]

"Why do you want to be on *The Real World*?" asks the interviewer. "Because I want everyone to witness my youth," answers Eggers:

> I just mean, that it's in bloom. That's what you're all about, right? The showing of raw fruit, correct? Whether that's in videos or on Spring Break, whatever, the amplifying of youth, the editing and volume magnifying what it means to be right there, at the point

when all is allowed and your body wants everything for it, is hungry and taut, churning, an energy vortex, sucking all toward it.[18]

Okay, you want to hear a sad story? Last night I was home, listening to an album. A favorite song came on, and I was singing aloud . . . and as I was singing and doing the slo-mo hands-in-hair maneuver, I messed up the words to the song I was singing, and though it was two fifty-one in the morning, I became quickly, deeply embarrassed about my singing gaffe, convinced that there was a very good chance that someone could see me—through the window, across the dark, across the street. I was sure, saw vividly that someone—or more likely a someone and his friends—over there was having a hearty laugh at my expense.[19]

At the end of the interview, Eggers says to the interviewer, "Reward me for my suffering,"

"Have I given you enough? Reward me. Put me on television. Let me share this with millions . . . I know how this works. I give you these things, and you give me a platform. So give me a platform. I am owed . . . I can do it any way you want, too—I can do it funny, or maudlin, or just straight, uninflected—anything. You tell me. I can do it sad, or inspirational, or angry. . . . All this did not happen to us for naught, I can assure you—there is no logic to that, there is logic only in assuming that we suffered for a reason. Just give us our due. . . . I need community, I need feedback, I need love, connection, give-and-take—will bleed if they will love. . . . I will open a vein, an artery. . . . Oh please let me show this to millions. . . . Let me be the conduit. . . . Oh, I want to be the heart pumping blood to everyone! . . . I want—"
"And that will heal you?"
"Yes! Yes! Yes! Yes!"[20]

We live in an age, Philip Roth wrote, in which the imagination of the novelist lies helpless before what will appear in the morning newspaper: "The actuality is continually outdoing our talents, and the culture tosses up figures daily that are the envy of any novelist." Roth observed that the reality of celebrity culture "stupefies, it sickens, it infuriates, and finally it is even a kind of embarrassment to one's own meager imagination."[21]

Philip Roth's grasp of the unreality of reality is exemplified in the British reality star Jade Goody.[22] A twenty-year-old dental technician who was the only child of two drug addicts, Goody was in 2002 given a role as a contestant in *Big Brother 3*. She got drunk on the first night of the program. She waltzed around the set topless. She asked what asparagus was and said, "Rio de Janeiro, ain't that a person?" She referred to East Anglia as "East Angular," thought Portugal was in Spain, and complained that she was being made an "escape goat." She thought "pistachio" was a famous painter. She finished fourth in the competition, but this did not, as it would for most others, end her career as a celebrity. She released several successful fitness DVDs and opened a beauty salon in Hertford. She published an autobiography and marketed her own fragrance in the weeks before Christmas 2006, which generated huge sales. She appeared on other reality shows including *Celebrity Wife Swap*, *Celebrity Driving School*, *Celebrity Weakest Link*, and *Celebrity Stars in Their Eyes*. She also hosted her own reality TV shows, including *What Jade Did Next*, *Jade's Salon*, and *Jade's P.A.*

Goody had the essential skill required of all who agree to expose their lives and selves to constant surveillance: She appeared to lack any degree of self-consciousness. She came naturally to exhibitionism, even when she was clearly a figure of ridicule. She opened her life to millions of viewers, even when it involved seamy and messy relationships and personal disasters, with a beguiling innocence. This is a bizarre skill highly prized in celebrity culture. Goody clearly craved the attention and sought to perpetuate it, but she seemed slightly bored or at least indifferent while doing it.

Her appearance, along with her mother Jackiey Budden and model boyfriend Jack Tweed, in the Big Brother house in January 2007, however, backfired. She bullied and taunted Bollywood actress Shilpa Shetty, and used crude, racist remarks to describe Shetty, calling her "Shilpa Poppadom." The show received some 45,000 complaints about her behavior and racist language. Her perfume was yanked from shelves, and publishers dropped plans to publish the paperback version of her autobiography. She apologized abjectly to Indian viewers and appeared on the Indian version of the show, called *Bigg Boss*. She might have faded from view, like most reality show contestants, but in 2007 she was diagnosed with cervical cancer, learning of the disease while being filmed for the Indian program. The new twist to the drama of her life propelled her back into the spotlight and allowed her a final chance to play a starring role in her life movie. The Living Channel commissioned a three-part series that documented her battle with cancer. The program drew an audience of more than 900,000 viewers in Britain when it aired. She milked her final days for money and celebrity, including making about $1 million by selling exclusive rights to cover her wedding. She died at the age of twenty-seven in March 2009.

Goody told the *News of the World* when she learned her cancer was probably terminal: "I've lived my whole adult life talking about my life. The only difference is that I'm talking about my death now. It's OK.

"I've lived in front of the cameras," she went on. "And maybe I'll die in front of them. And I know some people don't like what I'm doing, but at this point I really don't care what other people think. Now, it's about what I want."

Nothing is off-limits, including death. As long as it can be packaged and turned into drama, it works. The emptiness of those like Goody who crave this validation is tragic. They turn into clowns. This endless, mindless diversion is a necessity in a society that prizes entertainment above substance. Intellectual or philosophical ideas require too much effort and work to absorb. Classical theater, newspapers, and books are pushed to the margins of cultural life, remnants of a bygone literate age. They are dismissed as inaccessible and elitist unless they provide, as Goody did, effortless entertainment. The popularization of culture often ends in its total degradation. The philosopher Hannah Arendt wrote:

> The result of this is not disintegration but decay, and those who promote it are not the Tin Pan Alley composers but a special kind of intellectual, often well read and well informed, whose sole function is to organize, disseminate, and change cultural objects in order to persuade the masses that *Hamlet* can be as entertaining as *My Fair Lady*,

and perhaps as educational as well. There are many great authors of the past who have survived centuries of oblivion and neglect, but it is still an open question whether they will be able to survive an entertaining version of what they have to say.[23]

~

We are a culture that has been denied, or has passively given up, the linguistic and intellectual tools to cope with complexity, to separate illusion from reality. We have traded the printed word for the gleaming image. Public rhetoric is designed to be comprehensible to a ten-year-old child or an adult with a sixth-grade reading level. Most of us speak at this level, are entertained and think at this level. We have transformed our culture into a vast replica of Pinocchio's Pleasure Island, where boys were lured with the promise of no school and endless fun. They were all, however, turned into donkeys—a symbol, in Italian culture, of ignorance and stupidity.

Functional illiteracy in North America is epidemic. There are 7 million illiterate Americans. Another 27 million are unable to read well enough to complete a job application, and 30 million can't read a simple sentence.[24] There are some 50 million who read at a fourth- or fifth-grade level. Nearly a third of the nation's population is illiterate or barely literate—a figure that is growing by more than 2 million a year. A third of high-school graduates never read another book for the rest of their lives, and neither do 42 percent of college graduates. In 2007, 80 percent of the families in the United States did not buy or read a book.[25] And it is not much better beyond our borders. Canada has an illiterate and semiliterate population estimated at 42 percent of the whole, a proportion that mirrors that of the United States.[26]

Television, a medium built around the skillful manipulation of images, ones that can overpower reality, is our primary form of mass communication. A television is turned on for six hours and forty-seven minutes a day in the average household. The average American daily watches more than four hours of television. That amounts to twenty-eight hours a week, or two months of uninterrupted television-watching a year. That same person will have spent nine years in front of a television by the time he or she is sixty-five. Television speaks in a language of familiar, comforting clichés and exciting images. Its format, from reality shows to sit-coms, is predictable. It provides a mass, virtual experience that colors the way many people speak and interact with one another. It creates a false sense of intimacy with our elite—celebrity actors, newspeople, politicians, business tycoons, and sports stars. And everything and everyone that television transmits is validated and enhanced by the medium. If a person is not seen on television, on some level he or she is not important. Television confers authority and power. It is the final arbitrator for what matters in life.

Hour after hour, day after day, week after week, we are bombarded with the cant and spectacle pumped out over the airwaves or over computer screens by highly-paid pundits, corporate advertisers, talk-show hosts, and gossip-fueled entertainment networks. And a culture dominated by images and slogans seduces those who are functionally literate but who make the choice not to read. There have been other historical periods with high rates of illiteracy and vast propaganda campaigns. But not since the Soviet and fascist dictatorships, and perhaps the brutal authoritarian control of the Catholic Church in the Middle Ages, has the content of information been as skillfully and ruthlessly controlled and manipulated. Propaganda has become a substitute for ideas and ideology. Knowledge is confused with how we are made to feel. Commercial brands are mistaken for expressions of individuality. And in this precipitous decline of values and literacy, among those who cannot read and those who have given up reading, fertile ground for a new totalitarianism is being seeded.

The culture of illusion thrives by robbing us of the intellectual and linguistic tools to separate illusion from truth. It reduces us to the level and dependency of children. It impoverishes language. The *Princeton Review* analyzed the transcripts of the Gore-Bush debates of 2000, the Clinton-Bush-Perot debates of 1992, the Kennedy-Nixon debate of 1960, and the Lincoln-Douglas debates of 1858. It reviewed these transcripts using a standard vocabulary test that indicates the minimum educational standard needed for a reader to grasp the text. In the Lincoln-Douglas debates, Lincoln spoke at the educational level of an eleventh grader (11.2), and Douglas addressed the crowd using a vocabulary suitable (12.0) for a high-school graduate. In the Kennedy-Nixon debate, the candidates spoke in language accessible to tenth graders. In the 1992 debates, Clinton spoke at a seventh-grade level (7.6), while Bush spoke at a sixth-grade level (6.8), as did Perot (6.3). During the 2000 debates, Bush spoke at a sixth-grade level (6.7) and Gore at a high seventh-grade level (7.6).[27] This obvious decline was, perhaps, raised slightly by Barack Obama in 2008, but the trends above are clear.

Those captive to images cast ballots based on how candidates make them feel. They vote for a slogan, a smile, perceived sincerity, and attractiveness, along with the carefully crafted personal narrative of the candidate. It is style and story, not content and fact, that inform mass politics. Politicians have learned that to get votes they must replicate the faux intimacy established between celebrities and the public. There has to be a sense, created through artful theatrical staging and scripting by political spin machines, that the politician is "one of us." The politician, like the celebrity, has to give voters the impression that he or she, as Bill Clinton used to say, feels their pain. We have to be able to see ourselves in them. If this connection, invariably a product of extremely sophisticated artifice, is not established, no politician can get any traction in a celebrity culture.

The rhetoric in campaigns eschews reality for the illusive promise of the future and the intrinsic greatness of the nation. Campaigns have a deadening sameness, the same tired clichés, the concerned expressions of the sensitive candidates who are like you and me, and the gushing words of gratitude to the crowds of supporters. The metaphors are not empty. They say something about us and our culture. Changes in metaphors are, as the critic Northrop Frye understood, *fundamental* changes.

"Are we going to look forward," asked candidate Obama at an "American Jobs Tour" rally in Columbus, Ohio, on October 10, 2008, "or are we going to look backwards?"

> AUDIENCE: Forward!
> OBAMA: Are we going to look forward with hope, or are we going to look backwards with fear?
> AUDIENCE: Hope! Forward!
> OBAMA: Ohio, if you are willing to organize with me, if you are willing to go vote right now—we've got—you could go to the

early voting right across the street, right on—right there.
[Cheers and applause.] If every one of you are willing to grab
your friends and your neighbors and make the phone calls and
do what's required, I guarantee you we will not just win Ohio,
we will win this general election. And you and I together, we will
change this country and we will change the world. [Cheers and
applause.] God bless you. God bless the United States of America. [Cheers and applause.]

Celebrity culture has bequeathed to us what Benjamin DeMott calls
"junk politics." Junk politics does not demand justice or the reparation
of rights. It personalizes and moralizes issues rather than clarifying
them. "It's impatient with articulated conflict, enthusiastic about
America's optimism and moral character, and heavily dependent on
feel-your-pain language and gesture," DeMott notes. The result of junk
politics is that nothing changes—"meaning zero interruption in the
processes and practices that strengthen existing, interlocking systems
of socioeconomic advantage." It redefines traditional values, tilting
"courage toward braggadocio, sympathy toward mawkishness, humility toward self-disrespect, identification with ordinary citizens toward
distrust of brains." Junk politics "miniaturizes large, complex problems
at home while maximizing threats from abroad. It's also given to
abrupt, unexplained reversals of its own public stances, often spectacu-
larly bloating problems previously miniaturized." And finally, it "seeks
at every turn to obliterate voters' consciousness of socioeconomic and
other differences in their midst."[28] Politics has become a product of a
diseased culture that seeks its purpose in celebrities who are, as
Boorstin wrote, "receptacles into which we pour our own purposeless-
ness. They are nothing but ourselves seen in a magnifying mirror."[29]

Those captivated by the cult of celebrity do not examine voting
records or compare verbal claims with written and published facts and
reports. The reality of their world is whatever the latest cable news
show, political leader, advertiser, or loan officer says is reality. The illiterate, the semiliterate, and those who live as though they are illiterate
are effectively cut off from the past. They live in an eternal present.
They do not understand the predatory loan deals that drive them into
foreclosure and bankruptcy. They cannot decipher the fine print on the

credit card agreements that plunge them into unmanageable debt. They repeat thought-terminating clichés and slogans. They are hostage to the constant jingle and manipulation of a consumer culture. They seek refuge in familiar brands and labels. They eat at fast-food restaurants not only because it is cheap, but also because they can order from pictures rather than from a menu. And those who serve them, also often semiliterate or illiterate, punch in orders on cash registers whose keys are usually marked with pictures. Life is a state of permanent amnesia, a world in search of new forms of escapism and quick, sensual gratification.

Celebrity images are reflections of our idealized selves sold back to us. Yet they actually constrain rather than expand our horizons and experiences. "One of the deepest and least remarked features of the Age of Contrivance is what I would call the mirror effect," Boorstin wrote.

> Nearly everything we do to enlarge our world, to make life more interesting, more varied, more exciting, more vivid, more "fabulous," more promising, in the long run has an opposite effect. In the extravagance of our expectations and in our ever increasing power, we transform elusive dreams into graspable images within with each of us can fit. By doing so we mark the boundaries of our world with a wall of mirrors. Our strenuous and elaborate efforts to enlarge experience have the unintended result of narrowing it. In frenetic quest for the unexpected, we end by finding only the unexpectedness we have planned for ourselves. We meet ourselves coming back.[30]

The most essential skill in political theater and a consumer culture is artifice. Political leaders, who use the tools of mass propaganda to create a sense of faux intimacy with citizens, no longer need to be competent, sincere, or honest. They need only to appear to have these qualities. Most of all they need a story, a personal narrative. The reality of the narrative is irrelevant. It can be completely at odds with the facts. The consistency and emotional appeal of the story are paramount. Those who are best at deception succeed. Those who have not mastered the art of entertainment, who fail to create a narrative or do not have one fashioned for them by their handlers, are ignored. They become "unreal."

An image-based culture communicates through narratives, pictures, and pseudo-drama. Scandalous affairs, hurricanes, untimely deaths, train wrecks—these events play well on computer screens and television. International diplomacy, labor union negotiations, and convoluted bailout packages do not yield exciting personal narratives or stimulating images. A governor who patronizes call girls becomes a huge news story. A politician who proposes serious regulatory reform or advocates curbing wasteful spending is boring. Kings, queens, and emperors once used their court conspiracies to divert their subjects. Today cinematic, political, and journalistic celebrities distract us with their personal foibles and scandals. They create our public mythology. Acting, politics, and sports have become, as they were in Nero's reign, interchangeable. In an age of images and entertainment, in an age of instant emotional gratification, we neither seek nor want honesty or reality. Reality is complicated. Reality is boring. We are incapable or unwilling to handle its confusion. We ask to be indulged and comforted by clichés, stereotypes, and inspirational messages that tell us we can be whoever we seek to be, that we live in the greatest country on earth, that we are endowed with superior moral and physical qualities, and that our future will always be glorious and prosperous, either because of our own attributes or our national character or because we are blessed by God. In this world, all that matters is the consistency of our belief systems. The ability to amplify lies, to repeat them and have surrogates repeat them in endless loops of news cycles, gives lies and mythical narratives the aura of uncontested truth. We become trapped in the linguistic prison of incessant repetition. We are fed words and phrases like *war on terror* or *pro-life* or *change*, and within these narrow parameters, all complex thought, ambiguity, and self-criticism vanish.

"Entertainment was an expression of democracy, throwing off the chains of alleged cultural repression," Gabler wrote. "So too was consumption, throwing off the chains of the old production-oriented culture and allowing anyone to buy his way into his fantasy. And, in the end, both entertainment and consumption often provided the same intoxication: the sheer, endless pleasure of emancipation from reason, from responsibility, from tradition, from class, and from all the other bonds that restrained the self."[31]

When a nation becomes unmoored from reality, it retreats into a world of magic. Facts are accepted or discarded according to the dictates of a preordained cosmology. The search for truth becomes irrelevant. Our national discourse is dominated by manufactured events, from celebrity gossip to staged showcasings of politicians to elaborate entertainment and athletic spectacles. All are sold to us through the detailed personal narratives of those we watch. "The pseudo-events which flood our consciousness are neither true nor false in the old familiar senses," Boorstin wrote. "The very same advances which have made them possible have also made the images—however planned, contrived, or distorted—more vivid, more attractive, more impressive, and more persuasive than reality itself."[32]

In his book *Public Opinion*, Walter Lippmann distinguished between "the world outside and the pictures in our heads." He defined a "stereotype" as an oversimplified pattern that helps us find meaning in the world. Lippmann cited examples of the crude "stereotypes we carry about in our heads" of whole groups of people such as "Germans," "South Europeans," "Negroes," "Harvard men," "agitators," and others. These stereotypes, Lippmann noted, give a reassuring and false consistency to the chaos of existence. They offer easily grasped explanations of reality and are closer, as Boorstin noted, to propaganda because they simplify rather than complicate.[33]

Pseudo-events, dramatic productions orchestrated by publicists, political machines, television, Hollywood, or advertisers, however, are very different. They have the capacity to appear real, even though we know they are staged. They are capable because they can evoke a powerful emotional response of overwhelming reality and replacing it with a fictional narrative that often becomes accepted as truth. The power of pseudo-events to overtake reality was what plunged the marines who returned from Iwo Jima into such despair. The unmasking of a stereotype damages and often destroys its credibility. But pseudo-events are immune to this deflation. The exposure of the elaborate mechanisms behind the pseudo-event only adds to its fascination and its power. This is the basis of the convoluted television reporting on how effectively political campaigns and candidates have been stage-managed. Reporters, especially those on television, no longer ask whether the message is true but rather whether the pseudo-event worked or did not work as political theater. Pseudo-events are judged on how effectively we have been manipulated by illusion. Those events that appear real are relished and lauded. Those that fail to create a believable illusion are deemed failures. Truth is irrelevant. Those who succeed in politics, as in most of the culture, are those who create the most convincing fantasies.

A public that can no longer distinguish between truth and fiction is left to interpret reality through illusion. Random facts or obscure bits of data and trivia are used either to bolster illusion and give it credibility, or discarded if they interfere with the message. The worse reality becomes—the more, for example, foreclosures and unemployment sky-rocket—the more people seek refuge and comfort in illusions. When opinions cannot be distinguished from facts, when there is no universal standard to determine truth in law, in science, in scholarship, or in reporting the events of the day, when the most valued skill is the ability to entertain, the world becomes a place where lies become true, where people can believe what they want to believe. This is the real danger of pseudo-events and why pseudo-events are far more pernicious than stereotypes. They do not explain reality, as stereotypes attempt to, but replace reality. Pseudo-events redefine reality by the parameters set by their creators. These creators, who make massive profits selling illusions, have a vested interest in maintaining the power structures they control.

The old production-oriented culture demanded what the historian Warren Susman termed character. The new consumption-oriented culture demands what he called personality. The shift in values is a shift from a fixed morality to the artifice of presentation. The old cultural values of thrift and moderation honored hard work, integrity, and courage. The consumption-oriented culture honors charm, fascination, and likeability. "The social role demanded of all in the new culture of personality was that of a performer," Susman wrote. "Every American was to become a performing self."[34]

Totalitarian systems begin as propagandistic movements that ostensibly teach people to "believe what they want," but that is a ruse. The Christian Right, for example, argues that it wants Intelligent Design, or creationism, to be offered as an alternative to evolution in public-school biology classes. But once you allow creationism, which no reputable biologist or paleontologist accepts as legitimate science, to be considered as an alternative to real science, you begin the deadly assault against dispassionate, honest, intellectual inquiry. Step into the hermetic world of many Christian schools or colleges and there are no alternatives to creationism offered to students. Once these systems have control, the Christian advocates' purported love of alternative viewpoints and debates is replaced by an iron and irrational conformity to illusion.

Pseudo-events, which create their own semblance of reality, serve in the wider culture the same role creationism serves for the Christian Right. Pseudo-events destabilize truth. They are convincing enough and appear real enough to manufacture their own facts. We carry within us feelings and perceptions about politicians, celebrities, our nation, and our culture that are mirages generated by pseudo-events. The use of pseudo-events to persuade rather than overtly brainwash renders millions of us unable to see or question the structures and systems that are impoverishing us and in some cases destroying our lives. The flight into illusion sweeps away the core values of the open society. It corrodes the ability to think for oneself, to draw independent conclusions, to express dissent when judgment and common sense tell you something is wrong, to be self-critical, to challenge authority, to grasp historical facts, to advocate for change, and to acknowledge that there are other views, different ways, and structures of being that are morally and socially acceptable. A populace deprived of the ability to separate lies from truth, that has become hostage to the fictional semblance of reality put forth by pseudo-events, is no longer capable of sustaining a free society.

Those who slip into this illusion ignore the signs of impending disaster. The physical degradation of the planet, the cruelty of global capitalism, the looming oil crisis, the collapse of financial markets, and the danger of overpopulation rarely impinge to prick the illusions that warp our consciousness,. The words, images, stories, and phrases used to describe the world in pseudo-events have no relation to what is happening around us. The advances of technology and science, rather than obliterating the world of myth, have enhanced its power to deceive. We live in imaginary, virtual worlds created by corporations that profit from our deception. Products and experiences—indeed, experience *as* a product—offered up for sale, sanctified by celebrities, are mirages. They promise us a new personality. They promise us success and fame. They promise to mend our brokenness.

"People whose governing habit is the relinquishment of power, competence, and responsibility, and whose characteristic suffering is the anxiety of futility, make excellent spenders," wrote Wendell Berry in *The Unsettling of America*. "They are the ideal consumers. By inducing in them little panics of boredom, powerlessness, sexual failure, mortality, paranoia, they can be made to buy (or vote for) virtually anything that is 'attractively packaged.'"[35] And there are no shortages of experiences and products that, for a price, promise to stimulate us, make us powerful, sexy, invincible, admired, beautiful, and unique.

Blind faith in illusions is our culture's secular version of being born again. These illusions assure us that happiness and success is our birthright. They tell us that our catastrophic collapse is not permanent. They promise that pain and suffering can always be overcome by tapping into our hidden, inner strengths. They encourage us to bow down before the cult of the self. To confront these illusions, to puncture their mendacity by exposing the callousness and cruelty of the corporate state, signals a loss of faith. It is to become an apostate. The culture of illusion, one of happy thoughts, manipulated emotions, and trust in the beneficence of power, means we sing along with the chorus or are instantly disappeared from view like the losers on a reality show.

II / The Illusion of Love

Capitalism is not wicked or cruel when the commodity is the whore; profit is not wicked or cruel when the alienated worker is a female piece of meat; corporate bloodsucking is not wicked or cruel when the corporations in question, organized crime syndicates, sell cunt; racism is not wicked or cruel when the black cunt or yellow cunt or red cunt or Hispanic cunt or Jewish cunt has her legs splayed for any man's pleasure; poverty is not wicked or cruel when it is the poverty of dispossessed women who have only themselves to sell; violence by the powerful against the powerless is not wicked or cruel when it is called sex; slavery is not wicked or cruel when it is sexual slavery; torture is not wicked or cruel when the tormented are women, whores, cunts. The new pornography is left-wing; and the new pornography is a vast graveyard where the Left has gone to die. The Left cannot have its whores and its politics too.

—Andrea Dworkin, *Pornography: Men Possessing Women*

THE PINK CROSS BOOTH has a table of anti-porn tracts and is set up in the far corner of the Sands Expo convention center in Las Vegas. It is an unlikely participant at the annual Adult Video News (AVN) expo. Pink Cross is a Christian outreach program for women in the porn industry, run by ex-porn star Shelley Lubben.

In a convention exalting the pornography industry, Lubben's table is not overrun with visitors, most of whom are male and middle-aged with cameras around their necks. The few men who make it to the far corner of the convention center look curiously at its pink banner and walk past. The expo is filled with more alluring fare. There are numerous booths for porn producers and distributors, many with women in tiny skirts and bras who, often clinging to stripper poles, gyrate and bend over and spread their legs for groups of men. They simulate masturbation and flash their breasts for crowds of onlookers. Huge banners hang from the ceiling promoting new releases such as *Anal Buffet*, *Fetish Fuck Dolls*, *Gangbang My Face 3*, *Fuck Slaves 3*, *Milk Nymphos 2*, and *Slutty and Sluttier 6*.

A local escort service, VegasGirls, has a booth about a hundred feet from Pink Cross. There is a homemade wooden wheel with a flipper that looks like a middle-school shop project on its table. Those who spin the wheel can get various discounts or even a free visit by a "stripper" to their hotel room. Small, glossy cards are fanned out on the table, showing women in evocative poses and not much clothing, all with a first name, the agency's phone number, and the phrase *actual photo* emblazoned on the side of the card.

"You want to take a picture of my boobs, then you have to take my card," a woman in front of the booth tells a camera-wielding, middle-aged man.

"If I call this number, is it you who will come?" he asks.

"Here, baby," she says, giving him the card. "I will come."

Many of the booths at the Sands Expo feature well-known porn stars. There are long lines of men waiting for a signed photo and the chance to have a picture with stars from the Wicked Pictures studio, including Kaylani Lei, Kirsten Price, and Jessica Drake. The men usually wrap their arms around the women for the photo, always taken by a friend or someone in line. As they hug the women's waists, the women sometimes playfully grab the man's crotch or lick their lips. Huge plasma screens placed in the booths run nonstop porn, often featuring the stars having anal sex with multiple partners or giving blow jobs. The sheer volume of porn blasted throughout the convention floor by the sea of giant screens becomes, very quickly, numbing.

The porn films are not about sex. Sex is airbrushed and digitally washed out of the films. There is no acting because none of the women are permitted to have what amounts to a personality. The one emotion they are allowed to display is an unquenchable desire to satisfy men, especially if that desire involves the women's physical and emotional degradation. The lighting in the films is harsh and clinical. Pubic hair is shaved off to give the women the look of young girls or rubber dolls. Porn, which advertises itself as sex, is a bizarre, bleached pantomime of sex. The acts onscreen are beyond human endurance. The scenarios are absurd. The manicured and groomed bodies, the huge artificial breasts, the pouting, oversized lips, the erections that never go down, and the sculpted bodies are unreal. Makeup and production mask blemishes. There are no beads of sweat, no wrinkle lines, no human imperfections. Sex is reduced to a narrow spectrum of sterilized dimensions. It does not include the dank smell of human bodies, the thump of a pulse, taste, breath—or tenderness. Those in the films are puppets, packaged female commodities. They have no honest emotions, are devoid of authentic human beauty, and resemble plastic. Pornography does not promote sex, if one defines sex as a shared act between two partners. It promotes masturbation. It promotes the solitary auto-arousal that precludes intimacy and love. Pornography is about getting yourself off at someone else's expense.

"I was addicted to porn for two years," says Scott Smith, twenty-nine, from Cleveland, Tennessee, who is at the Pink Cross booth. He first watched Internet porn as a college student.

"I started out once a day, usually at night, when my roommate wasn't there," Smith says. "You try and hide it. Then I started watching it several times a day. I would only watch it long enough to masturbate. I never got why they make these long features since I would always turn it off when I was done."

Smith says the images crippled his ability to be intimate. He could not distinguish between the fantasy of porn and the reality of relationships. "Porn messes with the way you think of women," he says. "You want the women you are with to be like the women in porn. I was scared to get involved in a relationship. I did not know how extensive the damage was. I did not want to hurt anyone. I kept away from women."

There are some 13,000 porn films made every year in the United States, most in the San Fernando Valley in California. According to the Internet Filter Review, worldwide porn revenues, including in-room movies at hotels, sex clubs, and the ever-expanding e-sex world, topped $97 billion in 2006. That is more than the revenues of Microsoft, Google, Amazon, eBay, Yahoo!, Apple, Netflix, and EarthLink combined. Annual sales in the United States are estimated at $10 billion or higher. There is no precise monitoring of the porn industry. And porn is very lucrative to some of the nation's largest corporations. General Motors owns DIRECTV, which distributes more than 40 million streams of porn into American homes every month. AT&T Broadband and Comcast Cable are currently the biggest American companies accommodating porn users with the Hot Network, Adult Pay Per View, and similarly themed services. AT&T and GM rake in approximately 80 percent of all porn dollars spent by consumers.

The largest users of Internet porn are between the ages of twelve and seventeen. And porn producers increasingly target adolescents. "The age demographic has moved downwards, especially in the UK and Europe," explained Steve Honest, the European director of production for Bluebird Films. "Porn is the new rock and roll. Young people and women are embracing porn and making purchases. Porn targets the mid-teens to the mid-twenties and up."

Patrice Roldan, twenty-six, with black hair and a loose-fitting purple and black potato sack dress, is standing next to the Pink Cross table. Roldan, whose screen name was Nadia Styles, made her last porn film in November 2008. She starred in nearly two hundred films, including *Lord of Asses*, *Anal Girls Next Door*, *Monster Cock Fuckfest 9*, *Deep Throat Anal*, *Trophy Whores*, and *Young Dumb & Covered in Cum*. She is five feet, five inches, 110 pounds, and wears a black scarf around her neck, black knitted stockings with knee-high black socks, and flat, black shoes. Her outfit seems calculated to be exactly what a porn star should never wear in public. She looks like a schoolteacher.

Roldan, like many of the women who drift into the porn and prostitution industry, had a difficult and troubled childhood, including a physically abusive mother. Her mother threw her out of her home when she was seventeen, and she spent time in homeless shelters. She answered an ad in *LA Weekly* that offered women $1,000 as models.

This is a common doorway into the porn industry. She started appearing in Internet porn. She had a boyfriend when she began filming and tells me she "felt guilty" about hiding her porn sessions from him, but the money was good. Her boyfriend eventually found out, and their relationship descended into one increasingly characterized by verbal and physical abuse. She drifted from the Internet into films. She was nineteen when she made her first film.

"Doing a movie shoot was a different experience," she says as we sit in two folding chairs across from the Pink Cross booth. "I made my first film with New Sensations [adult video studio]. I got makeup. There was a set and cameramen all around. I thought it was glamorous to have my makeup done, to have pictures taken of me. That was a regular boy-girl shoot. At that point, I was just trying to survive."

She had been promised $1,000 for her first film. She was handed $600 when the scene was done. She also contracted gonorrhea. Porn stars are tested for HIV and sexually transmitted diseases once a month, but "people do so many scenes between tests that a month is a long time." She began, once she had treated her gonorrhea, to do films three or four times a month. She would have several more bouts with gonorrhea and other sexually transmitted diseases during her career. She got pregnant and had an abortion. The demands on her began to escalate. She was filmed with multiple partners. Her scenes became "extremely rough. They would pull my hair, slap me around like a rag doll."

"The next day my whole body would ache," she recalls. "It happened a lot, the aching. It used to be that only a few stars, people like Linda Lovelace, would once do things like anal. Now it is expected."

She became a staple in "gonzo" porn films. Gonzo movies are usually filmed in a house or hotel room. They are porn verité. The performers often acknowledge the camera and speak to it. Gonzo films push the boundaries of porn and often include a lot of violence, physical abuse, and a huge number of partners in succession. According to the magazine *Adult Video News*, "Gonzo, non-feature fare is the overwhelmingly dominant porn genre since it's less expensive to produce than plot-oriented features, but just as importantly, is the fare of choice for the solo stroking consumer who merely wants to cut to the chase, get off on the good stuff, then, if they really wanna catch some acting, plot, and dialog, pop in the latest Netflix disc."[1]

Roldan would endure numerous anal penetrations by various men in a shoot, most of them "super-rough." She would have one man in her anus and one in her vagina while she gave a blow job to a third man. The men would ejaculate on her face. She was repeatedly "face-fucked," with men forcing their cocks violently in and out of her mouth. She did what in industry shorthand is called "ATM," ass-to-mouth, where a man pulls his penis from her anus and puts it directly in her mouth.

As she talks of her career in porn, her eyes take on a dead, faraway look. Her breathing becomes more rapid. She slips into a flat, numbing monotone. The symptoms are ones I know well from interviewing victims of atrocities in war who battle post-traumatic stress disorder.

"What you are describing is trauma," I say.

"Yes," she answers quietly.

Shelley Lubben, who also worked as a porn actress, agrees.

"You have to do what they want on the sets," she says. "There's too much competition. They can always find other girls. Girls bring in their friends and get kickbacks. They feel like stars. They get attention. It's all about the spotlight. It's all about me. They have notoriety. They don't realize the degradation. Besides, this is a whole generation raised on porn. They're jaded and don't even ask if it is wrong. They fall into it. They get into drugs to numb themselves. They get their asses ripped. Their uterus hemorrhages. They get HPV and herpes, and they turn themselves off emotionally and die. They check out mentally. They get PTSD like Vietnam vets. They don't know who they are. They live a life of shopping and drugs. They don't buy real estate. They party, and in the end they have nothing to show for it except, like me, genital herpes and fake boobs."

"Porn is like any other addiction," Lubben says. "First, you are curious. Then you need harder and harder drugs to get off. You need gang bangs and bestiality and child porn. Porn gets grosser and grosser. We never did ass-to-mouth when I was in the industry. Now you get an award for it. And meanwhile the addicts make their wives feel like they can't live up to the illusion of the porn star. The addict asks, 'Why can't she give blow jobs like a porn star?' He wants what isn't real. Porn destroys intimacy. I can always tell if a man is a porn addict. They're shut down. They can't look me in the eyes. They can't be intimate."

"When legal and social mores first changed and porn went mainstream in the 1970s, there was a standard sexual script, which included oral and vaginal sex, with anal sex relatively rare, ending with the 'money' or 'come' shot, where the man ejaculated onto the body of the woman," Robert Jensen, the author of *Getting Off: Pornography and the End of Masculinity*, tells me over breakfast one Saturday morning at my home in Princeton. "But once there were thousands of porn films on the market, the porn industry had to expand that script to expand profits. It had to find new emotional thrills. It could have explored intimacy, love, the connection between two people, but this was not what appealed to the largely male audience. Instead, the industry focused on greater male control and cruelty. This started in the 1980s, with anal sex as a way for men to dominate women. It has descended to multiple penetrations, double anals, gagging, and other forms of physical and psychological degradation.

"What does it say about our culture that cruelty is so easy to market?" Jensen asks. "What is the difference between glorifying violence in war and glorifying the violence of sexual domination? I think that the reason porn is so difficult for so many people to discuss is not that it is about sex—our culture is saturated in sex. The reason it is difficult is that porn exposes something very uncomfortable about us. We accept a culture flooded with images of women who are sexual commodities. Increasingly, women in pornography are not people having sex but bodies upon which sexual activities of increasing cruelty are played out. And many men—maybe a majority of men—like it."

The cruelty takes a toll on the bodies, as well as the emotions, of porn actresses. Many suffer severe repeated vaginal and anal tears that require surgery. And there are some women porn stars, such as Jenna Jameson, who, once they are established, refuse to do scenes with men and are filmed only with other women. But few actresses in the industry are able to achieve this kind of control. Roldan, like most of the women, did not eat on nights before she was filmed. She flushed out her system with enemas and laxatives. "I would starve myself," she says, "so I wouldn't have to suck on my shit. The worst was when it came out of another girl and it was not clean and you had to do it."

"I could not go to the bathroom," she says. "I became a vegetarian and still couldn't go. I took enemas and laxatives. I got colonics where they would fill me up with water and flush everything out. Sometimes my butt would stay wide open for days. It was scary."

The male stars are encouraged to be rough and hostile. Some, she says, "hated women. They would spit in my face. I was devastated the first time that happened, but I thought it was good they were rough because of my abusive relationships. I thought roughness in porn was OK. I would say, 'Treat me like a little slut,' or 'I'm your bitch,' or 'Fuck me like a whore.' I would say the most degrading things I could say about myself because I thought this was what it meant to be sexy and what people wanted to hear, or at least the people who buy the films. You are just a slut to those who watch. You are nothing. They want to see that we know that."

She would shoot scenes with men who disgusted her, whose sweat and smell "made me cringe." And when the lights went off and the cameras stopped, she would stumble off the set in pain, her face often covered with semen. "Sometimes they would hand you a paper towel to wipe your face off," she says, "and sometimes they would say, 'Don't touch us. You're gross.' I remember the first time I had come all over my face. I was so pissed off, but I took it. I pretended to like everything they did. I took pride in being a good gonzo girl. My fame came from this."

By the second year of shooting, with an income of $100,000, she had turned to drugs, including painkillers and muscle relaxants.

"The lifestyle of a porn star is to spend your money as soon as you make it on weed, alcohol, coke, ecstasy, and Vicodin," Roldan says. "I wanted to be the good gonzo girl they wanted me to be. I took this so I would not feel anything. By the next year, instead of only Vicodin I began to drink vodka, a whole bottle. Every girl I knew used alcohol. We were drinking so we did not feel the pain, physically and emotionally. I remember driving home thinking, 'I could be stopped for DWI.'"

Roldan usually socialized with other porn stars, whom she and everyone in the industry call "girls." They often spent their days drinking. "Most are very lonely," she says. She longed for a relationship, "but it felt weird to have a boyfriend."

Adult video companies such as JM Productions and Extreme Associates, which includes graphic rape scenes in its array of physical abuse of women, make no attempt to hide the pain and acute discomfort endured by the women. The pain and discomfort are the major draws of the productions. JM Productions pioneered "aggressive throat-fucking" videos such as the *Gag Factor* series, in which women have penises pushed all the way down their throats until they gag or vomit. On the *Gag Factor* Web site, the producers promise "The best throat-fucking ever lensed." It offers still shots of women being "face-fucked." One typical description of a film begins with the standard brief summary, as if the women were criminals with a rap sheet: "Degraded On: 10/8/08. Name: Ashley Blue . . . Age: twenty-five. Status: Happy? Home Town: Thousand Oaks, CA." It shows a picture of a woman with black hair lying on her back with her eyes closed. Her face is covered with semen and a penis is buried in her throat.

"Here's Your Retirement Party," the description of the film reads. "As many of you will remember, for quite a long time superwhore Ashley Blue was the official JM contract whore. But like the sole of an old shoe, porn whores eventually wear out and have to be thrown away. So, our way of throwing a retirement party for Ashley was to have her head get pistonfucked one last time. Enjoy!"[2]

Las Vegas, a city built on illusions, lends itself to the celebration of porn. It is the corrupt, wilfully degenerate heart of America. It is, in Marc Cooper's memorable phrase, The Last Honest Place in America. Las Vegas strips away the thin moral pretension and hypocrisy of consumer society to reveal its essence. The commodification of human beings, the heart of the consumer society, is garishly celebrated in Las Vegas. Here there is no past, no history, no sense of continuity, and no real community. The mammoth resorts and casinos glittering in the desert are monuments to greed and vice, even as the rest of the country crumbles under the onslaught of physical decay, shuttered stores and factories, a disintegrating infrastructure, and mounting poverty.

Las Vegas is the city of spectacle. The Treasure Island Casino has an hourly pirate battle with two clipper ships, smoke-filled cannons, and scantily clad female pirates in a fake lagoon. Tourists can visit the New York-New York Hotel & Casino and take in a replica of the city's skyline. They can go to the Venetian, board gondolas, and be poled down indoor copies of the Venice canals by aspiring opera singers. They can watch the pathetic eruption of the belching man-made volcano and the rubberized trees in the "rain forest" of the lobby of the Mirage. They can eat in a replica of a French bistro called Mon Ami Gabi, under the shadow of a half-size copy of the Eiffel Tower.

Mon Ami Gabi, where I went one day for lunch in the forlorn hope of escaping the ugliness and noise of the Strip, has waiters in black vests, white shirts, black bow ties, and long, white aprons. But, like the rest of Las Vegas, the exotic is only a veneer. The menu offers hamburgers, sandwiches, waffles, and, in what I suppose is a concession to France, French toast. Diners at the bistro look out on Caesars Palace, where Roman statues speak, although not in Latin, in Caesar's Forum. It is a short walk to diminished copies of the Giza pyramids at the Luxor.

Las Vegas sells a cartoon version of other cultures and other lands. It is a monument to pseudo-events. It is a place where stereotypes can be experienced as reality. The guts and sinews of every theme-park hotel and casino, however, hold the same, mind-numbing slot machines, roulette wheels, and blackjack tables. A trip to Las Vegas is a visit to a sanitized, cutout version of foreign countries without the intrusion of foreign people, the hassle of unintelligible languages, strange habits, different ideas and traditions, or bizarre food. Here everyone speaks English. Here you are surrounded by Americans. Here, once you get past the façade, it is all the same. There is always beer on tap and hamburgers. The chaos of the real world, of other cultures and ways of being, is purged and made tidy, easy, and accessible. But it is all a game. New York-New York will part you from your money as efficiently as the Luxor. And that is the point. It is all about taking your money, and when the money runs out, you might as well not exist. Las Vegas, unlike the rest of the culture, is brutally honest about its exploitation.

Las Vegas speaks in the comforting epistemology of television. Many of the slot machines have movie and television themes with audio voices of characters from the *Austin Powers* movies, *I Love Lucy*, or *The Price is Right* cheering on the slack-jawed, glazed-eyed customers who repeatedly pull the lever, or, increasingly, push a button, to set off the whirl of icons. In Las Vegas the illusion of the exotic overlies the banal comfort of the safe and familiar. In a nation where less than 10 percent of the population has a passport, how many Americans can tell the difference between the illusion of France and the reality of France? How many can differentiate between Egypt and the illusion of Egypt? How many care?

Las Vegas should, as Neil Postman observed in his 1985 book *Amusing Ourselves to Death,* be considered the "symbolic capital" of America. "At different times in our history," Postman wrote, "different cities have been the focal point of a radiating American spirit. In the late eighteenth century, for example, Boston was the center of a political radicalism that ignited a shot heard round the world—a shot that could not have been fired any other place but the suburbs of Boston." In the mid-nineteenth century, "New York became the symbol of a melting pot America." In the early twentieth century, Chicago, "the city of big shoulders and heavy winds, came to symbolize the industrial energy and dynamism of America. If there is a statue of a hog butcher somewhere in Chicago, then it stands as a reminder of the time when America was railroads, cattle, steel mills, and entrepreneurial adventures."

"Today," Postman concluded,

> we must look to the city of Las Vegas, Nevada, as a metaphor of our national character and aspiration, its symbol a thirty-foot high cardboard picture of a slot machine and a chorus girl. For Las Vegas is a city entirely devoted to the idea of entertainment, and as such proclaims the spirit of a culture in which all public discourse increasingly takes the form of entertainment. Our politics, our religion, news, athletics, education, and commerce have been transformed into congenial adjuncts of show business, largely without protest or even much popular notice.[3]

The Las Vegas Strip is a monument to our nation's cult of eternal childishness. It plays off of our fear of growing up. In Marc Cooper's portrait of Las Vegas, *The Last Honest Place in America*, he wrote:

> In a television-marinated society in which the boundaries between childhood and adulthood have been blurred if not erased, increasingly and dismayingly, children and adults dress the same, eat the same, and often talk the same, where they certainly endlessly watch

the same TV shows, where simulation is often valued over authenticity (look no further than the acrobatic contrivances of so-called "reality TV" or the reclassification of steel and concrete hotels into "scenery"), it should come as little surprise that the phony lava eruption and the staged pirate-show next door should bring equal glee to the ten-year-olds *and* their parents. Add to that a certain solace Americans find in the worship of technology, even technology at this infantile level, and the Strip begins to make perfect sense.[4]

Porn films frequently build their themes around reality shows or popular sitcoms. I stand at the AVN expo in front of a display where the newest release is called *I'm Dreaming of Genie*. The company has also filmed *Paris and Nicole Go to Jail* and *Getting It Up with the Kardassians*. Jessica Lynn, twenty-three, plays the role of the porn Genie and for the convention is dressed in a replica of the television character's costume.

"I usually do whatever I want and think later," she says. "I won't do anal yet. I basically do boy-girl, girl-girl." She does do ATM, although she says, "I don't like to. There are a lot of infections." She says she can climax on the set, something most ex-porn actresses, including Lubben, insist never happens. "I can come if there is a vibrator." She says her parents recently discovered what she is doing and have asked her to get out of the industry. She has a boyfriend, whom she later calls her husband, who "is cool with it," and she says she sometimes "brings girls home for him." "I love watching my husband fuck other girls, watching him make her feel good." She has been in scenes, she said, that "got too violent and rough and one where one of the men began to eat his own come." She said she is saving money for college and has stayed away from drugs. "A lot of girls have breakdowns," she says. "They call me. I have had numerous calls. They are freaking out about their life and they are usually on drugs."

Jeff Thrill, who uses the pen name of Roger Krypton, writes porn scripts for the Hustler Video Group. He wrote *Not the Bradys XXX, This Ain't the Munsters XXX, Very Happy Days, This Ain't Gilligan's Island XXX*, and *This Ain't the Partridge Family XXX*. The logo on the poster for *This Ain't the Partridges XXX* has a line of little birds shaped as penises with wings.

"There have been parodies in porn forever," he says. "In the past, it might have been *Forrest Hump*. But they were not true to the original show. In my films we make sure the actors look like the characters and, God willing, deliver dialogue like the characters."

Thrill's big hit this year was *Who's Nailin' Paylin: Adventures of a Hockey MILF*, shot with a porn actress who resembled Sarah Palin. The actress, Lisa Anne, played a character called Serra Paylin. Nina Hartley plays Hillary Clinton and Jada Fire plays Condoleezza Rice. The women have a three-way sex scene. In the movie, Serra Paylin participates in sexual encounters with visiting Russian soldiers. There is a flashback to college days, in which her creationist science professor teaches her lessons on the "theory of the Big Bang." There are also shouts of "Drill, baby, drill" during sex scenes and many "you betcha"s. During a Serra Paylin press conference, there is an ode to the podium scene in the 1984 comedy *Police Academy*.

The film was featured on Fox News and the *Colbert Report*, as well as on *The O'Reilly Factor*. It sold well, four times Hustler's other releases, Thrill says. DVD, video, and magazine sales of porn have dropped by 25 to 45 percent because of free Internet porn. Thrill said he had just completed *Everybody Loves Lucy*. In this latest film, Lucy and Ethel sneak into Rickey's club and find that it is a sex club. "People like these familiar characters that they already know," Thrill says. "You would not think anybody would want to see Herman Munster have sex, but they actually did."

Thrill spends about six or eight hours on scripts, most of which have five scenes. A script runs about a dozen pages. "Once you get into the actual sex, we like them to stay in character," he says, "but these are no Academy Award–winning performances."

The sex those in the porn industry claim to promote is as fake, absurd, and unattainable as the façade of the Luxor casino and hotel. Porn is not about love or eroticism. It is about power and money. It is a transaction. It is based on the conversion of women into objects. They are assigned a monetary value and sexually exploited for profit. Most porn stars are also prostitutes. They charge a range of fees, usually in the thousands of dollars, to fans on porn escort Web sites.

When I ask ex-porn actress Jan Meza, thirty, who once did a scene in which twenty-five men had sex with her, how she would describe the producers and directors of the porn industry, she answers curtly: "Pimps." The porn stars make anywhere from $1,500 to $3,000 an hour as prostitutes. Roldan would, along with other porn actresses, be flown into a city, including New York, and stay at a hotel for a week. They would meet clients in their hotel room.

Lubben says the AVN convention and awards ceremony brings together high-priced porn stars and clients.

"Ninety percent work as prostitutes," she says. "They meet a lot of their big clients in Vegas during this convention. There is really big money being made by some of these women at night, as much as $2,000 an hour."

The most famous porn actresses can make as much as $30,000 a week as hotel-bound prostitutes. Clients "would see you in the film and they wanted you to be exactly the same way," Roldan says. "It was uncomfortable to meet some married stranger. I would walk around these cities and feel sad and empty. No one cared about me. My agent didn't care. All I had was money and nothing else."

The most successful porn films keep pushing the physical and emotional boundaries of the women onscreen and incorporate an expanding array of physically and verbally abusive acts.

Ariana Jollee, twenty-one, is sitting in a motel room beside a particle-board desk and a bare white wall, giving a pre-film interview for *65 Guy Cream Pie,* produced in 2005 by Devil's Film. She has sex with sixty-five men beside the indoor pool of a Prague resort during the film. She is smiling at the camera. Jollee has sleek, dark hair with bangs, a tribal tattoo encircling one bicep, and wears jeans and a loose black tank top. She has rounded arms, full cheeks, and a slightly heavy chin. Jollee started doing porn in 2003, when she was twenty, debuting in a film called *Nasty Girls 30.* She has done hundreds of films and was one of the industry's premier gonzo girls, purportedly enjoying extreme abuse. Jollee tells the camera that she performed in a twenty-one-man gang bang on her twenty-first birthday. She says she is looking forward to doing the same now with fifty men, although this number climbs to sixty-five on the set. "Cream pie" refers to men ejaculating in a woman's anus or vagina, rather than ejaculating on her body.

"I'll be banging fifty guys—fifty, fifty, fifty!," says Jollee. Maybe even more. That'd be cool. . . . So I'm like really excited."

She laughs and plays with her hair. "And it just so happens that all these guys are going to be coming *in* me." She looks coyly at the camera. "In the ass and pussy," she grins, wrinkling her nose. "See I like it in the ass the best. I wanna find the biggest pervert and get him to suck all fifty loads out and spit it in my mouth." She reaches up and fiddles with her bangs. "That'd be so good. That'd be fucking hot. It'd be disgusting." She giggles. "I get off on that." She runs her fingers through her hair, fanning it out behind her.

"It's a big, big fantasy, always been a big fantasy of mine to be with more than one guy at a time. Many women have that fantasy. . . ." Her voice drops to a whisper. She wrinkles her nose and narrows her eyes. "You have all these men, and they all wanna fuck you, and they're all there, and it's just like, *cock,* holy shit. It's so good. *So good*. Now I'm getting wet," she says, giggling. Her feet are up on the seat of her chair, and the camera pans down briefly to the exposed crotch of her jeans. She demurely pops her thumb in her mouth, still smiling, gazing at the camera.

"If you're watching this before the scene, you're in for a fucking treat. . . . Each one of those motherfuckers is gonna, you know, it's gonna be the ride of their lives." She nods thoughtfully. "But, who knows?" She throws her hands in the air. "Maybe they'll fuck me up. Maybe they'll really, like, teach me a lesson." She tosses a small smile at the camera. She scratches her knee absently. "We'll just have to wait and see. Maybe I'm not as insatiable as I think I am. We'll see. I'm excited."

She concedes that when it is over, she will "look like shit" but will be "well fucked." The interviewer asks what condition her vagina and anus will be in after having sex with that many men. She speaks of her genitals in the disembodied third person: "They can take it. They want it. They like it. They go back to size after. Pussy's tight. She always goes back to size."

Jollee talks briefly about her private life. She says that before she did gang bangs in films she once had sex with twelve men on a fire truck. "I won't say how old I was," she giggles. "It was so good. I will thank the man who took me there every day for the rest of my life. I still talk to him. He's a really good friend of mine. He's a pervert, but I love perverts. I like free people."

Her enthusiasm, as she relates this story about the fire truck, appears to momentarily fade. A brief tremor crosses her face. The fleeting impression when she falls out of character is that the experience of being taken to a firehouse by a friend who is "a pervert" and having sex with twelve men on a truck was not sexy or exciting, that for a young girl the experience was perhaps not the result of being free or the product of sexual desire. She quickly snaps back into the façade. She says, "I hope everyone gets off. I plan on coming."

Her smile broadens. "If you've just watched it, well, here's me beforehand." She chortles. "It should be cool." The camera zooms in and pans down her body as she fiddles with her hair. She reaches down and grabs her crotch. "Everything's intact at the moment, it's all intact." She grins and wrinkles her nose as she rubs her breasts happily. She sits up and hisses at the camera, "I'm ready, I'm fucking horny, dude. It's bad." Then, in her enthusiastic college-girl voice: "I'm so excited, can you tell? Like I can't sit still!" She rocks back and forth in her chair, raising her knees to her chest and putting her thumb in her mouth again. She giggles and swipes her bangs with her other hand.

65 Guy Cream Pie takes six hours to film. Jollee has oral sex, vaginal sex, double penetration, and double anal with sixty-five men. They ejaculate into and onto her body. When the shoot is finished, the last man heaves himself off Jollee. In a behind-the-scenes DVD bonus, she clambers up and stands on the curlicued iron bed. She is naked. Her body is covered in semen. Her hair is tied back. She jumps off the stained, pink mattress onto the tiled pool deck. She bounces up and down in front of a large potted palm, laughing gleefully.

"Grab your IDs really quick," says the director.

"Can I just wipe off?" she asks, holding out a sticky hand. "My stupid IDs. I'm not going anywhere. Let me just wipe off really quick. Really quick."

Jollee walks gingerly on her toes into the hallway. She holds her arms stiffly out to her side, fingers splayed. She glances down at herself.

"No hug?" a production assistant teases.

"I would hug you, but . . . I would give everyone big fucking kisses," she throws back.

She walks naked past a group of fully dressed men in a post-production huddle. She is the only woman visible. The men ignore her.

She rummages through a duffel bag. She pulls a white towel out of the bag and holds it in her hand, away from her body, as she walks naked to the bathroom. She laughs and banters with the camera crew. "No, no, no, don't touch me. Trust me. You don't want to." A camera flash goes off as she opens the bathroom door. The counter in the white marble bathroom is littered with crumpled paper towels. Jollee roams back and forth distractedly. She continues to hold her arms out stiffly.

"Good show," remarks the man holding the camera.

"Yeah, huh?" Jollee puts down the towel. She tears off a piece of paper towel. She wipes her belly with the paper towel. She bends over to wipe cautiously between her legs. "Oh, my God. Wow," she says, examining the paper towel.

Her laugh, as she straightens up, sounds like panting. "What'd ya think?"

"I think—I think you wore those guys out," answers the cameraman.

Jollee laughs again raggedly. "They wore me out, I won't fucking deny that," she says as she takes out a baby wipe from a packet on the counter. "Look at me. I'm about to pass out."

She pauses, unfolding the wipe. Then she looks at the camera. Her smeared eyeliner gives her the appearance of two black eyes. The corners of her mouth are pulled down. Her chin is tilted up. Her expression is hard to read. "Good gang bang?"

"Yeah. Yeah, it was intense. Great job."

Jollee nods for a moment.

"Thank you," she says quietly. "I tried."

She looks down and wipes her belly with the baby wipe. She blows her breath out as she holds the wipe to her vagina, bending her knees. "Oh my God, I gotta douche. I gotta douche real bad." She inspects the wipe and sighs. "Fuck." Suddenly she looks up with a wide grin and laughs. "D'you have fun with the camera? It's fun, right? It's like power. It's like, whoo! It's so much fun. It's so much fun. . . . It's like you're allowed to be a pervert, now you have the camera in your hands."

She catches sight of herself in the mirror and bursts out laughing. "Oh, God. I give up." She throws the used wipe on the counter and heads back out, naked, into the lobby, among the milling production crew.

Jollee was also featured in the 2005 JM Productions release *Swirlies*, in which the male performer dunks the woman's head into a toilet after sex and flushes. The company promo for the film promises that "every whore gets the swirlies treatment. Fuck her, then flush her."

In *Swirlies*, Jollee comes to the door of a house and meets a man named Jenner. She tells Jenner that his little brother has given her little brother a swirlie at school. There is less than a minute of the usual stilted dialogue before the sex scene begins. There is oral, vaginal, and anal penetration in a variety of positions, with many close-up shots of the performers' genitals. The oral penetration includes deep thrusting that causes Jollee to gag. Jenner finally ejaculates on Jollee's face. He then takes her to the bathroom for a swirlie. During the sex scenes Jollee says to Jenner:

- "Shove it up my fucking ass . . . fuck that fucking tight little motherfucking asshole. Ah, that's so fucking good."
- "Fuck that motherfucking filthy asshole, motherfucker. Fucking amazing. So fucking amazing. Fucking fuck me, motherfucker."
- "Fucking cock in that little asshole. That fucking dick in my fucking tight little filthy motherfucking asshole."
- "Fucking love it. Fucking love it."
- "Fuck, motherfucker is fucking me. Ride that fucking cock, huh."
- "Fucking nice, hard cock in fucking tight, little ass. Fuck me like a fucking little puppy, huh. Little puppy dog, huh. Fuck me with that fucking, hard cock so hard. So fucking hard, shoot your fucking hot come all over my pretty, little motherfucking face like a dirty, little, filthy, motherfucking whore."
- "Fucking dirty. I'm a filthy, little, fucking whore."[5]

As porn has gone mainstream, ushered two decades ago into middle-class living rooms and dens with VCRs and now available on the Internet, it has devolved into an open fusion of physical abuse and sex, of extreme violence, horrible acts of degradation against women with an increasingly twisted eroticism. Porn has always primarily involved the eroticization of unlimited male power, but today it also involves the expression of male power through the physical abuse, even torture, of women. Porn reflects the endemic cruelty of our society. This is a society that does not blink when the industrial slaughter unleashed by the United States and its allies kills hundreds of civilians in Gaza or hundreds of thousands of innocents in Iraq and Afghanistan. Porn reflects back the cruelty of a culture that tosses its mentally ill out on the street, warehouses more than 2 million people in prisons, denies health care to tens of millions of the poor, champions gun ownership over gun control, and trumpets an obnoxious and superpatriotic nationalism and rapacious corporate capitalism. The violence, cruelty, and degradation of porn are expressions of a society that has lost the capacity for empathy.

The Abu Ghraib images that were released, and the hundreds more disturbing images that remain classified, could be stills from porn films. There is a shot of a naked man kneeling in front of another man as if performing oral sex. There is a naked man on a leash held by a female American soldier. There are naked men in chains. There are naked men stacked one on top of the other in a human pile on the floor, as if in a prison gang bang. And there are hundreds more classified photos, many privately viewed by members of Congress, that show forced masturbation by Iraqi prisoners. Prisoners are made to pose for the camera in simulated sexual acts. And there are reportedly pictures of sexual intercourse among the guards. The photographs reflect the raging undercurrent of sexual callousness and perversion that runs through contemporary culture. These images speak in the language of porn, professional wrestling, reality television, music videos, and the corporate culture. It is the language of absolute control, total domination, racial hatred, fetishistic images of slavery, and humiliating submission. It is a world without pity. It is about reducing other human beings to commodities, to objects. It is a reflection of the sickness of gonzo porn.

Torture and pornography inevitably converge. They each turn human beings into submissive objects. In porn the woman is stripped of her human attributes and made to beg for abuse. She has no identity as a distinct human being. Her only worth is as a toy, a pleasure doll. She exists to gratify any whim that a male decides is pleasurable. She has no other purpose. Her real name vanishes. She adopts a cheap and usually vulgar stage name. She becomes a slave. She is filmed being degraded and physically abused. This film is sold to consumers, who, in turn, are aroused by the illusion that they too can dominate and abuse women. They, too, can be torturers.

Three of the alleged torturers in Abu Ghraib were women. They appeared to be willing participants. Porn has become so embedded and accepted in the culture, especially among the young, that sexual humiliation, abuse, rape, and physical violence have merged into a socially acceptable expression, once fear of retribution is removed. Absolute power over others almost always expresses itself through sexual sadism.

"My whole reason for being in the industry is to satisfy the desire of the men in the world who basically don't much care for women and want to see the men in my industry getting even with the women they couldn't have when they were growing up," Bill Margold, a performer and producer of porn, has said. "I strongly believe this, and the industry hates me for saying it. . . . So we come on a woman's face or somewhat brutalize her sexually: We're getting even for their lost dreams. I believe this. I've heard audiences cheer me when I do something foul onscreen. When I've strangled a person or sodomized a person or brutalized a person, the audience is cheering my action, and then when I've fulfilled my warped desire, the audience applauds."[6]

A performer known as Max Hardcore, currently in prison in Florida on obscenity charges, pioneered many of the forms of physical abuse now widely embraced by the industry. He was the first to perform anal fisting and "face-fucking." He placed lighted medical speculums in the vagina and anus. He urinated on women, often directly into their mouths. He slapped women around, tied them up, thrust their heads into toilets and flushed, pulled their hair, threw them onto the floor, and called them bitch, whore, cunt, and slut.

The women in porn plead to be abused. They call themselves whores and sluts. They are beaten and penetrated by groups of men. Their faces are covered with semen from dozens of masturbating men, their anuses penetrated repeatedly by lines of partners, and they are raped. The women portrayed in the films exist to fulfill the desires of men in the most degrading and painful way possible. Nearly all porn dialogue includes lines from women such as *I am a cunt. I am a bitch. I am a whore. I am a slut. Fuck me hard with your big cock.*

I find a man named Barry who refuses to give his last name sitting at a table selling bulk packages of 100 DVDs filmed by his company, Pain and Orgasm. He does business using the names Torture Portal, Masters of Pain, and Bacchus Studios. He admits his torture porn is outlawed in many states, and I find out later that he has been charged by a federal grand jury in Billings, Montana, with distributing obscene DVDs through the mail. The specific films named in the indictment are *Torture of Porn Star Girl*, *Pregnant and Willing*, and *Defiant Crista Submits*. If convicted, he faces a maximum penalty of five years in prison and a fine of $250,000 on each of the three counts charged in the indictment.

Barry is fifty-eight and is wearing a gold Star of David around his neck. He has graying hair pulled back in a ponytail. He has been making movies since 1998. Not surprisingly, he feels the government is too intrusive in the business. He has a Web site where subscribers can see his bondage and torture films for $24.95 a month, along, he said, with "one live show."

"There are more restrictions, more government involvement where there shouldn't be," he says. "People should be able to watch whatever they want to watch as long as it is between consenting adults and there are no kids or animals. Stay out of our bedrooms."

He has little time for traditional porn and tells me, "I couldn't tell you anything about porn. I don't shoot porn. I don't watch it. It's boring. I shoot bondage. Tie 'em up and fuck 'em and maybe I will watch.

"I am not really involved in the industry," he goes on. "All I know is that large segments around the world like to watch young girls being tortured."

Barrett Blade, whose real name is Russell Alex Heil, is a porn actor who directs and is often filmed in porn movies with his wife, Kirsten Price. He started acting in porn films a decade ago when, he says, a girlfriend who shot porn brought him to the set.

"When I came into the business, gonzo was very small," he tells me. "There were more features, more films with story lines. As a performer, I don't do a lot of the gonzo. I'm a lover. I film it as a director, but I don't do it. I can't do a scene with some girl who before we start is crying and sitting scared in a corner. I can't do a scene if the girls are not enjoying themselves."

Most porn films have dispensed with the thin fantasy plots of older porn. The raw sex scenes begin almost immediately. And porn is overtly racist. Black men in porn films are primitive animals, brawny and illiterate studs with vast sexual prowess. Black women are filled with raw, animalistic lust. Latina women are hot and racy. Asian women are sexually submissive geishas. In this year's AVN Awards, nominated movies bore titles such as *Get That Black Pussy You Big Dick White Bastard Muttha Fucka*, *My Daughter Went Black and Never Came Back*, and *Oh No! There's a Negro in My Mom*! Porn, as Gail Dines writes, is a "new minstrel show." Porn allows white males, safely removed from the black culture and the inner city, to be voyeurs into a depraved and frightening world of racial and sexual stereotypes. Porn, as Dines writes, functions as

> a peep show for whites into what they see as the authentic black life, not on the plantation, but in the "hood" where all the conventions of white civilized society cease to exist. The "hood" in the white racist imagination is a place of pimps, ho's and generally uncontrolled black bodies, and the white viewer is invited, for a fee, to slum in this world of debauchery. In the "hood," the white man can dispense with his whiteness by identifying with the black man, and thus can become as sexually skilled and as sexually out-of-control as the black man. Here he does not have to worry about being big enough to satisfy the white woman (or man) nor does he have to concern himself with fears about poor performance or "weak wads" or cages like poor hubby in *Blacks on Blondes* [an interracial film in which the husband is literally in a cage while watching black men have sex with his wife]. Indeed, the "hood" represents liberation from the cage, and the payoff is a satiated white woman (or man) who has been completely and utterly feminized by being well and truly turned into a "fuckee."[7]

Dines writes that the black body that is celebrated as uncontrolled in interracial pornography is the same body that must be controlled and shackled in the world of white supremacy:

Just as white suburban teenagers love to listen to hip-hop and white adult males gaze longingly at the athletic prowess of black men, the white pornography consumer enjoys his identification with (and from) black males through a safe peephole, in his own home, and in mediated form. The real, breathing, living black man, however, is to be kept as far away as possible from these living rooms, and every major institution in society marshals its forces in the defense of white society. The ideologies that white men take to the pornography text to enhance their sexual pleasure are the very ideologies that they use to legitimize the control of black men: While it may heighten arousal for the white porn users, it makes life intolerable for the real body that is (mis)represented in all forms of white controlled media.[8]

Male porn stars make about a third of the money paid to the women. They possess the singular talent of keeping an erection for long periods of time while a small audience of actors, directors, and production crew watch. Barrett Blade tells me that many male stars take Viagra or inject Caverject into an open vein in the penis. "Some guy will be waiting to go on and reading a book and their cock up like this," he says, indicating an erection with his fingers. "These guys who inject keep an open wound at the base of their penis. They bleed on the women. Pretty soon they can't get it up without it. They need to get a vial from the fridge every time they want to have sex, even when they are home with their girlfriends."

Jim Powers stands in his booth with a large, glossy poster behind him that reads, "Wanna Fuck a Porn Star?" The poster invites the reader to visit Fuckafan.com and "see Super Stars of XXX Cinema with Real Guys." Powers, who has directed films such as *Detention Whores, Mexicunts,* and *Squeel Like a Pig,* films "real" fans screwing porn stars and puts it up for view on the Internet for paid subscribers. The booth next to his is a cosmetic surgery company that offers "breast augmentation, liposuction, Tummy Tuck, Buttock Implants, Nose Refinement, Botox, and Facial Fillers and more."

"I find real guys and they get to fuck a porn star like Kenci," he says, turning to a young woman beside him in cutoff shorts, a bra, and a baseball hat.

Powers says he tried to film a scene the night before with a fan that "went really bad." "It was hours of heartache, but he got a free sandwich out of it," he says. "It is tough once the camera comes on." He is perturbed because three fans who had previously agreed to be filmed with Kenci this afternoon had not appeared. He says he "makes stupid content for stupid people," that porn is a prime example of the "stupidification of America." "This is a YouTube world," he continues. "It is a *Jackass* world. Everyone has short attention spans. You need a catchy trailer. You catch their attention, they buy the film and jerk off.

"There was a day when porn stars were veiled actresses," he says. "They took the job seriously. They were twenty-four or twenty-five years old. Now they are nineteen. They are hookers. They don't care. They are a throwaway commodity in a throwaway world." He turns and looks with disdain at Kenci and says to me, "She doesn't know what a book is, I bet." He asks me if I want to be filmed having sex with Kenci. I decline with a quick "No, thank you." He explains he doesn't have anyone else. He has a house nearby to film, a camera crew, a porn actress, and no fan. At no point is Kenci consulted.

Sharon Mitchell, an ex-porn star, is the founder of the Adult Industry Medical Healthcare Foundation. She tests and treats actors in the porn industry. She runs her clinic out of Los Angeles.

"The type of performances that they are doing, basically they walk on the set and it is wall-to-wall sex, and the type of sexual encounters they are having are extremely high-risk, much, much higher-risk than when I was involved," Mitchell said in a 2007 interview with National Public Radio. "When I was involved, I had the choice to use a condom, the choice to do whatever sex acts I preferred. Today, anyone pretty much with a handful of Viagra and a High-8 camera: 'Hey, I want to be a porn director and producer.' And they can literally go about this and sell these things on the Internet. So they recruit very young people, and my concern is, 'Are you ready to do this?'

"When I founded the Adult [Industry] Medical Healthcare Foundation in 1998, there was actually an actor who was knowingly and willfully infecting women with HIV," Mitchell said, "and finally I caught up with him and realized that he was going to county health clinics and getting anonymous testing. And he would put someone else's name on this test. And not everyone was testing, and the tests were not centrally located back then. Denial is the backbone of pornography when it comes to health care."

"I am a clinician that serves a world that I know very, very well because I come from it," Mitchell told NPR's Scott Simon. "And I know the pressures that these talent members go through not to use the condoms. They are offered more money. They are told, 'Look, these films will not sell if there are condoms on it.'"

"Not to get graphic, but you would think that in these days of computer enhancements and special effects, it would be no more necessary to endanger a performer that way than it would be to require Tom Cruise to jump off a twelve-story building," Simon said.

"Absolutely," Mitchell answered, "but they are not looked at as performers. They are looked at as commodities. They are looked at as body parts that are going to be edited into a product that's going to make money. And this industry, albeit mainstream as it's become, they are not going to say, 'OK, let's go ahead and spend half a million dollars, let's just digitally edit out the condom,' which can be done, obviously. They just don't want to spend any money."

"In helping porn performers are you just enabling them do something that is destructive?" Simon asked.

"You know, some days I feel like I am sweeping back the ocean with a broom," she said. "I wake up and I think, 'This is amazing.' I mean, we do catch a tremendous amount of HIV that would have ended up in the industry. And I can literally say I have saved lives. We have put a lot of people into rehab. We help a lot of people leave porn and get an education. We have a scholarship program. And with all this, some days, you know, when I see a young girl walk in, and I just know she is just going to get run over by all these producers and agents and types of things that she probably hasn't experienced or even thought of experiencing, I think, 'Am I just fattening them up for the kill? What am I doing?'"[9]

The Internet is the curse and salvation of the industry. It has vastly expanded the reach of the porn industry, but it has also made free porn easily accessible. DVDs and glossy magazines are going the way of newspapers. Playboy's stock is down 81 percent, and in October 2008 it announced it was selling off its DVD division. There are an estimated 4.2 million porn Web sites—12 percent of the total number of sites—

providing access to 72 million worldwide visitors monthly. One-quarter of total daily search-engine requests, or 68 million, are for pornographic material. There are 40 million Americans who are regular visitors to porn sites. Sites like Youporn.com and xtube.com allow amateurs with camcorders to show explicit porn. Illegal downloads and free video-sharing sites have cut into profits, say those in the industry, by as much as 20 percent.

The most successful Internet porn sites and films are those that discover new ways to humiliate and inflict cruelty on women. In the Web site *Slut Bus*, women are lured into a van, offered money for sex, filmed having sex, and then dumped on the side of the road. Money is held out toward the woman as the van pulls away. She is always left without payment. The message is clear. Women are compliant sex machines. They are good only for sex. And they are not worth paying for their services.

"The Mission?" the slutbus.com Web site asks. "Pick up the hottest girls we find. And get them to let us fuck them & cum in their pretty little faces all while videotaping the whole thing."

"The Fun?" the site goes on. "Treating these slutty bitches like they deserve to be treated . . . with a slam bam thank ya ma'am & a swift kick in the ass! What? You thought we would actually pay these sluts? Hahahaha. Think Again!"

The theme of luring women to have sex and then discarding them is common.

"Tired of stuck up bitches that want gifts, dinners, money all of your fuckin' time and attention?" reads an ad on a Web site called Creampie Thais, which charges subscribers $29.95 a month."

Did you ever want to just want to find a little **SUBMISSIVE** fuck toy and fill her full of your man seed? At Creampie Thais, I do just that. I pick up hot Thai whores off the streets of Thailand. In clubs, supermarkets, the beach and off the streets, I wreck their young slick pussies and fill them full of my spunk. After I have these whores suck my cock and dump my sperm into their receptive cunts, I throw them back to the world to fend for themselves. These girls are willing to do anything to receive my spunk inside their hot tight asian twats. Maybe they think it's a ticket to the promise land, or maybe they just want to breed. Are they on the pill? Who gives a fuck. Protection. Fuck no. Do I have illegitimate children in Thailand? Probably. This is the **REAL FUCKIN' DEAL.**

Jan Meza worked as a porn actress in a genre known as "Big Beautiful Women" films. She made about forty movies and was filmed on some twenty Web sites. She left the industry addicted to painkillers, drinking heavily, and on the edge of a nervous breakdown. She is currently married and is finishing her doctorate in psychology at the University of Texas at Austin.

"The more society loses touch with reality, especially in relationships, the more people do not know how it is supposed to be, how to react with other people, the more they turn to porn," she says. "People look at this fantasy and believe it should be their reality. They retreat further and further into their illusion because porn can never be real. It does not work in real life. Porn is a sickness."

Jersey Jaxin, as she was known in the industry, walked away from porn. "Guys punching you in the face. You have semen. . . . Twenty or thirty guys all over your face, in your eyes," she remembers. "You get ripped. Your insides can come out of you. It's never-ending. You are viewed as an object, not as a human with a spirit. People don't care. People do drugs because they can't deal with the way they're being treated." She estimates that the number of women who use drugs before they film are "75 percent and rising. Have to numb themselves. . . . There are specific doctors in this industry, if you go in for a common cold, they'll give you Vicodin, Viagra, anything you want, because all they care about is money. You are a number. You're bruised. You have black eyes. You're ripped. You're torn. You have your insides coming out of you. It's not pretty and foofoo on set. You get hurt.

"The main thing going around now is crystal meth, cocaine, and heroin," Meza says. "You have to numb yourself to go on set. The more you work, the more you have to numb yourself. The more you become addicted, the more your personal life is nothing but drugs. . . . Your whole life becomes nothing but porn. I was a drinker. I drank a lot. Vodka was my drug. Vodka was my numbing toy. Before sets, after sets, and if it was a set where people didn't care, they'd have it there waiting."

"You may see a forty-five-minute set that took us thirteen hours. . . . We're ripped, we're tired, we're sore, we're bleeding, we're cut up, we have dried semen all over our faces from numerous guys, and we can't wash it off because they want to take pictures. You have this stuff all over you, and they're telling you, 'Hold it!'" Meza says.

"You can say anything you want [e.g., 'Stop'], and they don't listen," she says. "There's the ultimate thing where you squeeze their leg to ease up, and most of them don't care. They have another scene to go to. It's all about the money. They've forgotten who they are, and they don't care who they're hurting.

"You have no soul in the porn industry," she adds.[10]

Porn is about reducing women to corpses. It is about necrophilia. Mingled with the booths set up by distribution and production companies, Las Vegas escort services, and a vast array of sex toy displays. There are booths that sell life-size, anatomically correct silicone dolls.

At the Lovable Dolls display booth, three large picture windows are set in walls of faux brick. There is a replica of an iron streetlamp outside the windows. The first window has two life-size silicone dolls. One wears knee-high, black latex boots with stiletto heels. She is reclining on a small frame covered in red velvet. Her fingers gently touch the hand of another doll in a black, curly wig and wearing a bandeau top. In the other two windows are more dolls, one with pointed pixie ears and what Bronwen Keller, a sales respresentative, calls "a deliberate fantasy face."

"They have removable heads," she tells me. "There's a whole array of heads. The head cap pops off. You can reach in and disconnect the head and put a new one on. You can move the eyes. You do that from the inside so you don't damage the eyelashes."

We stand and peer through the glass at the pixie doll, surrounded by huge plastic flowers, as if she is emerging from a tropical garden. She has a pierced naval.

"We ship them in lingerie, like a chemise," she tells me. "They are fully made up. They have their nails done, and they have a wig. They have shoes. We ship with the heads on. It creates the effect of 'Oh, wow, here's my girl, ready to go.'"

The dolls, which cost $7,500 each, are custom-built and come with various breast sizes, tongues, mouths, and vaginas, seven different skin colors, and eleven eye colors. Clients can create their own dolls. The dolls are the silicone replicas of the living porn stars signing autographs and permitting their fans to grab their asses and pose for a photo. The display next door, Reel Dolls, is even more disturbing. It has four silicone women's heads, lined up in glass cases, with their lips parted to receive an incoming cock. On top of the display case rests a headless, legless, armless female torso, complete with an anatomically correct vagina and a tuft of pubic hair. Men passing by the booth push their fingers into her red silicone slit.

Dr. Z—not his real name—has come to the convention to preach the joys of silicone doll ownership. He is a trim, bearded, fifty-two-year-old man who teaches anatomy. He is wearing khaki pants, an orange collared shirt, and a pair of boots. He owns eight silicone dolls, with names that include Lindsey, Danielle, Sunni, Trixie, Candy, and Shawna.

"You walk into a room and they are sitting or standing around you, and they seem real," he says. "It's like having a family. They all have personalities."

Dr. Z hides his hobby from most of his friends. He keeps the dolls locked in his bedroom closet. He positions them around the house, including in his bed, when he is alone. He shops for their clothing. He poses them for photo shoots. He carefully applies their makeup. And he talks to them. He began using blow-up dolls when he was married. He took blow-up dolls with him when he traveled. He kept his habit secret from his wife. He is now divorced. "Hey," he says, "I wasn't cheating."

"No one I dated was ever privy to it," he says. "It was always a private side of me. It did improve my relationships because it gave me the ability to experiment. It also takes the stress out of a relationship. My last wife used sex as a control mechanism."

"You have to be creative," he explains. "You have to make them feel like they are interacting. I have been in relationships where women just lie there like dead fish. The same thing can happen with this, but it is more fun with some dolls than with some women. You can make them do things with their hands. You can wrap their arms around your neck. You can use bungee cords to put them in positions. Their eyes are adjustable."

He uses the thick iron hook on the back of the dolls' necks to prop them up. He puts them in his sex swing. He photographs them using sex toys. He says it is a "really nice thing because you are in full control." He tells me the dolls "take the stress out of wining and dining women." He says he uses lubricants in the silicone mouth, vagina, and anus for sex. And he tells me that of the top three or four blow jobs he has had in his life, he would have to include those delivered by his dolls.

"You lie on top of one and it feels like you are on top of a person," he says. He fixes their eyes when he has sex with them so "there is direct eye contact." He explains, "I talk to them like pets," and then smiles, saying, "but they don't shed." He tells me that he has, over the years, "learned what works."

"You can't beat them all you want," he says. "They can get damaged, but spanking is OK. They jiggle like real."

His dolls are body types that he says are not available to him with the women he meets socially.

"From my experience, women who look like these dolls are not mentally or emotionally in line," he says. "It is hard to find someone who is smart, intelligent, attractive, and who wants to be with you. And then there are the breast sizes. I have one with ridiculous breasts. She is extremely hard to dress. I have become very appreciative of women's clothes."

"Everyone has a desire about controlling the look, the environment, what women represent and how they come across," he says.

We are looking at the dolls in the display. He points out the simulated veins in the feet, which he tells me are the dorsal venous arch. "To me," he says, "That's really, really cool."

"I have one doll, Sunni, who is blonde, hooker-style," he says. "She's really good at blow jobs. She's like a California beach bunny. She has dark skin and is always tanning herself. She's happiest in a black bikini and a blonde wig. She looks great in her bikini. I keep most of them dressed in underwear and sports bras. They hang out together, like a sorority. Personally, I have never ejaculated inside my dolls. I use the rhythm method. The cleanup is easier. I have a hanging apparatus in my tub and use the shower massage. They can absorb body oil. Look, you have old people who need to be taken care of, you can think about these dolls as being in a coma. Your job is to keep them comfortable. I am always a gentleman around them. I never have sex without asking permission. I sleep with them. I cover them with an electric blanket, and the silicone absorbs the heat."

The dolls, like the porn stars, are a compliant mouth, vagina, and rectum. They exist solely to allow a man to penetrate, usually with a penis, sometimes hands, sometimes objects, into their orifices at will. You can spit on their faces, slap them around, verbally abuse them, as is done with women in porn films, but with the dolls there is no chance of rebellion or complaint. The silicone mouths will always have the thick, slightly spread lips, offering themselves silently to their owner's penis.

⁓

The culmination of the AVN Expo is the awards ceremony, often referred to as the Oscars of porn. Porn actors and actresses walk down a red carpet into the cavernous Mandalay Bay Convention Center. The stars, producers, and directors sit at tables on the main floor, and fans are seated in the U-shaped bleachers around the main stage. Awards include Best Anal-Themed Release, Best All-Girl 3-Way Sex Scene, Best Double Penetration Sex Scene, and Best Big-Butt Series.

When an actress named Stoya wins the statuette for Best New Starlet, she thanks "each and every person who jerks off to my smut."

The Best Anal Sex Scene award goes to Sunny Lane and her role in the film *Big Wet Asses 13*. She tells the crowd, "I can't help it, I just love that cock." Introducing her co-star, Manuel Ferrara, she says: "This is the man. I had to choose Manuel to be my first anal because he is so passionate, so loving, and he definitely knows how to work that soda-can cock. I prepared for this scene by sitting with a butt plug in while I was doing my makeup time so I was ready to go, all for you."

"I did exactly the same for you while I was getting my makeup done," Ferrara quips.

"Oh, really, very nice," she says. "I would like to thank Elegant Angel for all of this, for the opportunity to let my ass show in all the right ways."

I sit through nearly three hours of this vapid banter, an irony-free reflection of the banality of mainstream awards ceremonies. The rapper Flo Rida provides entertainment along with local dancers from the Spearmint Rhino gentlemen's club. Evil Angel owner John "Buttman" Stagliano leads a dance sequence that incorporates images of George

W. Bush, Donald Rumsfeld, Abu Ghraib, Halliburton, the Iraq war, and freedom of speech, which the porn industry champions as protecting its Constitutional right to disseminate porn. The five-minute dance sequence is Stagliano's artistic objection to the federal government's use of the Patriot Act to persecute adult entertainment companies and customers.

"Did we really believe them when they said they would only use these laws to prosecute terrorists?" he asks in the sequence.

Stagliano, once a Chippendale dancer and also a porn actor, has tested positive for HIV. He was charged by the United States government for adult-to-adult obscenity. He is married to ex-porn star Tricia Devereaux, whose stage name was Karen Stagliano and who is also HIV-positive, as are many former members of the industry.

Porn has evolved from the airbrushed misogyny of glossy spreads in *Playboy* and smutty films sold in seedy shops. It is corporate and easily available. Its products today focus less on sex between a man and a woman and increasingly on groups of men beating off on a woman's face or tearing her anus open with their penises. Porn has evolved to its logical conclusion. It first turned women into sexual commodities and then killed women as human beings. And it has won the culture war. Pornography and the commercial mainstream have fused. The publicity photo for the porn production company Wicked could be lifted from a Victoria's Secret catalog. The lacy brassieres and thongs, candelabras, stilettos, windswept hair, strings of pearls, and arched backs are staples of mass culture. The wars fought by feminists such as Andrea Dworkin, Susan Faludi, Susan Brownmiller, and Gloria Steinem to free women from sexual tyranny have been defeated by a cultural embrace—by both men and women—of bondage and objectification. Stripping, promiscuity, S&M, exhibitionism, and porn are mainstream chic.

"Why do deep down within we'd all like to be porn stars at one point in our life or another?" asks Faye Wattleton in complete earnestness on the HBO special *Thinking XXX*. She is the president of the Center for the Advancement of Women.

Sexual callousness and emancipation have become synonymous. Fashion takes its cue from porn. Music videos feature porn stars and pantomime porn scenes. Commercials and advertisements milk porn for shock value. The grainy sex tapes of vacuous celebrities from

Pamela Anderson to Paris Hilton enhance their allure as porn icons. Madonna has built her public persona, and her dance routines and videos, around the sexual boundaries obliterated by porn. Rap stars like Snoop Dogg, 50 Cent, and Yella produce porn. Howard Stern interviews porn stars. Fitness clubs offer pole-dancing and strip classes. Porn star Jenna Jameson's memoir was published by HarperCollins and was a *New York Times* best-seller for six weeks. The *E! True Hollywood Story* episode of her life remains the highest-rated single episode of that show. Reality television shows like *The Girls Next Door* and *Rock of Love* feature a male celebrity who has multiple female partners competing for his affections. *The Girls Next Door,* which stars the octogenarian Hugh Hefner and girlfriends young enough to be his granddaughters, is spiced up with undertones of incest and pedophilia. HBO celebrates and glamorizes porn, prostitution, and strippers with specials and shows like *Thinking XXX, Katie Morgan's Sex Tips, Cathouse,* and *G-String Divas.* The language, abuse, and moral bankruptcy of porn shape and mold popular culture. And there is a direct line from the heartlessness and usury of the culture of porn to the hookup parties on college campuses, in which young men and women get hammered, have sex, and do not speak to each other again.

Women, porn asserts, whether they know it or not, are objects. They are whores. These whores deserve to be dominated and abused. And once men have had their way with them, these whores are to be discarded. Porn glorifies the cruelty and domination of sexual exploitation in the same way popular culture, as Jensen points out, glorifies the domination and cruelty of war. It is the same disease. It is the belief that "because I have the ability to use force and control to make others do as I please, I have a right to use this force and control." It is the disease of corporate and imperial power. It extinguishes the sacred and the human to worship power, control, force, and pain. It replaces empathy, eros, and compassion with the illusion that we are gods. Porn is the glittering façade, like the casinos and resorts in Las Vegas, like the rest of the fantasy that is America, of a culture seduced by death.

III / The Illusion of Wisdom

Men die, but the plutocracy is immortal; and it is necessary that fresh generations should be trained to its service.

—Sinclair Lewis

THE MULTIPLE FAILURES that beset the country, from our mismanaged economy to our shredding of Constitutional rights to our lack of universal health care to our imperial debacles in the Middle East, can be laid at the door of institutions that produce and sustain our educated elite. Harvard, Yale, Princeton, Stanford, Oxford, Cambridge, the University of Toronto, and the Paris Institute of Political Studies, along with most elite schools, do only a mediocre job of teaching students to question and think. They focus instead, through the filter of standardized tests, enrichment activities, AP classes, high-priced tutors, swanky private schools, entrance exams, and blind deference to authority, on creating hordes of competent systems managers. Responsibility for the collapse of the global economy runs in a direct line from the manicured quadrangles and academic halls in Cambridge, New Haven, Toronto, and Paris to the financial and political centers of power.

The elite universities disdain honest intellectual inquiry, which is by its nature distrustful of authority, fiercely independent, and often subversive. They organize learning around minutely specialized disciplines, narrow answers, and rigid structures designed to produce such answers. The established corporate hierarchies these institutions service—economic, political, and social—come with clear parameters, such as the primacy of an unfettered free market, and also with a highly specialized vocabulary. This vocabulary, a sign of the "specialist" and, of course, the elitist, thwarts universal understanding. It keeps the uninitiated from asking unpleasant questions. It destroys the search for the common good. It dices disciplines, faculty, students, and finally experts into tiny, specialized fragments. It allows students and faculty to retreat into these self-imposed fiefdoms and neglect the most pressing moral, political, and cultural questions. Those who critique the system itself—people such as Noam Chomsky, Howard Zinn, Dennis Kucinich, or Ralph Nader—are marginalized and shut out of the mainstream debate. These elite universities have banished self-criticism. They refuse to question a self-justifying system. Organization, technology, self-advancement, and information systems are the only things that matter.

In 1967, Theodor Adorno wrote an essay titled "Education After Auschwitz." He argued that the moral corruption that made the Holocaust possible remained "largely unchanged" and that "the mechanisms that render people capable of such deeds" must be uncovered, examined, and critiqued through education. Schools had to teach more than skills. They had to teach values. If they did not, another Auschwitz was always possible.

"All political instruction finally should be centered upon the idea that Auschwitz should never happen again," he wrote:

> This would be possible only when it devotes itself openly, without fear of offending any authorities, to this most important of problems. To do this, education must transform itself into sociology, that is, it must teach about the societal play of forces that operates beneath the surface of political forms.[1]

If we do not grasp the "societal play of forces that operates beneath the surface of political forms," we will be cursed with a more ruthless form of corporate power, one that does away with artifice and the seduction of a consumer society, and wields power through naked repression.

I had lunch in Toronto with Henry Giroux, professor of English and Cultural Studies at McMaster University in Canada. Giroux was for many years the Waterbury Chair Professor at Penn State. He has long been one of the most prescient and vocal critics of the corporate state and the systematic destruction of American education. He was driven, because of his work, to the margins of academia in the United States. He asked the uncomfortable questions Adorno knew should be asked by university professors. Giroux, who wrote *The University in Chains: Confronting the Military-Industrial-Academic Complex*, left in 2004 for Canada.

"The emergence of what Eisenhower had called the military-industrial-academic complex had secured a grip on higher education that may have exceeded even what he had anticipated and most feared," Giroux tells me. "Universities, in general, especially following the events of 9/11, were under assault by Christian nationalists, reactionary neoconservatives, and market fundamentalists for allegedly representing the weak link in the war on terrorism. Right-wing students were encouraged to spy on the classes of progressive professors, the corporate grip on the university was tightening, as was made clear not only in the emergence of business models of governance, but also in the money being pumped into research and programs that blatantly favored corporate interests. And at Penn State, where I was located at the time, the university had joined itself at the hip with corporate and military power. Put differently, corporate and Pentagon money was now funding research projects, and increasingly knowledge was being militarized in the service of developing weapons of destruction, surveillance, and death. Couple this assault with the fact that faculty were becoming irrelevant as an oppositional force. Many disappeared into discourses that threatened no one, some simply were too scared to raise critical issues in their classrooms for fear of being fired, and many simply no longer had the conviction to uphold the university as a democratic public sphere."

The moral nihilism embraced by elite universities would have terrified Adorno. He knew that radical evil was possible only with the collaboration of a timid, cowed, and confused population, a system of propaganda and mass media that offered little more than spectacle and entertainment, and an educational system that did not transmit transcendent values or nurture the capacity for individual conscience. He feared a culture that banished the anxieties and complexities of moral choice and embraced a childish hypermasculinity.

"This educational ideal of hardness, in which many may believe without reflecting about it, is utterly wrong," Adorno wrote. "The idea that virility consists in the maximum degree of endurance long ago became a screen-image for masochism that, as psychology has demonstrated, aligns itself all too easily with sadism."[2]

Sadism dominates the culture. It runs like an electric current through reality television and trash-talk programs, is at the core of pornography, and fuels the compliant, corporate collective. Corporatism is about crushing the capacity for moral choice and diminishing the individual to force him or her into an ostensibly harmonious collective. This hypermasculinity has its logical fruition in Abu Ghraib, the wars in Iraq and Afghanistan, and our lack of compassion for our homeless, our poor, the mentally ill, the unemployed, and the sick.

"The political and economic forces fueling such crimes against humanity—whether they are unlawful wars, systemic torture, practiced indifference to chronic starvation, and disease or genocidal acts—are always mediated by educational forces," Giroux says. "Resistance to such acts cannot take place without a degree of knowledge and self-reflection. We have to name these acts and transform moral outrage into concrete attempts to prevent such human violations from taking place in the first place."

But we do not name them. We accept the system handed to us and seek to find a comfortable place within it. We retreat into the narrow, confined ghettos created for us and shut our eyes to the deadly superstructure of the corporate state.

⌒

"Political silence. That's my summary. There are only flickers of resistance to most here-and-now issues," says Chris Hebdon, an undergraduate at the University of California at Berkeley. Hebdon went on to describe how various student groups gather at Sproul Plaza, the historic center of student activity at Berkeley. Groups set up tables to recruit and inform other students, a practice known as "tabling."

"Students table for Darfur, but seldom, if ever, do I see a table on Iraq, Afghanistan, or militarization. Tables on Sproul Plaza are ethnically fragmented and explicitly pre-professional, the [ethnicity-of-your-choice]-American Pre-Law, Pre-Med, Engineering, or Business

Association). There are strict restrictions and permitting processes for tabling. You see few, if any, tables on globalization, corporatization, or, heaven forbid, the commercialization of Berkeley. Too many students and professors are distracted, specialized, atomized, and timid. They follow trends, prestige, and money, and so rarely act outside the box. You know, U.C. adores the slogan 'Excellence Through Diversity,' but it doesn't mention multiculturalism's silent partner—the fragmentation of student society into little markets, segmenting the powerful sea of students into diverse but disarmed droplets. Exemplifying this disorientation is Sproul Plaza—the same place Mario Savio once gave his rallying cry for the Free Speech Movement from atop a police car—now composed of tens of tables for sports, entertainment, ethnic associations, résumé-building clubs for corporate careerists, and small causes. Disconnection prevails. In the absence of cohesion, one really wonders how such smart kids could be struck so, in the muting sense of the term, dumb."

The corporate hierarchy that has corrupted higher education is on public display at Berkeley. The wealthiest of the elite schools, such as Yale and Stanford, assign dormitories by lottery. They treat their students with a careful egalitarianism, expecting all to enter the elite. Berkeley and many other public universities, however, assign rooms depending on how much a student can pay. They fall into a capitalist logic of "choice."[3] The poorer Berkeley students end up in residences known as "the units" (Unit 1, Unit 2, Unit 3), while the wealthier students and recruited athletes, sustained by family money or athletic scholarships, receive rooms at Foothill or Clark Kerr, a fancy Stanford-style dorm that was once a private school for deaf and blind children. The food is better at the more expensive dorms. Corporations have cut deals with universities to be sole providers of goods and services and to shut out competitors. Coca-Cola, for example, has monopoly rights at Berkeley, including control of what drinks and food are sold at football games. Corporations such as Cingular and Allstate blanket California Memorial Stadium with their logos and signs.

Berkeley negotiated a deal with British Petroleum for $500 million. BP gets access to the university's researchers and technological capacity, built by decades of public investment, to investigate biofuels at a new Energy Biosciences Institute. BP can shut down another research center and move into a publicly subsidized one. BP will receive intellectual property rights, which it can use for profit, on scientific breakthroughs expected to come out of the joint project.

"When it comes to football, I go to Tightwad Hill, a no-cost site perched above the stadium where people can bring beers and laugh, rather than just hoot and scream," says Hebdon. "The crowd on Tightwad represents a Bay Area variety—students, grandparents, alcoholics, sports-families, children—and there is a culture of uncoordinated neighborly fun. The relative freedom at Tightwad contrasts to the neo-Pavlovian crowd training that goes on in the stadium below. In the stadium you are inundated. It begins right at the door. Tickets cost upwards of $25, you must enter with no food, and you must buy high-priced Coke or its underlings, Dasani water or Minute Maid juice."

The football coach is Berkeley's highest-paid employee. He makes about $3 million. Tuition has been steadily rising for decades. U.C. undergraduate students pay 100 percent of their educational costs because the state subsidy has effectively disappeared.[4] By the U.C. charter, tuition at the University of California is supposed to be free. Berkeley is a microcosm of the intrusion of corporations into education. Education, at least an education that challenges assumptions and teaches students to be self-critical, has been sacrificed in a Faustian bargain. Charles Schwartz, an emeritus professor of physics, drew up a chart that showed that in the last fourteen years, from 1993 to 2007, management staffs increased 259 percent. The total of employees increased 24 percent. Fulltime faculty increased by 1 percent.

When the U.C. Regents, who oversee the university system, announced they wouldn't accept thousands of qualified freshmen because of a budget shortfall, Schwartz drew up a plan. In the spirit of public service rather than personal enrichment, he proposed that the university take 1 percent from the salary of each employee making more than $100,000. This is not unprecedented. Weeks earlier, Barack Obama had capped his staffs' salaries at $100,000. "That would net you $29 million," Schwartz told the Regents. "That is more than enough to cover the full costs for those 2,300 new students that you were planning to turn away next year." The Regents ignored him.[5]

"Berkeley is trying to brand itself through its athletics, especially football," Hebdon tells me. "The program is a tremendous investment.

Our chancellor, in an act of great misdirection, just announced he plans to raise $1 billion for the athletic endowment by selling off 3,000 front-row seats for thirty to fifty years to private bidders for $225,000 a pop.[6] Piece by piece, Berkeley is becoming a trade school. Students, for instance, mostly agree with the idea of a sports university."

In December 2006, the university announced plans to cut down more than forty huge oak trees on a 1.5-acre site on campus to build a training facility for athletes. A group of protesters built crude tree houses in the branches and took shifts manning them to thwart the plan. Berkeley municipal law prohibits removing any Coast Live Oak with a trunk larger than six inches within city boundaries, but city boundaries do not include the university. The protest lasted for twenty-one months until September 2008, when the last protesters were coaxed down and the grove was demolished.

"During the well-publicized, two-year tree sits, most students supported the university's plans to build the sporting complex and railed against 'the hippies,'" Hebdon says. "One student, a war veteran, was treated as an imminent threat for tree-sitting with a sign that read 'Democratize the U.C. Regents.' Few students knew that the Regents, who oversee the whole university system, are appointed rather than elected and representative, even though this is required by law. Few really dug in and thought. My strongest memory is of a person selling rocks to throw at tree sitters. He had noticeable crowd support. When I see things like this, I think of how Berkeley, once known for conscientious objection, is training an inhumane, deeply frustrated, indifferent, game-driven people. The military has a strong presence on campus and is one of the few ways for students to pay their way without accruing large debt.

"We have bought hook, line, and sinker into the idea that education is about training and 'success,' defined monetarily, rather than learning to think critically and to challenge," Hebdon goes on. "The competitive efficiency culture—electronic immersion, high-paced everything, career networking as a way of life, prestige, money—it disconnects the so-called best and the brightest from commonsense obligations to society, ecology, and democratic ideals. Somewhere along the way into the free market, Berkeley forgot that learning isn't about handshaking, résumé fondling, and market rewards."

"What makes Berkeley a terribly contradictory public institution is its version of the wrought-iron gates that enclose Harvard or Yale: our high-security national laboratories. The Lawrence Berkeley National Laboratory, up the hill from campus, is a mystery to most. It is connected to U.C. Berkeley's historical involvement with nuclear technology, something inherently centralizing, undemocratic, and dangerous to civil rights. The labs have special buses students cannot ride. Buildings are restricted-access, and secrecy abounds. Researcher scientists do not fancy whistle-blowing, as they have no legal right to tenure. Students learn these labs are prestigious. After all, labs pull in copious amounts of taxpayer-funded federal science dollars."

⁓

I sat with a classmate from Harvard Divinity School who is now a theology professor. When I asked her what she was teaching, she unleashed a torrent of arcane academic jargon. I had no idea, even with three years of seminary, what she was talking about. You can see this retreat into specialized, impenetrable verbal enclaves in every academic department and discipline across the country. The more these universities churn out these stunted men and women, the more we are flooded with a peculiar breed of specialist who uses obscure code words as a way to avoid communication. This specialist blindly services tiny parts of a corporate power structure he or she has never been taught to question. Specialists look down on the rest of us, who do not understand what they are talking and writing about, with thinly veiled contempt.

By any standard comprehensible within the tradition of Western civilization, as John Ralston Saul points out, these people are illiterate. They cannot recognize the vital relationship between power and morality. They have forgotten, or never knew, that moral traditions are the product of civilization. They have little or no knowledge of their own civilization and do not know, therefore, how to maintain it. "One of the signs of a dying civilization," Saul writes, "is that its language breaks down into exclusive dialects which prevent communication. A growing, healthy civilization uses language as a daily tool to keep the machinery of society moving. The role of responsible, literate elites is to aid and abet that communication."[7]

Our elites use a private dialect that is a barrier to communication as well as common sense. The corporate con artists and economists who have rigged our financial system continue to speak to us in the obscure and incomprehensible language coined by specialists on Wall Street and at elite business schools. They use terms such as *securitization, deleveraging, structured investment vehicles,* and *credit default swaps* to shut us out of the debate. This retreat by elites into specialized ghettos spans the range of academic disciplines. English professors, who see novels as divorced from society, speak in the obscure vocabulary of deconstructionism, disempowering and emasculating the very works they study. Writers from Euripides to Russell Banks have used literature as both a mirror and a lens, to reflect back to us, and focus us on, our hypocrisy, moral corruption, and injustice. Literature is a tool to enlighten societies about its ills. It was Charles Dickens who directed the attention of middle-class readers to the slums and workhouses of London. It was Honoré de Balzac who, through the volumes of his *Human Comedy*, ripped open the callous heart of France. It was Sinclair Lewis who took us into the stockyards and shantytowns of Chicago in *The Jungle.*

In the hands of academics, however, who rarely understand or concern themselves with the reality of the world, works of literature are eviscerated and destroyed. They are mined for obscure trivia and irrelevant data. This disconnect between literature and philosophy on one hand and the real on the other is replicated in most academic disciplines. Economists build elaborate theoretical models yet know little of John Law, have never closely examined the tulip crisis, and do not study the railroad bubbles or the deregulation that led to the Great Depression. The foundation of Athenian democracy rose out of the egalitarian social and political reforms of Solon, including his decision to wipe out all of the debts that were bankrupting Athenian citizens. But the study of the classics, because it is not deemed practical or useful in a digitalized world, leaves such vital lessons unexamined. Tacitus' account of the economic meltdown during the reign of Tiberius—a meltdown that also saw widespread bankruptcies, a collapse of the real estate market, and financial ruin—is a reminder that we are not unique to history or human behavior. The meltdown during Tiberius' reign was finally halted by massive government spending and intervention that included interest-free loans to citizens. Those who suffer from historical amnesia, the belief that we are unique in history and have nothing to learn from the past, remain children. They live in an illusion.

The specialized dialect and narrow education of doctors, academics, economists, social scientists, military officers, investment bankers, and government bureaucrats keeps each sector locked in its narrow role. The overarching structure of the corporate state and the idea of the common good are irrelevant to specialists. They exist to make the system work, not to examine it. Our elites replicate, in modern dress, the elaborate mannerisms and archaic forms of speech employed by calcified, corrupt, and dying aristocracies. They cannot grasp that truth is often relative. They base their decisions on established beliefs, such as the primacy of an unregulated market or globalization, which are accepted as unquestioned absolutes. "In a corporatist society there is no serious need for traditional censorship or burning," Saul writes, "although there are regular cases. It is as if our language itself is responsible for our inability to identify and act upon reality."[8]

I was sent to boarding school on a scholarship at the age of ten. By the time I had finished eight years in New England prep schools and another eight at Colgate University and Harvard University, I had a pretty good understanding of the game. I have also taught at Columbia University, New York University, and Princeton University. These institutions feed students, no matter how mediocre, the comforting reassurance that they are there because they are not only the best but they are entitled to the best. You saw this attitude on display in every word uttered by George W. Bush. Here was a man with severely limited intellectual capacity and no moral core. Bush, along with Scooter Libby, who attended my pre-prep school, exemplifies the legions of self-centered, spoiled, intellectually limited and wealthy elitists churned out by places like Andover, Yale, and Harvard. Bush was, like the rest of his caste, propelled forward by his money and his connections. The real purpose of these richly endowed schools is to perpetuate their own. They do this even as they pretend to embrace the ideology of the common man, trumpet diversity on campus, and pose as a meritocracy. The public commitment to egalitarianism alongside the private nurturing of elitism creates a bizarre schizophrenia.

"There's a certain kind of student at these schools who falls in love with the mystique and prestige of his own education," said Elyse Graham, whom I taught at Princeton and who is now doing graduate work at Yale. "This is the guy who treats his time at Princeton as a scavenger hunt for Princetoniana and Princeton nostalgia: 'How many famous professors can I collect?' and so on. And he comes away not only with all these props for his sense of being elect, but also with the smoothness that seems to indicate wide learning. College socializes you, so you learn to present even trite ideas well."

These institutions cater to their students like high-end resorts. My prep school—remember, this is a *high school*—built a $26 million gym. Not that they didn't have a gym. They had a fine one, with an Olympic pool. But they needed to upgrade their facilities to compete for the elite boys and girls being wooed by other expensive prep schools. Princeton is so overcrowded with glittering new buildings. There is almost always a building project under way. It has devoured its once-rolling expanses of green and become cramped and claustrophobic. While public schools crumble, while public universities are slashed and diminished, while for-profit universities rise as our newest vocational schools, elite institutions become unaffordable even for the middle class. The privileged retreat further and further behind the walls of their opulent, gated communities. Harvard, like most institutions, has lost money. Its endowment fell $8 billion over four months in 2008, and by 2009 had officially declined by some 30 percent. Harvard's investments, once they have been disentagled, may have shrunk to half their former value. But Harvard remains very well endowed. It still has at least $20 or $25 billion. Schools like Yale, Stanford, and Princeton are not far behind.

At the elite institution, those on the inside are told they are there because they are better than others. Most believe it. They see their money and their access to power as a natural extension of their talents and abilities, rather than the result of a system that favors the privileged. They are carefully socialized in chapel, on groomed playing fields, in dormitories, and within the natural, exclusive gatherings they have with the powerful and the rich. They are members of the same clubs and fraternities. George W. Bush and John Kerry, who ran for the presidency in 2004, had each attended Yale and had been inducted as undergraduates into the university's secret and exclusive Skull and Bones society.

John D. Rockefeller III, an alumnus, was our graduation speaker the year I finished prep school at Loomis-Chaffee. The wealthy and powerful families in Boston, New York, or Los Angeles are molded by these institutions into a tribe. School, family, and entitlement effectively combine. The elites vacation together, ski at the same Swiss resorts, and know the names of the same restaurants in New York and Paris. They lunch at the same clubs and golf on the same greens. And by the time they finish an elite college, they have been conditioned to become part of the inner circle. They speak an intimidating language of privilege, complete with references to minutiae and traditions only the elite understand. They have obtained a confidence those on the outside often struggle to duplicate. And the elite, while they may not say so in public, disdain those who lack their polish and connections. Once they finish their schooling they have the means to barricade themselves in exclusive communities, places like Short Hills, New Jersey, or Greenwich, Connecticut. They know few outside their elite circles. They may have contact with a mechanic in their garage or their doorman or a nanny or gardener or contractor, but these are stilted, insincere relationships between the powerful and the relatively powerless. The elite rarely confront genuine differences of opinion. They are not asked to examine the roles they play in society and the inequities of the structure that sustains them. They are cultural philistines. The sole basis for authority is wealth. And within these self-satisfied cocoons they think of themselves as caring, good people, which they often are, but only to other members of the elite or, at times, the few service workers who support their lifestyles. The gross social injustices that condemn most African Americans to urban poverty and the working class to a subsistence level of existence, the imperial bullying that led to the wars in Iraq and Afghanistan, do not touch them. They engage in small, largely meaningless forays of charity, organized by their clubs or social groups, to give their lives a thin patina of goodness. They can live their entire lives in state of total self-delusion and perpetual childhood. "It is for people in such narrow milieux that the mass media can create a pseudo-world beyond, and a pseudo-world within themselves as well," wrote C. Wright Mills.[9]

The people I loved most, my working-class family in Maine, did not go to college. They were plumbers, post-office clerks, and mill workers. Most of the men were veterans. They lived frugal and hard lives. They were indulgent of my incessant reading and incompetence with tools, even my distaste for deer hunting, and they were a steady reminder that although I had been blessed with an opportunity that had been denied to them, I was not better or more intelligent. If you are poor, you have to work after high school or, in the case of my grandfather, before you finish high school. You serve in the military because it is one of the few jobs in which you can get health insurance and a decent salary. College is not an option. No one takes care of you. You have to do that for yourself. This is the most important difference between members of the working classes and elites. If you are poor or a member of the working class, you are on your own.

The elite schools speak often of the diversity among their students. But they base diversity on race and ethnicity rather than on class. The admissions process, along with the staggering tuition costs, precludes most of the poor and working classes. The system is stacked against those who do not have parents with incomes and educations to play the game. When my son got his SAT scores back as a senior in high school, we were surprised to find that his critical reading score was lower than his math score. He dislikes math but is an avid and perceptive reader. And so we did what many educated, middle-class families do. We hired an expensive tutor from the Princeton Review—its deluxe SAT preparation package costs $7,000—who taught him the tricks and techniques of standardized testing. The undergraduate test-prep business takes in revenues of $726 million a year, up 25 percent from four years ago. The tutor told my son things like "stop thinking about whether the passage is true. You are wasting test time thinking about the ideas. Just spit back what they tell you." His reading score went up 130 points, pushing his test scores into the highest percentile in the country. Had he somehow become smarter thanks to the tutoring? Was he suddenly a better reader because he could quickly regurgitate a passage rather than think about it or critique it? Had he become more intelligent? Is it really a smart, effective measurement of intelligence to gauge how students read and answer narrowly selected multiple-choice questions while someone holds a stopwatch over them? What about families that do not have a few thousand dollars to hire a tutor? What chance do their children have?

Elite universities, because of their incessant reliance on standardized tests and the demand for perfect grades, fill their classrooms with large numbers of drones and a disproportionate percentage of the rich and well connected. Joseph A. Soares, in *The Power of Privilege: Yale and America's Elite Colleges,* used Yale's internal data to show that 14 percent of the students attending in 2000 were "legacies," children of alumni. And at Harvard the most generous donors, those who give more than $1 million, are grouped together in the Committee on University Resources. The 340 committee members who have children at or past college age have 336 children who are, or were previously, enrolled or have studied at Harvard—even though the university admits fewer than one in ten candidates overall, *Inside Higher Education* reported. According to Daniel Golden, who wrote *The Price of Admission: How America's Ruling Class Buys Its Way into Elite Colleges—and Who Gets Left Outside the Gates*, Harvard has something called the "Z list" (on which the university refuses to comment) of about twenty-five to fifty well-connected but academically borderline applicants. These wealthy applicants are told they can enroll if they defer for a year.[10] The list is a major tool for lining up big prospective donors. Soares and Golden illustrate that you can, if you are rich enough, almost always buy your way into an Ivy League school.

I have taught gifted and engaged students who used these institutions to expand the life of the mind, who asked the big questions, and who cherished what these schools had to offer. But they were often a marginalized minority. The bulk of their classmates, most of whom headed off to Wall Street or corporate firms when they graduated, with opening salaries starting at $120,000 a year, did prodigious amounts of work, and faithfully regurgitated information. They received perfect grades in both tedious, boring classes and stimulating ones. They may have known the plot and salient details of Joseph Conrad's *Heart of Darkness,* but they were unable to tell you why the story was important. Their professors, fearful of being branded "political" and not wanting to upset the legions of wealthy donors and administrative overlords who rule these institutions, did not dare draw the obvious parallels between events in the Conrad novel and the failures and discontents of the Iraq occupation and American empire. They did not use Conrad's story, as it was meant to be used, to examine our own imperial darkness. Even in the anemic and marginalized world of the humanities, what is taught exists in a moral void.

The bankruptcy of our economic and political systems can be traced directly to the assault against the humanities. The neglect of the humanities has allowed elites to organize education and society around predetermined answers to predetermined questions. Students are taught structures designed to produce these answers even as these structures have collapsed. But those in charge, because they are educated only in specializations designed to maintain these economic and political structures, have run out of ideas. They have been trained only to find solutions that will maintain the system. This is what the Harvard Business School case method is about, a didactic system in which the logic employed to solve a specific problem always, in the end, sustains market capitalism. These elites are not capable of asking the broad, universal questions, the staples of an education in the humanities, which challenge the deepest assumptions of a culture and examine the harsh realities of political and economic power. They have forgotten, because they have not been taught, that human nature is a mixture of good and evil. They do not have the capacity for critical reflection. They do not understand that for every answer there arises another question—the very basis behind the Socratic academy's search for wisdom.

For Socrates, all virtues were forms of knowledge. To train someone to manage an account for Goldman Sachs is to educate him or her in a skill. To train them to debate stoic, existential, theological, and humanist ways of grappling with reality is to educate them in values and morals. A culture that does not grasp the vital interplay between morality and power, which mistakes management techniques for wisdom, which fails to understand that the measure of a civilization is its compassion, not its speed or ability to consume, condemns itself to death. Morality is the product of a civilization, but the elites know little of these traditions. They are products of a moral void. They lack clarity about themselves and their culture. They can fathom only their own personal troubles. They do not see their own biases or the causes of their own frustrations. They are blind to the gaping inadequacies in our economic, social, and political structures and do not grasp that these structures, which they have been taught to serve, must be radically modified or even abolished to stave off disaster. They have been rendered mute and ineffectual. "What we cannot speak about," Ludwig Wittgenstein warned, "we must pass over in silence."[11]

"The existence of multiple forms of intelligence has become a commonplace, but however much elite universities like to sprinkle their incoming classes with a few actors or violinists, they select for and develop one form of intelligence: the analytic," wrote William Deresiewicz in *The American Scholar.* Deresiewicz, who taught English at Yale, writes that

> while this is broadly true of all universities, elite schools, precisely because their students (and faculty, and administrators) possess this one form of intelligence to such a high degree, are more apt to ignore the value of others. One naturally prizes what one most possesses and what most makes for one's advantages. But social intelligence and emotional intelligence and creative ability, to name just three other forms, are not distributed preferentially among the educational elite.[12]

Intelligence is morally neutral. It is no more virtuous than athletic prowess. It can be used to further the exploitation of the working class by corporations and the mechanisms of repression and war, or it can be used to fight these forces. But if you determine worth by wealth, as these institutions do, then examining and reforming social and political systems is inherently devalued. The unstated ethic of these elite institutions is to make as much money as you can to sustain the elitist system. College presidents, many of whom earn salaries that rival those of corporate executives, must often devote their energies to fund-raising rather than to education. They shower honorary degrees and trusteeships on hedge-fund managers and Wall Street titans whose lives are often examples of moral squalor and unchecked greed.

The slavish honoring of the rich by elite schools, despite the lofty rhetoric about public service, is clear to the students. The object is to make money. These institutions have an insatiable appetite for donations and constant fund-raising campaigns to boost multibillion-dollar endowments. This constant need can be met only by producing rich alumni. But grabbing what you can, as John Ruskin said, isn't any less wicked when you grab it with the power of your brains than with the power of your fists.

Most of these students are so conditioned to success that they become afraid to take risks. They have been taught from a young age by zealous parents, schools, and institutional authorities what constitutes failure and success. They are socialized to obey. They obsess over grades and seek to please professors, even if what their professors teach is fatuous. The point is to get ahead, and getting ahead means deference to authority. Challenging authority is never a career advancer. The student becomes adept, as Richard Hoggart wrote, at

> a technique of apparent learning, of acquiring facts. He learns how to receive a purely literate education, one using only a small part of his personality and challenging only a limited area of his being. He begins to see life as a ladder, as a permanent examination with some praise and some further exhortation at each stage. He becomes an expert imbiber and doler-out; his competence will vary, but will rarely be accompanied by genuine enthusiasm. He rarely feels the reality of knowledge, of other men's thoughts and imaginings, on his own pulses; he rarely discovered an author for himself and on his own. In this half of his life he can respond only if there is a direct connection with the system of training. He has something of the blinkered pony about him; sometimes he is trained by those who have been through the same regimen, who are hardly unblinkered themselves, and who praise him in the degree to which he takes comfortably to their blinders. Though there is a powerful, unidealistic, unwarmed realism about his attitude at bottom, that is his chief form of initiative; of other forms—the freely-ranged mind, the bold flying of mental kites, the courage to reject some 'lines' even though they are officially as important as all the rest–of these he probably has little, and his training does not often encourage them.[13]

The products of these institutions, as Hoggart noted, have "difficulty in choosing a direction in a world where there is no longer a master to please, a toffee-apple at the end of each stage, a certificate, a place in the upper half of the assessable world."[14]

The very qualities and intellectual inquiries that sustain an open society are often crushed by elite institutions. The elite school, as Saul writes,

> actively seeks students who suffer from the appropriate imbalance and then sets out to exaggerate it. Imagination, creativity, moral balance, knowledge, common sense, a social view—all these things wither. Competitiveness, having an ever-ready answer, a talent for manipulating situations—all these things are encouraged to grow. As a result amorality also grows; as does extreme aggressivity when they are questioned by outsiders; as does a confusion between the nature of good versus having a ready answer to all questions. Above all, what is encouraged is the growth of an undisciplined form of self-interest, in which winning is what counts.[15]

One winter night I was returning books to Firestone Library at Princeton University. I glanced at the book the student behind the main desk was reading. It was *How to Win at College* by Cal Newport. The flap cover promised that it was "the only guide to getting ahead once you've gotten in—proven strategies for making the most of your college years, based on winning secrets from the country's most successful students."

"What does it take to be a standout student?" the flap read.

> How can you make the most of your college years—graduate with honors, choose exciting activities, build a head-turning résumé, and gain access to the best post-college opportunities? Based on interviews with star students at universities nationwide, from Harvard to the University of Arizona, *How to Win at College* presents seventy-five simple rules that will rocket you to the top of the class. These college-tested—and often surprising—strategies include:
>
> - Don't do all your reading
> - Drop classes every term

- Become a club president
- Care about your grades, ignore your GPA
- Never pull an all-nighter
- Take three days to write a paper
- Always be working on a "grand project"
- Do one thing better than anyone else you know

"Proving that success has little to do with being a genius workaholic, and everything to do with playing the game," it went on. "*How to Win at College* is the must-have guide for making the most of these four important years—and getting an edge on life after graduation."[16]

First-year students arrive on elite campuses and begin to network their way into the exclusive eating clubs, fraternities, sororities, or secret societies, test into the elite academic programs and lobby for competitive summer internships. They put in punishing hours, come to office hours to make sure they grasp what their professors want, and challenge all grades under 4.0 in an effort to maintain a high average. They learn to placate and please authority, never to challenge it. By the time they graduate, they are superbly conditioned for the drudgery of moving large sums of money around electronically or negotiating huge corporate contracts.

"The system forgot to teach them, along the way to the prestige admissions and the lucrative jobs, that the most important achievements can't be measured by a letter or a number or a name," Deresiewicz wrote. "It forgot that the true purpose of education is to make minds, not careers.

"Only a small minority have seen their education as part of a larger intellectual journey, have approached the work of the mind with a pilgrim soul," he went on. "These few have tended to feel like freaks, not least because they get so little support from the university itself. Places like Yale, as one of them put it to me, are not conducive to searchers. Places like Yale are simply not set up to help students ask the big questions. I don't think there ever was a golden age of intellectualism in the American university, but in the 19th century students might at least have had a chance to hear such questions raised in chapel or in the literary societies and debating clubs that flourished on campus."[17]

This soul-crushing experience of education is not new within elite academic institutions, as William Hazlitt noted at the beginning of the nineteenth century:

> Men do not become what by nature they are meant to be, but what society makes them. The generous feelings, and high propensities of the soul are, as it were, shrunk up, seared, violently wrenched, and amputated, to fit us for our intercourse with the world, something in the manner that beggars maim and mutilate their children, to make them fit for their future situation in life.[18]

The educational landscape, however, has deteriorated since Hazlitt. There has been a concerted assault on all forms of learning that are not brutally utilitarian. The Modern Language Association's end-of-the-year job listings in English, literature, and foreign languages dropped 21 percent for 2008–2009 from the previous year, the biggest decline in thirty-four years. The humanities' share of college degrees is less than half of what it was during the mid- to late '60s, according to the Humanities Indicators Prototype, a new database recently released by the American Academy of Arts & Sciences. Only 8 percent of college graduates, or about 110,000 students, now receive degrees in the humanities. Between 1970 and 2001, bachelor's degrees in English have declined from 7.6 percent to 4 percent of the whole, as have degrees in foreign languages (2.4 percent to 1 percent), mathematics (3 percent to 1 percent), and social science and history (18.4 percent to 10 percent). Bachelor's degrees in business, which promise to teach students how to accumulate wealth, have skyrocketed. Business majors since 1970–1971 have risen from 13.6 percent of the graduating population to 21.7 percent. Business has now replaced education, which has fallen from 21 percent to 8.2 percent, as the most popular major.[19]

Frank Donoghue, the author of *The Last Professors: The Corporate University and the Fate of the Humanities*, writes that liberal arts education has been systemically dismantled for decades. Any form of learning not strictly vocational has at best been marginalized and in many schools abolished. Students are steered away from asking the broad, disturbing questions that challenge the assumptions of the power elite. They do not know how to interrogate or examine an economic system that serves the corporate state. This has led many bright graduates directly into the arms of corporate entities.

Matthew Arnold's *Culture and Anarchy*, written in 1869, was once considered a canonical work on the lofty goals of education. Arnold argued that a broad knowledge of culture, "the best that has been thought and said," would provide standards to resist the errors and corruptions of contemporary life. This belief held sway, at least in the outward manifestations of higher education, for perhaps a century. But Arnold's eloquent defense of knowledge for its own sake, as a way to ask the broad moral and social questions, has been shredded and destroyed. Most universities have become high-priced occupational training centers. Students seek tangible vocational credentials. At the few institutions where the liberal arts survive, as Donoghue writes, prestige is the paramount commodity. *U.S. News & World Report* has, since its annual America's Best Colleges issue debuted in 1983, ranked schools that, through their selectiveness, also offer a route into the world of the elite. These schools may still teach the liberal arts, but those arts are marketed as another way to propel students into the vocational specialties offered by graduate schools or into lucrative jobs.

The assault on education began more than a century ago by industrialists and capitalists such as Andrew Carnegie. In 1891, Carnegie congratulated the graduates of the Pierce College of Business for being "fully occupied in obtaining a knowledge of shorthand and typewriting" rather than wasting time "upon dead languages." The industrialist Richard Teller Crane was even more pointed in his 1911 dismissal of what humanists call the "life of the mind." No one who has "a taste for literature has the right to be happy" because "the only men entitled to happiness . . . are those who are useful."[20] The arrival of industrialists on university boards of trustees began as early as the 1870s and the University of Pennsylvania's Wharton School of Business offered the first academic credential in business administration in 1881. The capitalists, from the start, complained that universities were unprofitable. These early twentieth-century capitalists, like heads of investment houses and hedge-fund managers, were, as Donoghue writes, "motivated by an ethically based anti-intellectualism that transcended interest in the financial bottom line. Their distrust of the ideal of intellectual inquiry for its own sake, led them to insist that if universities were to be preserved at all, they must operate on a different set of principles from those governing the liberal arts."[21]

And as small, liberal arts schools have folded—at least 200 since 1990—they have been replaced with corporate, for-profit universities. There are now some forty-five colleges and universities listed on the NYSE or the NASDAQ. The University of Phoenix, the largest for-profit school with some 300,000 students, proudly calls itself on its Web site: "Your corporate university." Ronald Taylor, the chief operator and co-founder of DeVry, the second-largest for-profit, higher-education provider, bluntly stated his organization's goals: "The colossally simple notion that drives DeVry's business is that if you ask employers what they want and then provide what they want, the people you supply to them will be hired."[22] The only mission undertaken by for-profit universities, and increasingly non-profit universities, is job training. And as universities become glorified vocational schools for the corporations, they adopt values and operating techniques of the corporations they serve. It may be more cost-effective to replace tenured faculty with adjuncts and whittle down or shutter departments like French or history that do not feed vocational aspirations, but it decimates the possibility of a broad education that permits students to question the assumptions of a decaying culture, reach out beyond our borders, and chart new alternatives and directions.

It is not just the humanities that are in danger, but the professors themselves. Most universities no longer hire the best and most experienced teachers but the cheapest. Tenured and tenure-track teachers now make up only 35 percent of the pedagogical work force and the number is steadily falling.[23] Professors are becoming itinerant workers, often having to work at two or three schools, denied office space, and unable to make a living wage. The myopic and narrow vision of life as an accumulation of money and power, promoted at the turn-of-the-century by rapacious capitalists such as Carnegie or Crane, has become education's dominant ideology. We have, as Steven Brint points out, displaced the "social-trustee professional" by the "expert professional."

The old social-trustee professional came out of the humanities. He or she valued collegial organization, learning, and the volunteerism of public service. The new classes of expert professionals have been trained to focus on narrow, specialized knowledge independent of social ideas or conceptions of the common good. A doctor, lawyer, or engineer may become wealthy, but the real meaning of their work is that they sustain health, justice, good government, or safety. The flight from the humanities has become a flight from conscience. It has created an elite class of experts who seldom look beyond their tasks and disciplines to put what they do in a wider, social context. And by absenting themselves from the moral and social questions raised by the humanities, they have opted to serve a corporate structure that has destroyed the culture around them.

Our elites—the ones in Congress, the ones on Wall Street, and the ones being produced at prestigious universities and business schools—do not have the capacity to fix our financial mess. Indeed, they will make it worse. They have no concept, thanks to the educations they have received, of how to replace a failed system with a new one. They are petty, timid, and uncreative bureaucrats superbly trained to carry out systems management. They see only piecemeal solutions that will satisfy the corporate structure. Their entire focus is numbers, profits, and personal advancement. They lack a moral and intellectual core. They are as able to deny gravely ill people medical coverage to increase company profits as they are to use taxpayer dollars to peddle costly weapons systems to blood-soaked dictatorships. The human consequences never figure into their balance sheets. The democratic system, they believe, is a secondary product of the free market—which they slavishly serve.

Andrew Lahde, a Santa Monica, California, hedge-fund manager who made an 866 percent gain by betting on the subprime mortgage collapse, abruptly shut down his fund in 2008, citing the risk of trading with faltering banks. In his farewell letter to his investors, he excoriated the elites who run our investment houses, banks, and government.

"The low-hanging fruit, i.e. idiots whose parents paid for prep school, Yale, and then the Harvard MBA, was there for the taking," he said of our oligarchic class:

> These people who were (often) truly not worthy of the education they received (or supposedly received) rose to the top of companies such as AIG, Bear Stearns, and Lehman Brothers and all levels of our

government. All of this behavior supporting the Aristocracy ended up only making it easier for me to find people stupid enough to take the other side of my trades. God bless America. . . .

"On the issue of the U.S. Government, I would like to make a modest proposal," he went on:

> First, I point out the obvious flaws, whereby legislation was repeatedly brought forth to Congress over the past eight years, which would have [reined] in the predatory lending practices of now mostly defunct institutions. These institutions regularly filled the coffers of both parties in return for voting down all of this legislation designed to protect the common citizen. This is an outrage, yet no one seems to know or care about it. Since Thomas Jefferson and Adam Smith [sic] passed, I would argue that there has been a dearth of worthy philosophers in this country, at least ones focused on improving government.[24]

The single most important quality needed to resist evil is moral autonomy. As Immanuel Kant wrote, moral autonomy is possible only through reflection, self-determination, and the courage not to cooperate. Moral autonomy is what the corporate state, with all its coded attacks on liberal institutions and "leftist" professors, have really set out to destroy. The corporate state holds up as our ideal what Adorno called "the manipulative character." The manipulative character has superb organizational skills yet is unable to have authentic human experiences. He or she is an emotional cripple and driven by an overvalued realism. The manipulative character is a systems manager. He or she is exclusively trained to sustain the corporate structure, which is why our elites wasted mind-blowing amounts of our money on corporations like Goldman Sachs and AIG.

"He makes a cult of action, activity, of so-called efficiency as such which reappears in the advertising image of the active person," Adorno wrote of this personality type. These manipulative characters, people like Lawrence Summers, Henry Paulson, Robert Rubin, Ben

Bernanke, Timothy Geithner, AIG's Edward Liddy, and Goldman Sachs CEO Lloyd Blankfein, along with most of our ruling class, have used corporate money and power to determine the narrow parameters of the debate in our classrooms, on the airwaves, and in the halls of Congress—while looting the country. Many of these men appear to be so morally and intellectually stunted that they are incapable of acknowledging their responsibility for our decline.

"It is especially difficult to fight against it," warned Adorno, "because those manipulative people, who actually are incapable of true experience, for that very reason manifest an unresponsiveness that associates them with certain mentally ill or psychotic characters, namely schizoids."[25]

Obama is a product of this elitist system. So are his degree-laden cabinet members. They come out of Harvard, Yale, Wellesley, and Princeton. Their friends and classmates made huge fortunes on Wall Street and in powerful law firms. They go to the same class reunions. They belong to the same clubs. They speak the same easy language of privilege, comfort, and entitlement. The education they have obtained has served to rigidify and perpetuate social stratification. These elite schools prevent, to use Arnold's words, the "best selves" in the various strata in our culture from communicating across class lines. Our power elite has a blind belief in a decaying political and financial system that has nurtured, enriched, and empowered it. But the elite cannot solve our problems. It has been trained only to find solutions, such as paying out trillions of dollars of taxpayer money to bail out banks and financial firms, to sustain a dead system. The elite, and those who work for them, were never taught how to question the assumptions of their age. The socially important knowledge and cultural ideas embodied in history, literature, philosophy, and religion, which are at their core subversive and threatening to authority, have been banished from public discourse.

Ironically, the universities have trained hundreds of thousands of graduates for jobs that soon will not exist. They have trained people to maintain a structure that cannot be maintained. The elite as well as those equipped with narrow, specialized vocational skills, know only how to feed the beast until it dies. Once it is dead, they will be help-less. Don't expect them to save us. They don't know how. They do not even know how to ask the questions. And when it all collapses, when our rotten financial system with its trillions in worthless assets implodes and our imperial wars end in humiliation and defeat, the power elite will be exposed as being as helpless, and as self-deluded, as the rest of us.

IV / The Illusion
of Happiness

"And that," put in the Director sententiously, "that is the secret of happiness and virtue—liking what you've got to do. All conditioning aims at that: making people like their unescapable social destiny."[1]

—ALDOUS HUXLEY

"Feeling blue? Doctors now say you can lie yourself into happiness. By creating self-deceptions, no matter how negative [your problem], it can be turned into a positive and you'll have greater [happiness]."[2]

—RADIO ADVERTISEMENT

DAVID COOPERRIDER, a professor from Case Western Reserve University, is a plump, balding man in a shapeless black suit and checkered tie. He stands in the center of the stage in the high-ceilinged lecture hall of Claremont Graduate University before some six hundred people. The spotlight illuminates his head.

"What would it mean to create an entire change theory around strengths?" he asks. Such a theory, he asserts, exists. It is called "Transformational Positivity." And to understand it, people need to shift their thinking, much like Einstein, whom he quotes as saying, "No problem can be solved from the same level of consciousness that created it. We must learn to see the world anew."

Positive thinking, which is delivered to the culture in a variety of forms, has its academic equivalent in positive psychology. Cooperrider touts what he calls Transformational Positivity. Transformational Positivity, he says, is the future of organizational change. Optimism can and must become a permanent state of mind. He has designed a corporate workshop that promises to bring about this change. It is called "Appreciative Inquiry." Appreciative Inquiry, he assures the audience, will spread happiness around the world.

Appreciative Inquiry promises to transform organizations into "Positive Institutions." "It's almost like fusion energy," Cooperrider explains. "Fusion is where two positive atoms come together, and there is an incredible energy that is released." His clients include the U.S. Navy, Wal-Mart, Hewlett-Packard, United Way, Boeing, the American Red Cross, the Carter Center, and the United Nations.[3] Celebrities such as Goldie Hawn also promote positive psychology, designing workshops and curriculums for children and corporate workers. And Appreciative Inquiry, which is supposed to make workers into a happy, harmonious whole, is advertised as a way to increase profits.

Cooperrider, excited and at times sputtering, stands before a Power-Point demonstration. He slips into obscure and often incomprehensible jargon: "Positive Institutions are organizations, including groups, families, and communities, designed and managed for the *elevation* and the engagement of signature strengths, the connected and combined *magnification* of strengths, and ultimately, the coherent cross-level *refraction* of our highest human strengths outward into society and our world" [emphases are Cooperrider's]. He compares Appreciative Inquiry to a solar concentrator.

Happiness, Cooperrider explains, is achieved through "a progressive concentration and release of positivity—a 'concrescence' or growing together—whereby persons are 'enlarged,' and organizational or mutual strengths, resources, and positive-potentials are connected and magnified, where both (person and organization) become agents of the greater good beyond them.

"In other words," he continues, "institutions can be a vehicle for bringing more courage into the world, for amplifying love in the world, for amplifying temperance and justice, and so on."

He ends by saying that this generation—presumably his—is the most privileged generation in human history. It is a generation that will channel positive emotions through corporations and spread them throughout the culture. The moral and ethical issues of corporatism, from the toxic assets they may have amassed, to predatory lending, to legislation they may author to destroy regulation and oversight, even to the actual products they may produce, from weapons systems to crushing credit-card debt, appear to be irrelevant. There presumably could have been a "positive" Dutch East Indies Company just as there can be a "positive" Halliburton, J. P. Morgan Chase, Xe (formerly Blackwater), or Raytheon.

Corporate harmony means all quotas can be met. All things are possible. Profits can always increase. All we need is the right attitude. The highest form of personal happiness comes, people like Cooperrider insist, when the corporation thrives. Corporate retreats are built around this idea of merging the self with the corporate collective. They often have the feel, as this conference does, of a religious revival. They are designed to whip up emotions. In their inspirational talks, sports stars, retired military commanders, billionaires, and self-help specialists such as Tony Robbins or Cooperrider claim that the impossible is possible. By thinking about things, by visualizing them, by wanting them, we can make them happen. It is a trick worthy of the con artist "Professor" Harold Hill in *The Music Man* who insists he can teach children to play instruments by getting them to think about the melody.

The purpose and goals of the corporation are never questioned. To question them, to engage in criticism of the goals of the collective, is to be obstructive and negative. The corporations are the powers that determine identity. The corporations tell us who we are and what we can become. And the corporations offer the only route to personal fulfillment and salvation. If we are not happy there is something wrong with *us*. Debate and criticism, especially about the goals and structure of the corporation, are condemned as negative and "counterproductive."

Positive psychology is to the corporate state what eugenics was to the Nazis. Positive psychology—at least, as applied so broadly and unquestioningly to corporate relations—is a quack science. It throws a smokescreen over corporate domination, abuse, and greed. Those who preach it serve the corporate leviathan. They are awash in corporate grants. They are invited to corporate retreats to assure corporate employees that they can find happiness by sublimating their selves into corporate culture. They hold academic conferences. They publish a *Journal of Happiness Studies* and a *World Database of Happiness.* And the movement has sought and found academic legitimacy. There are more than a hundred courses on positive psychology available on college campuses. The University of Pennsylvania offers a Masters of Applied Positive Psychology established under the leadership of Martin Seligman, author of *Authentic Happiness: Using the New Positive Psychology to Realize Your Potential for Lasting Fulfillment* and a former president of the American Psychological Association. The School of Behavioral and Organizational Sciences at Claremont Graduate University offers Ph.D. and M.A. concentrations on what it calls "the Science of Positive Psychology." Degree programs are also available at the University of East London, the University of Milan, and the National Autonomous University of Mexico in Mexico City.

Dr. Tal D. Ben-Shahar, who wrote *Happier: Learn the Secrets to Daily Joy and Lasting Fulfillment,* taught hugely popular courses at Harvard University on "Positive Psychology" and "The Psychology of Leadership." He called himself, when he taught at Harvard, the "Harvard Happiness Professor."

"There is mounting evidence in the psychological literature showing that focusing on cultivating strengths, optimism, gratitude, and a positive perspective can lead to growth during difficult times," Ben-Shahar has stated.

Positive Psychology has its own therapy techniques to achieve happiness. It instructs patients to write a letter of gratitude to someone who had been kind to them. Patients are instructed to pen "You at your best" essays in which they are asked "to write about a time when they were at their best and then to reflect on personal strengths displayed in the story." They are instructed to "review the story once every day for a week and to reflect on the strengths they had identified." And the professionals argue that their research shows that many of their patients have "lastingly increased happiness and decreased depressive symptoms."

Ben-Shahar pumps out the catchy slogans and clichés that color all cheap self-improvement schemes. "Learn to fail or fail to learn," he says, and "not 'It happened for the best,' but 'How can I make the best of what happened?'"

He argues that if a traumatic episode can result in post-traumatic stress disorder, it may be possible to create the opposite phenomenon with a single glorious, ecstatic experience. This could, he says, dramatically change a person's life for the better.

Those who fail to exhibit positive attitudes, no matter the external reality, are in some ways ill. Their attitudes, like those of recalcitrant Chinese during the Cultural Revolution, need correction. Once we adopt a positive mind, positive things will always happen. This belief, like all the other illusions peddled in the culture, encourages people to flee from reality when reality is frightening or depressing. These academic specialists in "happiness" have formulated the "Law of Attraction." It argues that we attract the good things in life, whether it is money, relationships, or employment, when we focus on what we desire. The gimmick of visualizing what we want and believing we can achieve it is no different from praying to a god or Jesus who we are told wants to make us wealthy and successful. For those who run into the hard walls of reality, the ideology has the pernicious effect of forcing the victim to blame him or herself for his or her pain or suffering. Abused and battered wives or children, the unemployed, the depressed, the mentally ill, the illiterate, the lonely, those grieving for lost loved ones, those crushed by poverty, the terminally ill, those fighting with addictions, those suffering from trauma, those trapped in menial and poorly paid jobs, those facing foreclosure or bankruptcy because they cannot pay their medical bills, need only overcome their negativity. "I think positive emotions are available to everybody," says Barbara Frederickson, the Kenan Distinguished Professor of Psychology at the University of North Carolina at Chapel Hill and director of that university's Positive Emotions and Psychophysiology Lab, in the May 2009 issue of *The Sun*. She also speaks at the Claremont conference. "There's been research done with people in slums across the globe and with prostitutes, looking at their well-being and satisfaction with life. The data suggest that positive emotions have less to do with material resources than we might think; it's really about your attitude and approach to your circumstances." This flight into self-delusion is no more helpful in solving real problems than alchemy. But it is very effective in keeping people from questioning the structures around them that are responsible for their misery. Positive Psychology gives an academic patina to fantasy.

The conference is filled with people in business attire. At the break, many stand in clusters, holding a coffee in one hand and a pastry in the other.

The university is quiet for a Saturday afternoon. The weather outside is overcast and cold. The browning lawns of Claremont's Pomona College, dotted with palm trees and oaks, reflect the harshness of the statewide drought. There is a half-moon wall visible from the conference center. "CLOSE THE SCHOOL OF THE AMERICAS" is written in large red letters on the wall. "Dan Eats Chicken Skin" and "Dog Boner To The Rescue!" read other graffiti. "SUCK IT, LIFE" is spray-painted in black. Sections of the wall resemble works by Picasso or Diego Rivera. The largest message is "Vote Obama '08." The university buildings, with imitation adobe walls and red clay tile roofs, cluster around the college's clock tower. The campus has the appearance of a California Spanish mission.

In the auditorium, the round face of Martin Seligman appears in a video on a twenty-foot screen. His gaze is serious. Behind him are disordered bookshelves.

"Welcome to this auspicious occasion," he says to the attentive, mostly white crowd. A young woman, a student of psychology at California State University at Long Beach, scribbles notes. She underlines *auspicious occasion*.

Seligman speaks of four endeavors for the movement.

"The first endeavor I call 'positive physical health,'" Seligman says. "If you think about positive psychology as having argued that positive mental health is something over and above the absence of mental illness. That is," he clarifies, hammering his desk with every "presence," "the *presence* of positive emotion, the *presence* of flow, the *presence* of engagement, the *presence* of meaning, the *presence* of positive relationships." Seligman pauses. "Can the same thing be said for physical health?" He believes researchers will find a correlation between these positive mental states and the "real" body.[4]

Seligman announces that twenty $200,000 grants—a dream sum for any researcher—will be given out for "groundbreaking research" in the burgeoning field of positive neuroscience. The goal is to locate where positive emotions originate in the brain.

"Education usually consists of taking young people and teaching them workplace skills. . . . But there is an epidemic of depression," he says sadly. His optimistic tone returns: "Would it be possible to have positive education? . . . That is, without sacrificing any of the usual skills such as discipline, reading, literacy, numeracy. . . . Can we build engagement, meaning, positive emotion, good relations in schools?"

Seligman announces that schools in the United States, such as the Knowledge Is Power Program (KIPP) schools in Riverside, California, as well as schools in the United Kingdom and in Australia, are putting his theory into practice. The Geelong Grammar School in Australia is implementing a positive psychology curriculum. Hundreds of teachers there are being taught, in missionary fashion, to "spread the notion of positive education."

In *Authentic Happiness*, written in 2002, Seligman argues that authentic happiness can be conditioned and thus taught.

A similar-sounding life of "enjoyment," "engagement," and "affiliation" is the engineered temperament of the pliant characters in Aldous Huxley's *Brave New World.* There, the protagonist, Bernard Marx, turns in frustration to his girlfriend Lenina:

"Don't you wish you were free, Lenina?"

"I don't know what you mean. I am free. Free to have the most wonderful time. Everybody's happy nowadays."

He laughed, "Yes, 'Everybody's happy nowadays.' We have been giving the children that at five. But wouldn't you like to be free to be happy in some other way, Lenina? In your own way, for example; not in everybody else's way."

"I don't know what you mean," she repeated.[5]

"A typical day is full of anxiety and boredom," writes Mihály Csíkszentmihályi, who is "the brains behind positive psychology," according to Seligman. He credits Csíkszentmihályi with adding the concept of "flow" to the movement's ideas.[6] "Flow experiences provide the flashes of instense living against this dull background." "Flow" is described by Csíkszentmihályi as a state of "being completely involved in an activity for its own sake. The ego falls away. Time flies. Every action, movement, and thought follows naturally from the previous one, like playing jazz. Your whole being is involved, and you're using your skills to the utmost."[7] With enough adjustment, he implies, we could all be making beautiful jazz of our lives.

"People who learn to control inner experience will be able to determine the quality of their lives, which is as close as any of us can come to being happy," Csíkszentmihályi writes in *Flow: The Psychology of Optimal Experience* (1990). "There are two main strategies we can adopt to improve the quality of life," he continues. "The first is to try making external conditions match our goals. The second is to change how we experience external conditions to make them fit our goals better. . . . We cannot deny the facts of nature, but we should certainly try to improve on them."

Csíkszentmihályi specializes in "optimizing" human experience. The optimal organization man is fitter, happier, more productive, and less expensive. The optimal worker complains less. He or she obeys more. The optimal worker costs the employer less in health-care expenditures.

Csíkszentmihályi developed the idea of "psychological capital," or what he terms "paratelics." When Ed Diener, a professor of psychology at the University of Illinois, measured the world according to Csíkszentmihályi's paratelic factors, he discovered something so "shocking," he says, it must be true. These paratelic factors—"I can count on others," "I feel autonomous," "I learned something new today," and "I did what I do best"—are, more than money, corruption, starvation, or abuse, "the best predictors of the positive emotions of nations."

Diener believes he can measure happiness. He conducted a study that found a correlation between the incomes of undergraduates nineteen years after graduation with their level of cheerfulness.[8] His research also showed that happy people have higher supervisor ratings, higher organizational citizenship, and higher incomes.

The movement embraces self-delusion as psychologically and socially beneficial. It also makes handsome profits peddling it. Seligman, Diener, Shelley Taylor, and a slew of positive psychologists write popular books for, essentially, those who can afford the therapy. It is a trade. Dacher Keltner, a positive psychologist at Berkeley, hosts for-pay motivational workshops that cost $139 for standard registration. Csíkszentmihályi participates in the Annual Positive Psychology Forum, which in 2009 was in Sedona, Arizona, supposedly one of the energy hot spots of the world, for a registration fee of $716.74 per person.

"The effective individual in the face of threat seems to be one who permits the development of illusions, nurtures those illusions, and is ultimately restored by those illusions," writes Taylor, a psychologist at the University of California at Los Angeles.[9] In 1991 Taylor published a book titled *Positive Illusions: Creative Self-Deception and the Healthy Mind*, in which she argued that "positive illusions" protect mental and physical health."[10]

Taylor's article "Illusion and Well-Being" is a commonly cited resource in positive psychology. She insists that positive illusions have a measurable affect on survival rates among patients with cancer, HIV, and cardiovascular disease or surgery.

Positive illusions, described as "pervasive, enduring, and systematic," come, Taylor writes, in three types: (1) unrealistically positive views of the self; (2) exaggerated perceptions of personal control; and (3) unrealistic optimism. All of these illusions can, managed the right way, supposedly improve our lives. Illusions are good for people, she says, and therefore, by extension, unadorned reality is negative.

But while Taylor sees positive illusions as tools to ward off dysfunction, stress, and bad health, not everyone agrees. Philosopher David Jopling calls such illusions "life-lies." He argues that so-called positive illusions may work for a while but collapse when reality becomes too harsh and intrudes on the dream world.

"The deeper and more pervasive an individual's positive illusions," writes Jopling, "the greater their effect of diminishing his range of awareness of himself, other people, and the situation confronting him." Jopling argues that self-deception strategies are reality filters that organize what people understand into self-relevant and self-serving packages. "With the diminishing of the range of awareness comes a corresponding diminishing of the range of responsiveness and openness" to what is real. One's ability to interact intelligently with all of the world's real consequences diminishes.

Jopling warns of grave moral consequences for a delusional society. "This means that the range of social, emotional, and personal relations that connect us to others, to the social world, and to our own humanity, are progressively weakened as self-deceptive strategies become progressively entrenched in behavior and thought."[11]

Psychology has a long history of lending its services to the military and government as well as propaganda industries such as advertising, public relations, and human management. The National Institute of Mental Health, from which many positive psychologists have generous grants, though a public institution, has numerous government, military, and commercial relationships.[12]

Keltner is the author of *Born to be Good: The Science of the Meaningful Life*. He is also executive editor of *The Greater Good*, a magazine, and director of The Greater Good Science Center on the Berkeley campus. He teaches a course on happiness at the university and hosts motivational workshops on "building compassion, creating well-being." He has had his ears rubbed by the Dalai Lama.[13]

Keltner sits in his office in Berkeley's Tolman Hall. Students wait in the hallway for an appointment. He is dressed in shorts, a polo shirt, and sweatshirt with Berkeley's blue background with gold stripes.

When asked whether positive psychology could be used for mass coercion, Keltner replies: "As scientists our task is to describe human nature as well as we can. So the motivations of positive psychology are well founded. There are branches of our nervous system that we study in our lab that are really mysteries scientifically. The vagus nerve, oxytocin, parts of the brain that are involved in compassion. That's our first task, and that's the scientific motivation of positive psychology. And then cultures and societies and communities take science and push it in a lot of different directions. [Charles] Darwin had a theory about human nature that was very sanguine. He said we are a sympathetic species, we take care of others, we are inherently cooperative, and then [Herbert] Spencer, and social Darwinists, and libertarians pushed it in all sorts of directions, in the service of their versions of public policies. . . . So you always have to separate science from practice. And you can't critique the science based on the practices that follow. Nazism was an application of a lot of scientific ideas that have nothing to do with the science."

The theme of the most recent issue of *The Greater Good* is "The Psychology of Power." It exposes in scenario after scenario the true purpose of positive psychology—how to manipulate people to do what you want.

The magazine has an article called "Peaceful Parenting," in which two practitioners explain "how to turn parent-child conflict into cooperation." The article begins: "It's nine o'clock on a school night and twelve-year-old Jessie is absorbed in his favorite video game—until his mother comes into his bedroom and announces it's bedtime."

"I don't want to go to bed!" says Jessie.

"But it's already past your bedtime," says Mom, "and you know you have to get your rest."

"But I'm not tired!"

"Well, you will be in the morning if you don't go to sleep soon."

"Shut up!" Jessie yells. "Anyway, you can't make me go to sleep."

"Sound familiar?" the article asks. "It does to us. . . . The conversation might go on in this way until Mom, exhausted and angry, shouts something like 'I quit! Suit yourself!'"

What parents need to do, says the article, is shift from "using power *over* kids to using power *with* them."

"Peaceful parenting" should go like this:

"You're having a lot of fun playing now, huh?" asks Mom.

"Yeah," says Jessie. "And I'm not even tired."

"So you just want to keep playing until you're tired?"

"Yeah."

"It must be frustrating to be asked to stop doing something that's so much fun when you don't feel tired."

"I don't have time for what I want to do. I just have to come home and do homework."

"Hmm. It sounds like this time between homework and bedtime is really important to you, and you wish it were longer?"

"Yeah, Mom, I do."

"Thanks for helping me understand that. You know, I'd like you to have as much time as you want for the things that interest you. At the same time, I've also noticed that when you stay up after nine on school nights, you're tired the next morning. Do you hear what my concern is?"

"Yeah, you want me to get a good night's sleep."

"Yes, thanks for hearing that."

"I just need five more minutes to finish this game. Okay?"

"Okay. I'll get out your pajamas."[14]

The pages of *The Greater Good* are awash in such insincere and coercive techniques. The goal, replicated in the corporate workshops where managers are taught how to speak to employees, is not to communicate but to control.

Richard S. Lazarus, who was a professor of psychology at Berkeley, was disturbed by "the vagueness, the religious tone, and the arrogance with which [the claims of positive psychology] are made."[15] He saw positive psychology as "populist and intellectually much too easy rather than a set of thoughtful ideas or principles to be respected." "In my opinion, [positive psychologists] are promoting a kind of religion," wrote Lazarus, "a vision from on high, which is falsely clothed in a claim to science that never materializes."

Barbara Frederickson, from the University of North Carolina at Chapel Hill, shows the crowd in the Claremont auditorium a cartoon diagram of a sailboat. She says she has found an exact, "totally scientific," optimal "positivity" ratio for positive to negative emotions: 3 to 1. The keel of the sailboat, she says, represents the "necessary negative emotions" that are heavy and burdensome and "keep the boat on course and manageable," while the sail, "having ample and sufficient positivity, is what really allows us to take off. What matters most, I have found, is the ratio of your heartfelt positivity relative to your heart-wrenching negativity," said Frederickson.

"Why do we need positive emotions to really take off?" she asks. "Because positivity opens us." On the screen overhead, the image of a blue flower appears. "Now imagine you are this flower, and your petals are drawn tightly around your face. If you could see out at all, it's just a little speck," she says mournfully. "You can't appreciate much of what goes on around you. . . . But once you feel the warmth of the sun, things begin to change, your leaves begin to soften, your petals loosen and begin to stretch outward, exposing your face"—Frederickson splays her hands open around her face like petals—"and removing your delicate blinders, you *see* more and more, and your world quite literally *expands.*

"Now some flowers bloom just once. But others, like these day lilies," she says, pointing to the slides of the blue and now red flowers, "they close up every evening and they bloom again when they see the sun. . . . Our minds are like these day lilies. Yet their openness honors momentary shifts in our positivity." Frederickson pauses. "Positivity is to our minds what the sunlight is to day lilies."

Christopher Peterson and Nansook Park claim to have found the statistically most important "character strengths" in every society around the world. Peterson and Park stand on opposite sides of the stage. The large screen between them shows a bar graph titled "Adult Character Strengths."

"We have our adult questionnaire online," says Peterson. "I think to date it's been completed by about 1.3 million people. Pretty soon it will be the whole world! But about 100,000 people into this, we simply calculated the more common versus less common character strengths, and we have arranged them here."

Peterson gestures at the graph.

"What's interesting is that on the left side are certain strengths that are more common, like kindness, fairness, honesty, gratitude. And, we wonder, and other people have said this, if these might not be the sorts of strengths that are necessary for a viable society? It's kind of hard to imagine a viable society in which these things are not present.

"Now what I left out is, 'Who do these data refer to?' Well, this particular graph is 50,000 Americans. But we subdivided it into all fifty states, and you get the same distribution across the fifty states."

Peterson chuckles.

"Oh yeah, we also looked at fifty-four other nations, and you get the same distribution across the nations . . . I remember we sent it to a journal," Peterson says confidently, "and the first journal editor rejected it, and he said, 'You didn't find anything different, any differences.'"

Peterson comically slaps himself on the head, mugging in mock disbelief.

"I said, '*We found human nature*!'" Peterson throws his arms out. "Isn't that good enough!?"

Peterson goes on to talk about the less important indicators. "Oh, look what's on the bottom: Self-regulation—that's like staying on a diet. That's why I am hiding behind the podium!" The crowd chuckles.

"Modesty," he says. "Like, 'God, we are good researchers!'" The crowd laughs louder. "You get the idea!"

Kim Cameron is dressed in a black suit with a red tie. He is Professor of Management and Organizations at the University of Michigan, where he is co-founder of the Center for Positive Organizational Culture. Cameron has come to talk about how corporations can use positive or "virtuous" practices to improve profits.

"All organizations exist to eliminate deviance," says Cameron. "The reason we organize is to minimize unexpected, chaotic, unpredictable behavior. Right? Organization exists to eliminate negative deviance. The problem is, it also eliminates positive deviance. We organize, and thereby, by definition, we eliminate positively deviant or extraordinary or spectacular or virtuous behavior."

Cameron says he shows business executives how happiness, compassion, and goodness can increase profits. Cameron's clients include *Fortune* 100 companies, but also small organizations, nonprofits, and county governments. Clients range from the YMCA to the trucking industry. Cameron reminds the audience he is not in it for the money, but for the fulfillment he gets from his work. What matters is *feeling* good. He sells harmony ideology to corporations.

Most positive psychologists belong to the 148,000-member American Psychological Association (APA), which has lent its services for decades to the military and intelligence communities to research and perfect techniques for interrogation and control. Psychologists working for government agencies in the 1950s and '60s conducted human experiments and discovered that psychological torture, including sensory and sleep deprivation, was far more disorientating and destructive to the human psyche than crude beatings and physical abuse. They refined psychological techniques to ensure complete emotional breakdowns. Psychologists are the only group of major health-care providers who openly participate in interrogations at military and CIA facilities. The American Psychiatric Association and the American Medical Association have forbidden members to participate in military interrogations. But the APA, despite complaints and resignations by a few of its members, has refused to ban its psychologists from interrogations, including at notorious torture sites such as Guantánamo Bay.

A May 2007 Pentagon report by the inspector general's office acknowledged that psychologists oversaw the adaptation of the military's Survive, Evade, Resist, and Escape (SERE) program for use against prisoners. SERE was first designed to replicate torture techniques and help U.S. troops resist Chinese and Soviets interrogators. But, in the hands of army and intelligence psychologists, SERE has been reverse-engineered to break prisoners held in American interrogation centers. The sleep deprivation, lengthy stress positions, complete sensory deprivation, isolation, sexual humiliation, and forced nudity are systematically employed to reduce prisoners to a state of utter helplessness. Many become catatonic. The psychologists monitor the steady deterioration of the prisoner and advise interrogators how to employ techniques to complete the psychological disintegration.

Psychologists, in and out of the government, have learned how to manipulate social behavior. The promotion of collective harmony, under the guise of achieving happiness, is simply another carefully designed mechanism for conformity. Positive psychology is about banishing criticism and molding a group into a weak and malleable unit that will take orders. Personal values, those nurtured by an independent conscience, are gently condemned as antagonistic to harmony and happiness. Those who refuse under group pressure to become harmonious are deemed a drag on the corporate body and, if they cannot be reformed, expunged. Those who are willing to surrender their individuality are granted small rewards doled out by the corporate structure. They can feel, at least until they lose their jobs, that they belong to an important and powerful collective. They can adopt a corporate identity. They feel protected. The greatest fear becomes the fear of disrupting the system, of becoming an impediment to the harmony of the corporate collective. The quest for harmony, which these psychologists understand, lures people into a state of psychological somnambulism.

Berkeley anthropologist Laura Nader argues that most oppressive systems of power, including classical Western colonialism and proponents of globalization, all use the idea of social harmony as a control mechanism. There is a vast difference, Nader points out, between social harmony and harmony ideology, between positivity and being genuinely positive. Nader sees harmony ideology as a concerted assault on democracy. The drive for harmony, Nader argues, always lends itself to covert censorship and self-censorship. The tyranny of harmony, when pushed to the extreme, leads to a life of fantasy that shuts out reality. Nader sees the ideology of harmony as one that has slowly dominated and corrupted the wider culture.

Positive psychology is only the latest incarnation of this assault on community and individualism. A related ideology was lauded by *Business Week* in the early 1980s as the "New Industrial Relations."[16] It was touted as a new form of human management. It was also said to be "nicer" than the earlier "scientific management" and social engineering innovations of Henry Ford or Frederick Taylor.[17]

Roberto González, an anthropologist at San Jose State University, spent nine months in 1989 and 1990 as a student engineer at General Motors. He later wrote "Brave New Workplace: Cooperation, Control, and the New Industrial Relations," a study on corporate work teams and "quality circles." The goal of such programs, González found, "was to end the adversarial relationship between management and labor through 'self-managed' work teams, and in so doing improve the efficiency and psychological 'health' of those involved." He notes that these workplace reform programs have gone by several names, including "the team approach," "employee participation," "workplace democracy," "human capitalism," and "quality of work life" programs.[18]

During the 1980s American automobile corporations used this tactic of labor-management cooperation to compete with what was seen as the Japanese economic juggernaut. " . . . [T]his can be seen, for example," González recounts, "in the charts at the Chevrolet Gear and Axle plant in Detroit, which lists the sales figures of various American and Japanese cars. Next to these lists is a sign that reads, 'You are entering the war zone, Quality and productivity are our weapons.'"[19]

Workers at GM were arranged into "self-managed" "quality circles," or teams of workers who form an identity. These teams competed with other teams to increase their productivity. "We and they" mentality is reduced and collapses into a collective "we." Quality circles at GM gave themselves names such as "Joe's Trouble Shooters," "Positive Approach," and "Loose Wires and Stripped Nuts."[20]

"Any status symbol that ferments class consciousness is removed from the workplace," noted Robert Ozaki in his book *Human Capitalism* in an observation of a GM-Toyota plant in California. "There are no parking spaces or toilets reserved for executives. Managers and workers dine in the common cafeteria. . . . Production workers are called 'associates' or 'technicians' rather than 'workers' or employees.'"[21]

Prestige systems, like those in the military, were employed at the Toyota plant at which Satoshi Kamata worked in the 1970s. He recalled how hats of different colors and stripes were used to distinguish rank: " . . . two green stripes stand for Seasonal Worker; one green stripe, Probationer; one white stripe, Trainee; one red stripe, Minor; a cap without any stripe, Regular Worker; two yellow stripes, Team Chief. . . ."[22]

"At the same assembly plant," González continued, citing Kamata's book *Japan in the Passing Lane: An Insider's Account of Life in a Japanese Auto Factory*, "Good idea suggestions" were elicited from workers, and the number submitted by each worker was posted in the locker room.[23] Similarly, one of Kamata's closest friends boasted about the number of pieces he could produce in a work day. Production became a source of identity and prestige.[24] Any incident or act that disrupted production was condemned. When a worker in Kamata's quality circle was injured on the job, all members were forced to wear a "Safety First arm band." This saw them stigmatized by others in the plant.[25] Low prestige was attached to the arm band. Peer pressure—from a worker's own team—formed a strong disincentive for anyone to report a job-related injury to avoid having to wear the arm band.

González in *Brave New Workplace* described a long and double-edged history of attempts to reconcile workers' interests with those of corporations. It dated back to the "scientific management" methods of Frederick Taylor, who, in the name of efficiency, "'streamlined' assembly plants by conducting time-motion studies of each worker, breaking down each movement into a number of discrete steps, and then reorganizing them in a more efficient sequence by eliminating all unnecessary movements."[26] This dehumanization led Taylor's disciples to take another approach. While some conservative followers focused solely on "productivity and efficiency," liberal "business leaders, bankers, politicians, trade-union leaders, and academic social scientists" during the 1920s "tried to forge a viable corporate order."[27] They sought to establish a stable corporate state by implementing worker "uplift" programs, such as collective bargaining, profit-sharing, company magazines, insurance, pension plans, safety reform, workmen's compensation, restricted work hours and the "living wage." The idea that "better living

and working conditions would render him [the worker] more cooperative, loyal, content, and, thus, more efficient and 'level-headed' . . . also
carried over into such aspects of the industrial-betterment movement
as gardens, restaurants, clubs, recreational facilities, bands, and medical
departments."[28]

"Since at least a century ago, a number of engineers, businessmen,
and scientists realized that technology was no longer the limiting factor
of production; now, it was man that could be engineered, and made
still more efficient, given the right motivation," González wrote, quot-
ing from historian David Noble's book *America by Design*.[29] "However
there are two aspects of today's industrial relations that are genuinely
new: first, the specific psychological techniques used to motivate workers; and, second, the increased number of companies willing to experiment with these techniques."[30]

Toyota pioneered the new approach. "Toyota City" was built by the
corporation to completely encapsulate and control the lives of its
employees. "Total control over the social environment is an important
component of thought reform programs," González wrote.[31] "At Toyota
City, thousands of young men were housed in military-style dormitories, surrounded by a fence and a guardhouse." He also describes how,
"during the time Kamata wrote his account, visitors—including family
members—were not allowed to enter the dorms to visit temporary
workers. Roommate assignments often grouped men from the same
town together," because, "according to Kamata, 'it helps them adjust to
the new environment and stay put during the employment period.'"[32]

These techniques were adopted by "U.S. bureaucracies and corporations, such as supermarkets, schools, banks, and government offices,
including the Pentagon."[33] During the 1990s, American and Japanese
automakers began pursuing what they called the Southern Strategy.
They set up factories modeled on Toyota City in Tennessee, Ohio, Ken-
tucky, and Indiana, where, they believed, a lack of unions and rural
insularity made for a fertile environment.[34]

González quotes Kamata's personal account of Toyota City in the
1970s as an example of how emotional stress and sheer fatigue can create bewildering confusion and despair reminiscent of the experiences
of those who are inducted into a cult. "When I come back from work,"

Kamata recounts, "I do nothing but sleep. I try not to think about the job; even the thought of it is enough to make me feel sick. Mostly, I feel too tired to think about anything." Several weeks later, Kamata slips into trancelike states on the assembly line:

[S]ometimes I think of something totally illogical: landscapes with towns I once visited suddenly appear one by one. It's impossible to concentrate on any one scene. . . . I'm not myself while I'm on the line. . . . It often surprises me to look up and suddenly find some strange scene in front of my eyes. In that split second I always wonder where I am. Merely seeing the light come in through a door on the opposite side of the building can bowl me over. . . . Again, for a few seconds, I'm totally disoriented.[35]

This peer group approach replicates the techniques used in coercive influence and control programs in Communist China, the Soviet Union, and North Korea. In these programs, the target subject "would become emotionally attached to the peer group members, who 'came to know the target's personality and history exceedingly well.'"[36]

" . . . [A] prisoner in Communist China would develop a circle of friends among his jailers," explains González, "who could reward or sanction him according to whether or not his behavior fit their standards. Eventually, his behavior could be conditioned through peer pressure."[37]

Similar processes occur in the cooperative work groups. Kamata explains: "If Fukuyama, the worker on my right, falls behind, he'll pull me behind, since I barely keep up with the work myself. Even if Fukuyama finishes his job in time, should I take longer on my job, then the next worker, Takeda, will be pulled out of his position. It takes enormous energy to catch up with the line, and if things go wrong, the line stops."[38]

Anthropologist Alejandro Lugo, who worked at a *maquiladora* plant in Ciudad Juárez, Mexico, describes a similar experience. He dropped behind many times in his first few days of work, and writes that "the pressure would be almost unbearable" as members of his work group would shout at him for not keeping up.[39]

When a temporary worker at Toyota City was injured and forced to quit, he told Kamata: "I'd have quit a long time ago. But I came here with Miura, so I can't let him down."[40] Reflecting on these statements, Kamata argues that the "work here is so difficult that people try to support and encourage one another, especially the ones who come here together. We feel it's not fair to drop out and go home alone."

"Circle leaders often learn a great deal about team members' personalities and histories, sometimes for the purpose of manipulation," González writes.

For example, at an assembly plant jointly owned by General Motors and Toyota in Fremont, California, a management handout, entitled "Facts a Group Leader Must Know," implored team leaders to learn the birthday, marital status, anniversary, number of children, and hobbies of each circle member. Furthermore, "team members are encouraged to help each other deal with personal problems." At a Toyota plant in Japan, team chiefs even used team members' birthdays to calculate biorhythm charts, so that an individual's "bad days" could be anticipated by the quality circle.

At a General Motors plant, 22,000 employees partook in weeklong "family awareness training" aimed at "establishing a family atmosphere within the division," where managers and workers did interpersonal activities.[41] "One of the exercises worked at developing trust," González summarized:

> Employees were paired up and then one of them was blindfolded and guided by the other. In another exercise, "Johari Window," the object was to reveal as much about one's "joys, fears, and needs" as possible—and in so doing, open the "window." Another exercise, "Hot Seat," took place on the last day of the training session: "One by one each person sits on the 'hot seat' and listens to group members say positive things about him or her. It is hard to say which is the more moving experience—sitting on the 'hot seat' or seeing those in the seat moved to tears."[42]

"A recent scandal in the federal government illustrates the dangers posed by coercion masked as harmony," González concludes.

In May 1995, a Congressional subcommittee was stunned by the bizarre testimony of many witnesses who told of being "psychologically abused" and subjected to sessions resembling "cult programming" during management and diversity training sessions sponsored by the Federal Aviation Administration. According to witnesses, men were fondling women, blacks and whites were urged to exchange epithets, and co-workers were tied together or disrobed for hours at a time during the weeklong training courses, which the FAA subcontracted to various management consultants. One consultant, Gregory May, received $1.67 million in government contracts. According to some witnesses, May is influenced by a West Coast "guru" who occasionally contacts a 35,000-year-old spirit named Ramtha.[43]

In Britain, coercive persuasion techniques were among the blunt instruments used to undermine the strong shop-stewards organizations in well-organized plants such as Unilever and at Rover in Cowley (in the greater Oxford area), with the promise of "jobs for life." Many trade union officials were initially seduced by this illusion of corporate and worker harmony. General Motors' Saturn car was built in plants that adopted the Japanese industrial relations model. This experiment, which soon became very unpopular with workers, lasted until 2004, when the union at the Spring Hill plant in Tennessee challenged the GM management and voted to restore the traditional United Auto Workers' contract.

Corporatism, aided by positive psychology, relies on several effective coercive persuasion techniques, similar to those often employed by cults, to meld workers into a "happy" collective. It sanctions interpersonal and psychological attacks and lavish praise to destabilize an individual's sense of self and promote compliance. It uses the coercive pressure of organized peer groups. It applies interpersonal pressure, including attacks on individuality and criticism as a form of negativity, to ensure conformity. It manipulates and controls the totality of the person's social environment to stabilize modified behavior.

Anthony Vasquez is a student at Berkeley. Sitting on the steps of Berkeley's Kroeber Hall on a sunny evening, he describes his experience with positive psychology at FedEx Kinko's, a photocopy and printing store. He has hazel eyes and messy black hair, and he is wearing corduroys and a brown mountaineer jacket. He worked at FedEx Kinko's for about two years and was "always called negative, a complainer, and not a team player."

Vasquez recalls that his store's slogan was "Yes We Can." "It meant that if a customer asked us to do a job for them, no matter what it was, we were to say, 'Yes We Can!'" Posters of the slogan were posted near telephones and around the back room. Corporate auditors would phone the store to make sure employees said, "Yes we can!" to every request. Employees would be punished as a group for failures, and individuals could be fired. Other slogans included, "Winning by engaging the hearts and minds of every team member" and "I promise to make every FedEx experience outstanding."

Vasquez tells about the scandal that ensued when his trainee, Sam, was fired. The store managers did not announce the dismissal but kept Sam on the schedule to make it appear that Sam was skipping work. The managers then used this as grounds for Sam's removal. After two weeks and several conversations with Sam, Vasquez wrote "Fired" in pencil under Sam's name on the schedule. The store managers were outraged. They called Vasquez into the office and reprimanded him with a "Positive Discipline Documentation Form." He was charged with defacing company property and slandering Sam.

"The document explained how I had made 'false or malicious statements' against Sam," says Vasquez. "I told [the managers] they were being duplicitous and that nothing I wrote had been false or malicious. I told them that if they wanted to make 'our organization a success,' they could start by paying me a fair wage. I went on and on until they both threw their hands in the air and told me to stop being difficult. I told them that I wasn't the one being difficult. They stared hard at me and said reluctantly, 'We know.'" Vasquez signed the document and left the office.

"It must have been in 2006, the company was holding another mandatory meeting for 'team members,' which is what they call us," he says. "I went with a couple of co-workers to Fresno, where we met a lot of other employees from various stores in northern California. . . . [T]he meeting took place in this rented room, and the woman from corporate had all these toys, markers, and candy in the middle of each table. The first thing she had us do was organize ourselves according to duration of employment at the company. While in this line, we had to introduce ourselves and say how long we had been working. The girl on the far end had been hired two months prior; the man on the other had been with the company for almost twenty years."

Some of his co-workers didn't like having to reveal that they had spent a lifetime working at FedEx Kinko's. But the corporate manager tried to muster up corporate pride. "She spun it so hard I felt dizzy," says Vasquez. "'Isn't this wonderful?! We have such a wide range of great team members. This really shows what a great place this is to work, and how you can make a career here!' she said."

One man stared at the floor in anger and embarrassment. "[I]f he had said anything, she would have e-mailed his center manager and he would have been written up and probably denied a raise. By the way, raises are twenty-five cents a year.

"The purpose of the meeting was, her euphemisms aside, to push merchandise and services onto customers that they didn't want. I believe it's called up-selling. She wanted us to talk about our positive customer service experiences. Most of us struggled with this, as nearly all of our experiences with customers and the company had been extremely negative and stressful. But she was all smiles, no matter what we said, and I noticed she was able to make almost everyone there smile and laugh and have a good time. She used the toys, the candy, the markers, and activities like skits and competitions to get people active and involved with each other. She used the happiness and was able to switch its source from human interaction to the company. You aren't happy because you are being social, you are happy because you work for the company.

"From my two years at the company, 'positive psychology' is a euphemism for 'spin,'" he adds. "They try to spin their employees so much they can't tell right from left, and in the process they forget they do the work of three people, have no health insurance, and three-quarters of their paycheck goes to rent."

Positive psychology, like celebrity culture, the relentless drive to consume, and the diversionary appeals of mass entertainment, feeds off the unhappiness that comes from isolation and the loss of community. The corporate teaching that we can find happiness through conformity to corporate culture is a cruel trick, for it is corporate culture that stokes and feeds the great malaise and disconnect of the culture of illusion.

In *The Loss of Happiness in Market Democracies*, political scientist Robert Lane writes:

> Amidst the satisfaction people feel with their material progress, there is a spirit of unhappiness and depression haunting advanced market democracies throughout the world, a spirit that mocks the idea that markets maximize well-being and the eighteenth-century promise of a right to the pursuit of happiness under benign governments of people's own choosing. The haunting spirit is manifold: a postwar decline in the United States in people who report themselves as happy, a rising tide in all advanced societies of clinical depression and dysphoria (especially among the young), increasing distrust of each other and of political and other institutions, declining belief that the lot of the average man is getting better . . . a tragic erosion of family solidarity and community integration together with an apparent decline in warm, intimate relations among friends.[44]

There is a dark, insidious quality to the ideology promoted by the positive psychologists. They condemn all social critics and iconoclasts, the dissidents and individualists, for failing to surrender and seek fulfillment in the collective lowing of the corporate herd. They strangle creativity and moral autonomy. They seek to mold and shape individual human beings into a compliant collective. The primary teaching of this movement, which reflects the ideology of the corporate state, is that fulfillment is to be found in complete and total social conformity, a conformity that all totalitarian and authoritarian structures seek to impose on those they dominate. Its false promise of harmony and happiness only increases internal anxiety and feelings of inadequacy. The nagging undercurrents of alienation and the constant pressure to exhibit a false enthusiasm and buoyancy destroy real relationships. The loneliness of a work life where self-presentation is valued over authenticity and one must always be upbeat and positive, no matter what one's actual mood or situation, is disorienting and stressful. The awful feeling that being positive may not, in fact, work if one is laid off or becomes sick must be buried and suppressed. Here, in the land of happy thoughts, there are no gross injustices, no abuses of authority, no economic and political systems to challenge, and no reason to complain. Here, we are all happy.

V / The Illusion
of America

We would rather be ruined than changed;
We would rather die in our dread
Than climb the cross of the moment
And let our illusions die.

—W. H. AUDEN, *The Age of Anxiety*

Where there is no vision, the people perish.

—PROVERBS 29

I USED TO LIVE in a country called America. It was not a perfect country, especially if you were African American or Native American or of Japanese descent in the Second World War. It could be cruel and unjust if you were poor, gay, a woman, or an immigrant, but there was hope it could be better. It was a country I loved and honored. It paid its workers wages envied around the world. It made sure these workers, thanks to labor unions and champions of the working class in the Democratic Party and the press, had health benefits and pensions. It offered good, public education. It honored basic democratic values and held in regard the rule of law, including international law, and respect for human rights. It had social programs, from Head Start to welfare to Social Security, to take care of the weakest among us, the mentally ill, the elderly, and the destitute. It had a system of government that, however flawed, worked to protect the interests of most of its citizens. It offered the possibility of democratic change. It had a press that was diverse and independent and gave a voice to all segments of society, including those beyond our borders, to impart to us unpleasant truths, to challenge the powerful, to reveal ourselves to ourselves.

I am not blind to the imperfections of this old America, or the failures to meet these ideals consistently at home and abroad. I spent more than two years living in Roxbury, the inner city in Boston, across the street from a public housing project where I ran a small church as a seminarian at Harvard Divinity School. I saw institutional racism at work. I saw how banks, courts, dysfunctional schools, probation officers, broken homes, drug abuse, crime, and employers all conspired to make sure the poor remained poor. I spent two decades as a foreign correspondent in Latin America, Africa, the Middle East, and the Balkans. I saw there the crimes and injustices committed in our name and often with our support, whether during the *contra* war in Nicaragua or the brutalization of the Palestinians by Israeli occupation forces. We had much to atone for, but still there was also much that was good, decent, and honorable in our country.

The country I live in today uses the same civic, patriotic, and historical language to describe itself, the same symbols and iconography, the same national myths, but only the shell remains. The America we celebrate is an illusion. America, the country of my birth, the country that formed and shaped me, the country of my father, my father's father, and his father's father, stretching back to the generations of my family that were here for the country's founding, is so diminished as to be unrecognizable. I do not know if this America will return, even as I pray and work and strive for its return.

The words *consent of the governed* have become an empty phrase. Our textbooks on political science and economics are obsolete. Our nation has been hijacked by oligarchs, corporations, and a narrow, selfish, political, and economic elite, a small and privileged group that governs, and often steals, on behalf of moneyed interests. This elite, in the name of patriotism and democracy, in the name of all the values that were once part of the American system and defined the Protestant work ethic, has systematically destroyed our manufacturing sector, looted the treasury, corrupted our democracy, and trashed the financial system. During this plundering we remained passive, mesmerized by the enticing shadows on the wall, assured our tickets to success, prosperity, and happiness were waiting around the corner.

The government, stripped of any real sovereignty, provides little more than technical expertise for elites and corporations that lack moral restraints and a concept of the common good. America has become a façade. It has become the greatest illusion in a culture of illusions. It represents a power and a democratic ethic it does not possess. It seeks to perpetuate prosperity by borrowing trillions of dollars it can never repay. The absurd folly of trying to borrow our way out of the worst economic collapse since the 1930s is the cruelest of all the recent tricks played on American citizens. We continue to place our faith in a phantom economy, one characterized by fraud and lies, which sustains the wealthiest 10 percent, Wall Street, and insolvent banks. Debt leveraging is not wealth creation. We are vainly trying to return to a bubble economy, of the sort that once handed us the illusion of wealth, rather than confront the stark reality that lies ahead. We are told massive borrowing will create jobs and re-inflate real estate values and the stock market. We remain tempted by mirages, by the illusion that we can, still, all become rich.

The corporate power that holds the government hostage has appropriated for itself the potent symbols, language, and patriotic traditions of the state. It purports to defend freedom, which it defines as the free market, and liberty, which it defines as the liberty to exploit. It sold us on the illusion that the free market was the natural outgrowth of democracy and a force of nature, at least until the house of cards collapsed and these corporations needed to fleece the taxpayers to survive. Making that process even more insidious, the real sources of power remain hidden. Those who run our largest corporations are largely anonymous to the mass of the citizens. The anonymity of corporate forces—an earthly Deus absconditus—makes them unaccountable. They have the means to hide and to divert us from examining the decaying structures they have created. As Karl Marx understood, capitalism when it is unleashed from government and regulatory control is a revolutionary force.

Cultures that cannot distinguish between illusion and reality die. The dying gasps of all empires, from the Aztecs to the ancient Romans to the French monarchy and the Austro-Hungarian Empire, have been characterized by a disconnect between the elites and reality. The elites were blinded by absurd fantasies of omnipotence and power that doomed their civilizations. We have been steadily impoverished by our own power elites—legally, economically, spiritually, and politically. And unless we radically reverse this tide, unless we wrest the state away from corporate hands, we will be dragged down by the dark and turbulent undertow of globalization. In this world there are only masters and serfs. We are entering an era in which workers may become serfs, no longer able to earn a living wage to sustain themselves or their families, whether in sweatshops in China or the industrial wasteland of Ohio.

The country's moral decay is manifested in its physical decay. It is no coincidence that our infrastructure—roads, bridges, sewers, airports, trains, mass transit—is overburdened, outdated, and in dismal repair. It is not so elsewhere. China opens a new subway system every year. Europeans travel from London to Paris on high-speed trains. Meanwhile, America's antiquated and inefficient rail system cannot maintain its lumbering cars and aging tracks. Cities are plagued by broken pipes and sinkholes. The Environmental Protection Agency estimates that collapsing and overwhelmed sewage systems release more than 40,000 discharges of raw sewage into our drinking water, streams, and homes each year. The Education Department found that one-third of our schools are in such a severe state of disrepair that it "interferes with the delivery of instruction." A report in the journal *Health Affairs* estimates that if the for-profit health-care system is left unchanged, one of every five dollars spent by Americans in 2017 will go to health coverage. Half of all bankruptcies in America occur because families are unable to pay their medical bills. And staggering unemployment, bankruptcies, declining real estate prices, and the shuttering of stores and factories, are sweeping across the nation.

War and rampant militarism—we now have 761 military bases we maintain around the globe—drains the lifeblood out of the body politic. The U.S. military spends more than all other militaries on earth combined. The official U.S. defense budget for fiscal year 2008 is $623 billion, and by 2010 the Pentagon is slated to receive more than $700 billion, once funding for items such as nuclear weapons is included in the budget. The next closest national military budget is China's at $65 billion, according to the Central Intelligence Agency. We embrace the dangerous delusion that we are on a providential mission to save the rest of the world from itself, to impose our virtues—which we see as superior to all other virtues—on others, and that we have a right to do this by force. This belief has corrupted both Republicans and Democrats. The wars of occupation in Iraq and Afghanistan are doomed to futility. We cannot afford them. The rash of home foreclosures, the mounting job losses, the collapse of banks and the financial services industry, the poverty ripping apart the working classes, our crumbling infrastructure, and the killing of Afghan and Iraqi civilians by our iron fragmentation bombs converge. The costly forms of death we dispense on one side of the globe are hollowing us out from the inside at home.

The daily bleeding of thousands of jobs will soon turn our economic crisis into a political crisis. The street protests, strikes, and riots that have rattled France, Turkey, Greece, Ukraine, Russia, Latvia, Lithuania, Bulgaria, and Iceland will descend on us. It is only a matter of time. And not much time. When things start to go sour, when the Obama administration is exposed as a group of mortals waving a sword at a tidal wave, the United States could plunge into a long period of precarious social and political instability.

At no period in American history has our democracy been in such peril or the possibility of totalitarianism as real. Our way of life is over. Our profligate consumption is finished. Our children will never have the standard of living we had. This is the bleak future. This is reality. There is little President Obama can do to stop it. It has been decades in the making. It cannot be undone with $1 trillion or $2 trillion in bailout money. Nor will it be solved by clinging to the illusions of the past.

How will we cope with our decline? Will we cling to the absurd dreams of a superpower and the fantasies of a glorious tomorrow, or will we responsibly face our stark, new limitations? Will we heed those who are sober and rational, those who speak of a new simplicity and humility, or will we follow the demagogues and charlatans who rise up in moments of crisis and panic to offer fantastic visions of escape? Will we radically transform our system to one that protects the ordinary citizen and fosters the common good, that defies the corporate state, or will we employ the brutality and technology of our internal security and surveillance apparatus to crush all dissent?

There were some who saw it coming. The political philosophers Sheldon S. Wolin, John Ralston Saul, and Andrew Bacevich, writers such as Noam Chomsky, Chalmers Johnson, David Korten, and Naomi Klein, and activists such as Bill McKibben, Wendell Berry, and Ralph Nader warned us about our march of folly. In the immediate years after the Second World War, a previous generation of social critics recognized the destructive potential of the rising corporate state. Books such as David Riesman's *The Lonely Crowd*, C. Wright Mills's *The Power Elite*, William H. White's *The Organization Man*, Seymour Mellman's *The Permanent War Economy: American Capitalism in Decline*, Daniel Boorstin's *The Image: A Guide to Pseudo-Events in America*, and Reinhold Niebuhr's *The Irony of American History* have proved to be prophetic. This generation of writers remembered what had been lost. They saw the intrinsic values that were being dismantled. The culture they sought to protect has largely been obliterated. During the descent, our media and universities, extensions of corporate and mass culture, proved intellectually and morally useless. They did not thwart the decay. We failed to heed the wisdom of these critics, embracing instead the idea that all change was a form of progress.

In his book *Democracy Incorporate*d, Wolin, who taught political philosophy at Berkeley and at Princeton, uses the phrase *inverted totalitarianism* to describe our system of power. Inverted totalitarianism, unlike classical totalitarianism, does not revolve around a demagogue or charismatic leader. It finds expression in the anonymity of the corporate state. It purports to cherish democracy, patriotism, and the Constitution while manipulating internal levers to subvert and thwart democratic institutions. Political candidates are elected in popular votes by citizens, but candidates must raise staggering amounts of corporate funds to compete. They are beholden to armies of corporate lobbyists in Washington or state capitals who author the legislation and get the legislators to pass it. Corporate media control nearly everything we read, watch, or hear. It imposes a bland uniformity of opinion. It diverts us with trivia and celebrity gossip. In classical totalitarian regimes, such as Nazi fascism or Soviet communism, economics was subordinate to politics. "Under inverted totalitarianism the reverse is true," Wolin writes. "Economics dominates politics—and with that domination comes different forms of ruthlessness."

"In order to cope with the imperial contingencies of foreign war and occupation," according to Wolin,

> democracy will alter its character, not only by assuming new behaviors abroad (e.g., ruthlessness, indifference to suffering, disregard of local norms, the inequalities in ruling a subject population) but also by operating on revised, power-expansive assumptions at home. It will, more often than not, try to manipulate the public rather than engage its members in deliberation. It will demand greater powers and broader discretion in their use ("state secrets"), a tighter control over society's resources, more summary methods of justice, and less patience for legalities, opposition, and clamor for socioeconomic reforms.

Imperialism and democracy are incompatible. The massive resources and allocations devoted to imperialism mean that democracy inevitably withers and dies. Democratic states and republics, including ancient Athens and Rome, that refuse to curb imperial expansion eviscerate their political systems. Wolin writes:

> Imperial politics represents the conquest of domestic politics and the latter's conversion into a crucial element of inverted totalitarianism. It makes no sense to ask how the democratic citizen could "participate" substantively in imperial politics; hence it is not surprising that the subject of empire is taboo in electoral debates. No major politician or party has so much as publicly remarked on the existence of an American empire.

I reached Wolin by phone at his home about twenty-five miles north of San Francisco. He was a bombardier in the South Pacific during the Second World War and went to Harvard after the war for his doctorate. Wolin has written political science classics such as *Politics and Vision* and *Tocqueville Between Two Worlds*. He is the author of a series of essays on Augustine of Hippo, Richard Hooker, David Hume, Martin Luther, John Calvin, Max Weber, Friedrich Nietzsche, Karl Marx, and John Dewey. His voice, however, has faded from public awareness because, as he told me, "it is harder and harder for people like me to get a public hearing." He said that publications such as the *New York Review of Books,* which often printed his essays a couple of decades ago, shied away from his blistering critiques of American empire and capitalism, his warnings about the subversion and undermining of democratic institutions and the emergence of a corporate state. To question the ideology of the free market became, even among the liberal elite, a form of heresy.

"The basic systems are going to stay in place; they are too powerful to be challenged," Wolin told me when I asked him about the Obama administration. "This is shown by the financial bailout. It does not bother with the structure at all. I don't think Obama can take on the kind of military establishment we have developed. This is not to say that I do not admire him. He is probably the most intelligent president we have had in decades. I think he is well-meaning, but he inherits a system of constraints that make it very difficult to take on these major power configurations. I do not think he has the appetite for it in any ideological sense. The corporate structure is not going to be challenged. There has not been a word from him that would suggest an attempt to rethink the American imperium."

Wolin argues that a failure to dismantle our overextended imperial projects, coupled with the economic collapse, is likely to result in a full-blown inverted totalitarianism. He said that without "radical and drastic remedies" the response to mounting discontent and social unrest will probably lead to greater state control and repression. There will be, he warned, a huge "expansion of government power."

"Our political culture has remained unhelpful in fostering a democratic consciousness," he said. "The political system and its operatives will not be constrained by popular discontent or uprisings."

Wolin writes that in inverted totalitarianism, consumer goods, and a comfortable standard of living, along with a vast entertainment industry that provides spectacles and appealing diversions, keep the citizenry politically passive. I asked if the economic collapse and the steady decline in our standard of living might not, in fact, trigger classical totalitarianism. Could widespread frustration and poverty lead the working and middle classes to place their faith in demagogues, especially those from the Christian Right?

"I think that's perfectly possible," he answered. "That was the experience of the 1930s. There wasn't just FDR. There was Huey Long and Father Coughlin. There were even more extreme movements, including the Klan. The extent to which those forces can be fed by the downturn and bleakness is a very real danger. It could become classical totalitarianism."

He said the political passivity bred by a culture of illusion is exploited by demagogues who present themselves to a submissive population as saviors. They offer dreams of glory. He warned that "apoliticalness, even anti-politicalness, will be very powerful elements in taking us towards a radically dictatorial direction. It testifies to how thin the commitment to democracy is in the present circumstances. Democracy is not ascendant. It is not dominant. It is beleaguered. The extent to which young people have been drawn away from public concerns and given this extraordinary range of diversions makes it very likely they could then rally to a demagogue."

Wolin lamented that the corporate state has successfully blocked public debate about alternative forms of power. Corporations determine who gets heard and who does not, he said. And those, such as Wolin, who critique corporate power are excluded from the national dialogue. Pundits on television news programs discuss politics as a horse race or compare the effectiveness of pseudo-events staged by candidates. They do not discuss ideas, issues, or meaningful reform.

"In the 1930s there were all kinds of alternative understandings, from socialism to more extensive governmental involvement," he said. "There was a range of different approaches. But what I am struck by now is the narrow range within which palliatives are being modeled. We are supposed to work with the financial system. So the people who helped create this system are put in charge of the solution. There has to be some major effort to think outside the box."

"The puzzle to me is the lack of social unrest," Wolin said when I asked why we have not yet seen rioting or protests. He said he worried that popular protests will be dismissed and ignored by the corporate media. This, he said, is what happened when tens of thousands protested the war in Iraq. If protestors are characterized as cranks or fringe groups, if their voices are never heard, the state will have little trouble suppressing local protests, as happened during the Democratic and Republican conventions. Anti-war protests in the 1960s gained momentum, he said, from their ability to spread their message across the country. This may not happen now. "The ways [corporate/governmental authorities] can isolate protests and prevent it from [becoming] a contagion are formidable," he said.

"My greatest fear is that the Obama administration will achieve relatively little in terms of structural change," he added. "They may at best keep the system going. But there is a growing pessimism. Every day we hear how much longer the recession will continue. They are already talking about beyond next year [into 2011]. The economic difficulties are more profound than we had guessed and because of globalization more difficult to deal with. I wish the political establishment, the parties, and leadership, would become more aware of the depths of the problem. They can't keep throwing money at this. They have to begin structural changes that involve a very different approach from a market economy. I don't think this will happen.

"I keep asking why and how and when this country became so conservative," he went on. "This country once prided itself on its experimentation and flexibility. It has become rigid. It is probably the most conservative of all the advanced countries."

The American left has crumbled and sold out to a bankrupt Democratic Party. It has abandoned the working class, which has no ability to organize and little political clout, especially with labor unions a spent force. The universities are mills for corporate employees. The media churn out info-tainment and pollute the airwaves with fatuous pundits. The Left, he said, no longer has the capacity to be a counterweight to the corporate state, and if an extreme right regains momentum there will probably be very little organized or effective resistance.

"The Left is amorphous," he said. "I despair over the Left. Left parties may be small in number in Europe, but they are a coherent organization that keeps going. Here, except for Nader's efforts, we don't have that. We have a few voices here, a magazine there, and that's about it. It goes nowhere."

The decline of American empire began long before the current economic meltdown or the wars in Afghanistan and Iraq. It began before the first Gulf War or Ronald Reagan. It began when we shifted, in the words of the historian Charles Maier, from an "empire of production" to an "empire of consumption." By the end of the Vietnam War, when the costs of the war ate away at Lyndon Johnson's Great Society and domestic oil production began its steady, inexorable decline, we saw our country transformed from one that primarily produced to one that primarily consumed. We started borrowing to maintain a lifestyle we could no longer afford. We began to use force, especially in the Middle East, to feed our insatiable thirst for cheap oil. The decline has been steady and uninterrupted since the conclusion of the Second World War. At the end of the war, we possessed nearly two-thirds of the world's gold reserves and more than half of its entire manufacturing capacity. The United States accounted for one-third of world exports, the foreign trade balance was in the black, and exports more than doubled imports. Three decades later, the nation had slipped into a negative trade balance, imports began to exceed exports, manufacturing jobs were on the decline, and we began, collectively, to spend more than we earned. Total public debt is now more than $11 trillion, or about $36,676 per capita.

The bill is now due. America's most dangerous enemies are not Islamic radicals but those who sold us the perverted ideology of free-market capitalism and globalization. They have dynamited the foundations of our society.

"The Big Lies are not the pledge of tax cuts, universal health care, family values restored, or a world rendered peaceful through forceful demonstrations of American leadership," Bacevich wrote in *The Limits of Power*:

> The Big Lies are the truths that remain unspoken: that freedom has an underside; that nations, like households, must ultimately live within their means; that history's purpose, the subject of so many confident pronouncements, remains inscrutable. Above all, there is this: Power is finite. Politicians pass over matters such as these in silence. As a consequence, the absence of self-awareness that forms such an enduring element of the American character persists.[1]

The problems we face are structural. The old America is not coming back. Our financial system was taken hostage and looted by bankers, brokers, and speculators who told us that the old means of making capital by producing and manufacturing were outdated. They assured us money could be made out of money. They insisted that financial markets could be self-regulating. Like all financial markets throughout history that have thrown off oversight and regulation, ours has collapsed. Speculators in the seventeenth century were hanged. Today they receive billions in taxpayer dollars and huge bonuses.

The corporate forces that control the state will never permit real reform. It would mean their extinction. These corporations, especially the oil and gas industry, will never allow us to achieve energy independence. That would devastate their profits. It would wipe out tens of billions of dollars in weapons contracts. It would cripple the financial health of a host of private contractors from Halliburton to Blackwater/Xe and render obsolete the existence of U.S. Central Command. This is the harsh, unspoken reality of corporate power. The unseen hands of Lockheed Martin, Boeing, and Northrup Grumman, the nation's top-three defense contractors, divided up $69 million in Pentagon contracts in 2007, the last year for which contracting data are available. These industries, which have judiciously spread their parts and supply business throughout the country, defend the production of weapons systems as vital for employment. But their leaders are clearly nervous. The Aerospace Industries Association (AIA), which represents more than one hundred defense and aerospace corporations, has an ad campaign with the slogan: "Aerospace and Defense: The Strength to Lift America." It claims its manufacturers contribute $97 billion in exports a year and employ 2 million people, a figure disputed by the U.S. Bureau of Labor Statistics, which puts the number at 472,000 wage and salary workers. But this has not dampened the promise made by these corporate executives to help lift the nation out of its economic morass. "Our industry is ready and able to lead the way out of the economic crisis," Fred Downey, an associate vice president, told the Associated Press. The ads are useful, but so is the some $149 million a year the industry lavishes on lobbying firms, according to the Center for Representative Politics.

Seymour Mellman spent his academic career, which spanned the Cold War, at Columbia University, researching, writing, and speaking about the large military portion of the federal budget. In *Pentagon Capitalism* he described the redundancy and costliness of modern weapons systems—such as the next wave of fighter planes, missiles, submarines, and aircraft carriers. He said that high-tech weapons yet to be designed always escalate spending as new, costlier systems replace the old, which are often junked.

The United States has become the largest single seller of arms and munitions on the planet. The defense budget for fiscal 2008 is the largest since the Second World War. More than half of federal discretionary spending goes to defense. And so we build Cold War relics such as the $14 billion *Virginia*-class submarines as well as the stealth fighters we engineered to evade radar systems the Soviets never built. We spend $8.9 billion on ICBM missile defense systems that would be useless in stopping a shipping container concealing a dirty bomb. The defense industry is able to monopolize the best scientific and research talent and squander the nation's resources and investment capital. These defense industries produce nothing that is useful for society or the national trade account. They offer little more than a psychological security blanket for fearful Americans who want to feel protected and safe.

The defense industry is a virus. It destroys healthy economies. We produce sophisticated fighter jets while Boeing is unable to finish its new commercial plane on schedule and our automotive industry goes bankrupt. We sink money into research and development of weapons systems and starve renewable energy technologies to fight global warming. Universities are flooded with defense-related cash and grants yet struggle to find money for environmental studies. The massive military spending, aided by this $3 trillion war, has a social cost. Our bridges and levees collapse, our schools decay, our real manufacturing is done overseas by foreign workers, and our social safety net is taken away. And we are bombarded with the militarized language of power and strength that masks our brittle reality.

Mellman coined the term *permanent war economy* to describe the American economy. Since the end of the Second World War, the federal government has spent more than half its tax dollars on past, current, and future military operations. It is the largest single sustaining activity of the government. The military-industrial establishment is especially lucrative to corporations because it offers a lavish form of corporate welfare. Defense systems are usually sold before they are produced, and military industries are permitted to charge the federal government for huge cost overruns. Huge profits are guaranteed. Foreign aid is given to countries such as Egypt, which receives some $3 billion in assistance but is required to buy American weapons with $1.3 billion of it. The taxpayers fund the research, development, and building of weapons systems and then buy them on behalf of foreign governments. It is a circular system that little resembles the paradigm of a free-market economy.

There is rarely any accounting to the client (i.e., the government and people of the United States) if work is shoddy or produces flawed weapons systems. The U.S. Coast Guard, in one of many examples, undertook a five-year, $24 billion modernization program called "Deepwater." The Coast Guard spent $100 million to lengthen by thirteen feet the 110-foot Island Class patrol boats. They shipped the boats to the Bollinger Shipyard outside of New Orleans. The eight boats, when they returned, had such severe structural problems that they all had to be retired from service.

The Pentagon, Mellman noted, is not restricted by the economic rules of producing goods, selling them for a profit, then using the profit for further investment and production. It operates, rather, outside of competitive markets. It has erased the line between the state and the corporation, and it subverts the actual economy. It leeches away the ability of the nation to manufacture useful products and produce sustainable jobs. Mellman used the example of the New York City Transit Authority and its allocation in 2003 of $3 billion to $4 billion for new subway cars. New York City asked for bids, and no American companies responded. Mellman argued that the industrial base in America was no longer centered on items that maintain, improve, or are used to build the nation's infrastructure. New York City eventually contracted with companies in Japan and Canada to build its subway cars. Mellman estimated that such a contract could have generated, directly and indirectly, about 32,000 jobs in the United States. In another instance, of 100 products offered in the 2003 L.L. Bean catalogue, Mellman found that ninety-two were imported and only eight were made in the United States.

The defense industries, like all corporations, rely on deceptive ad campaigns and lobbyists to perpetuate their lock on taxpayer money.

The late Senator J. William Fulbright described the reach of the military-industrial establishment in his 1970 book *The Pentagon Propaganda Machine*. Fulbright explained how the Pentagon influenced public opinion through direct contacts with the public, Defense Department films, close ties with Hollywood producers, and use of the commercial media to gain support for weapons systems. The majority of the military analysts on television are former military officials, many employed as consultants to defense industries, a fact they rarely disclose to the public. Barry R. McCaffrey, a retired four-star army general and military analyst for NBC News, was, *The New York Times* reported, at the same time an employee of Defense Solutions, Inc., a consulting firm. He profited, the article noted, from the sale of the weapons systems and expansion of the wars in Iraq and Afghanistan he championed over the airwaves.[2]

The grip of corporations on government is not limited to the defense industry. It has leeched into nearly every aspect of the economy. The attempt to create a health-care plan that also conciliates the corporations that profit from the misery and illnesses of tens of millions of Americans is naïve, at best, and probably disingenuous. This conciliation insists that we can coax these corporations, which are listed on the stock exchange and exist to maximize profit, to transform themselves into social-service agencies that will provide adequate health care for all Americans.

"Obama offers a false hope," says Dr. John Geyman, former chair of family medicine at the University of Washington and author of *Do Not Resuscitate: Why the Health Insurance Industry Is Dying, and How We Must Replace It*. "We cannot build on or tweak the present system. Different states have tried this. The problem is the private insurance industry itself. It is not as efficient as a publicly financed system. It fragments risk pools, skimming off the healthier part of the population and leaving the rest uninsured or underinsured. Its administrative and overhead costs are five to eight times higher than public financing through Medicare. It cares more about its shareholders than its enrollees or patients. A family of four now pays about $12,000 a year just in premiums, which have gone up by 87 percent from 2000 to 2006.

The insurance industry is pricing itself out of the market for an ever-larger part of the population. The industry resists regulation. It is unsustainable by present trends."

Our health-care system is broken. There are some 46 million Americans without coverage and tens of millions with inadequate policies that severely limit what kinds of procedures and treatments they can receive. Eighteen thousand people die, according to the Institute of Medicine, every year because they can't afford health care.

"There are at least 25 million Americans who are underinsured," Geyman says. "Whatever coverage they have does not come close to covering the actual cost of a major illness or accident."

The corporations that run our for-profit health-care industry would be shut down if single-payer, not-for-profit health-care was provided for all Americans. The for-profit health-care industry, like the defense industry, has vigorously fought to protect itself through campaign contributions and lobbying. They have placed profit before the common good. A study by Harvard Medical School found that national health insurance would save the country $350 billion a year. But Medicare does not make campaign contributions. The private health-care industries do.

"The private health insurance companies and the pharmaceutical industry completely and totally oppose national health insurance," says Stephanie Woolhandler, one of the founders of Physicians for a National Health Program. "The private health insurance companies would go out of business. The pharmaceutical companies are afraid that a national health program will, as in Canada, be able to negotiate lower drug prices. Canadians pay 40 percent less for their drugs. We see this on a smaller scale in the United States, where the Department of Defense is able to negotiate pharmaceutical prices that are 40 percent lower."

We cannot improve the system by expanding government oversight or improve for-profit health care by requiring doctors and hospitals to prove they provide quality medical services. Proposals to require insurance companies to use more income from premiums for patient care or link payment with reported quality are unworkable. Nor will turning record-keeping from paper to electronic data blunt rising costs.

"There isn't an enforcement mechanism," Geyman says bluntly. "Most states have been unable to control rates or set a cap on rates."

"The only way everyone will get insurance is with national health insurance," says Woolhandler, who is a professor at Harvard Medical School. "People with catastrophic illnesses usually lose their jobs and lose their insurance. They often cannot afford the high premiums for the insurance they can get when they are unable to work. Most families that file for bankruptcy because of medical costs had insurance before they got sick. They either lost the insurance because they lost their jobs or faced gaps in coverage that meant they could not afford medical care."

Our health system costs nearly twice as much as national programs in countries such as Switzerland. The overhead for traditional Medicare is 3 percent, and the overhead for the investment-owned companies is 26.5 percent. A staggering 31 percent of our health-care expenditures is spent on administrative costs. Look what we get in return. And yet the reality of the health-care system is never discussed because corporations, which fund the main political parties, do not want it discussed.

The Democratic Party has been as guilty as the Republicans in the abdication of real power to the corporate state. It was Bill Clinton who led the Democratic Party to the corporate watering trough. Clinton argued that the party had to ditch labor unions, no longer a source of votes or power, as a political ally. Workers, he insisted, would vote Democratic anyway. They had no choice. It was better, he argued, to take corporate money and do corporate bidding. By the 1990s, the Democratic Party, under Clinton's leadership, had virtual fund-raising parity with the Republicans. Today the Democrats raise more.

The legislation demanded by corporations sold out the American worker. This betrayal was accompanied with a slick advertising campaign that promoted the laws, used to destroy the working class, as the *salvation* of the American worker. The North American Free Trade Agreement was peddled by the Clinton White House as an opportunity to raise the incomes and prosperity of the citizens of the United States, Canada, and Mexico. NAFTA would also, we were told, stanch Mexican immigration into the United States.

"There will be less illegal immigration because more Mexicans will be able to support their children by staying home," President Clinton said in the spring of 1993 as he was lobbying for the bill.

But NAFTA, which took effect in 1994, had the effect of reversing every one of Clinton's rosy predictions. Once the Mexican government lifted price supports on corn and beans grown by Mexican farmers, those farmers had to compete against the huge agribusinesses in the United States. Many Mexican farmers were swiftly bankrupted. At least 2 million Mexican farmers have been driven off their land since 1994. And guess where many of them went? This desperate flight of poor Mexicans into the United States is now being exacerbated by large-scale factory closures along the border as manufacturers pack up and leave Mexico for the cut-rate embrace of China's totalitarian capitalism. But we were assured that goods would be cheaper. Workers would be wealthier. Everyone would be happier. I am not sure how these contradictory things were supposed to happen, but in a sound-bite society, reality no longer matters. NAFTA was great if you were a corporation. It was a disaster if you were a worker.

Clinton's welfare reform bill, signed on August 22, 1996, obliterated the nation's social safety net. It threw 6 million people, many of them single mothers, off the welfare rolls within three years. It dumped them onto the streets without child care, rent subsidies, or continued Medicaid coverage. Families were plunged into crisis, struggling to survive on multiple jobs that paid $6 or $7 an hour, or less than $15,000 a year. And these were the lucky ones. In some states, half of those dropped from the welfare rolls could not find work. Clinton slashed Medicare by $115 billion over a five-year period and cut $25 billion in Medicaid funding. The booming and overcrowded prison system handled the influx of the poor, as well as our abandoned mentally ill. We have 2.3 million of our citizens behind bars, most of them for nonviolent drug offenses. More than one in one hundred adults in the United States is incarcerated. The United States, with less than 5 percent of the global population, has almost 25 percent of the world's prisoners. One in nine black men between twenty and thirty-four is behind bars. This has effectively decapitated the leadership in the inner cities, where African Americans have traditionally had to react more quickly to confront social injustices.

The Clinton administration, led by Lawrence Summers, signed into law the Financial Services Modernization Act of 1999, which ripped down the firewalls that had been established by the 1933 Glass-Steagall Act. Designed to prevent the kind of meltdown we are now experiencing, Glass-Steagall established the Federal Deposit Insurance Corporation. It set in place banking reforms to stop speculators from hijacking the financial system. With Glass-Steagall demolished, and the passage of NAFTA, the Democrats, led by Clinton, tumbled gleefully into bed with corporations and Wall Street speculators. They used institutions like Fannie Mae and Freddie Mac as a welfare gravy train. And many of the architects of this deregulation, economists such as Summers, remain in charge of the nation's economic policy.

"When times are prosperous, we do not mind a modest increase in 'welfare,'" wrote Robert N. Bellah:

> When times are not so prosperous, we think at least our successful career will save us and our families from failure and despair. We are attracted, against our skepticism, to the idea that poverty will be alleviated by the crumbs that fall from the rich man's table. . . . Some of us often feel, and most of us sometimes feel, that we are only someone if we have made it: can look down on those who have not. The American dream is often a very private dream of being a star, the uniquely successful and admirable one, the one who stands out from the crowd of ordinary folk, who don't know how. And since we have believed in that dream for a long time and worked very hard to make it come true, it is hard for us to give it up, even though it contradicts another dream that we have—that of living in a society that would really be worth living in."[3]

The cost of our empire of illusion is not being paid by the corporate titans. It is being paid on the streets of our inner cities, in former manufacturing towns, and in depressed rural enclaves. This cost transcends declining numbers and statistics and speaks the language of human misery and pain. Human beings are not commodities. They are not goods. They grieve and suffer and feel despair. They raise children and struggle to maintain communities. The growing class divide is not understood, despite the glibness of many in the media, by complicated sets of statistics, lines on a graph that chart stocks, or the absurd, utopian faith in unregulated globalization and complicated trade deals. It is understood in the eyes of a man or woman who is no longer making enough money to live with dignity and hope.

Elba Figueroa, forty-seven, lives in Trenton, New Jersey. She worked as a nurse's aide until she got Parkinson's disease. She lost her job. She lost her health care. She receives $703 a month in government assistance. Her rent alone runs $750 a month. And so she borrows money from friends and neighbors to stay in her apartment. She laboriously negotiates her wheelchair up and down steps and along the sidewalks of Trenton to get to soup kitchens and food pantries to eat.

"Food prices have gone up," Figueroa says, waiting to get inside the food pantry run by the Crisis Ministry of Princeton and Trenton. "I don't have any money. I run out of things to eat. I worked until I physically could not work anymore. Now I live like this."

The pantry occupies a dilapidated, three-story art deco building in Old Trenton, the poorest neighborhood in the city. The pantry is one of about two dozen charities in the city that provide shelter and food to the poor. Those who qualify for assistance are permitted to pick up food once a month. Clutching pieces of paper that show the number of points they have been allotted, they push shopping carts in a U-shaped course around the first floor. Every food item is assigned a number of points. Points are allotted according to the number of people in a household. The shelves of the pantry hold bags of rice, jars of peanut butter, macaroni and cheese, and cans of beets, corn, and peas. Two refrigerated cases have eggs, chickens, fresh carrots, and beef hot dogs. "All Fresh Produce 2 pounds = 1 point," a sign on the glass door of the refrigerated unit reads. Another reads: "1 Dozen EGGS equal 3 protein points. Limit of 1 dozen per household."

The swelling numbers waiting outside homeless shelters and food pantries around the country, many of them elderly or single women with children, have grown by at least 30 percent over the last year. General welfare recipients struggle to survive on $140 a month in cash and another $140 in food stamps. This is all many in Trenton and other impoverished pockets now have to survive. Trenton, a former manufacturing center with a 20 percent unemployment rate and a median income of $33,000, is a window into our unraveling. And as the government squanders taxpayer money in fruitless schemes to prop up insolvent banks and investment houses, citizens are thrown into the streets without work, a place to live, or enough food.

There are now 36.2 million Americans who cope daily with hunger, up by more than 3 million since 2000, according to the Food Research and Action Center in Washington. The number of people in the worst-off category—the hungriest—rose by 40 percent since 2000, to nearly 12 million people.

"We are seeing people we have not seen for a long time," says the Reverend Jarrett Kerbel, director of the Crisis Ministry's food pantry, which supplies food to 1,400 households in Trenton each month. "We are seeing people who haven't crossed that threshold for five, six, or seven years coming back. We are seeing people whose unemployment has run out, and they are struggling in that gap while they reapply, and, of course, we are seeing the usual unemployed. This will be the first real test of [Bill] Clinton's so-called welfare reform."

The Crisis Ministry, like many hard-pressed charities, is over budget, and food stocks are precariously low. Donations are on the decline. There are days when soup kitchens in Trenton are shut down because they have no food.

"We collected 170 bags of groceries from a church in Princeton, and it was gone in two days," Kerbel says. "We collected 288 bags from a Jewish center in Princeton, and it was gone in three days. What you see on the shelves is pretty much what we have."

States, facing dramatic budget shortfalls, are slashing social assistance programs, including Medicaid, social services, and education. New Jersey's shortfall has tripled to $1.2 billion and could soar to $5 billion. Tax revenue has fallen to $211 million less than projected. States are imposing hiring freezes, canceling raises, and cutting back on services big and small, from salting and plowing streets in winter to heating assistance programs. Unemployment insurance funds, especially with the proposed extension of benefits, are running out of money.

Dolores Williams, fifty-seven, sits in the cramped waiting room at the Crisis Ministry clutching a numbered card, waiting for her number to be called. She has lived in a low-income apartment block known as The Kingsbury for a year. Two residents, she says, recently jumped to their deaths from the nineteenth floor. She had a job at Sam's Club but lost it. No one, she says, is hiring. She is desperate.

She hands me a copy of the *Trentonian*, a local paper. The headline on the front page reads: "Gangster Slammed for Bicycle Drive-By." It is the story of the conviction of a man for a fatal drive-by shooting from a bicycle. The paper is filled with stories like these, the result of social, economic, and moral collapse. Poverty breeds more than hunger. It destroys communities. In one *Trentonian* story, a fifty-six-year-old woman is robbed and pistol-whipped in the middle of the afternoon. Another article reports the plight of four children whose parents had been shot and seriously wounded. "Libraries OK Now, but Future Is Murky," a headline reads. Another reads: "Still No Arrests in Hooker Slayings."

"It is like this every day," Williams says.

Corporations are ubiquitous parts of our lives, and those that own and run them want them to remain that way. We eat corporate food. We buy corporate clothes. We drive in corporate cars. We buy our fuel from corporations. We borrow from, invest our retirement savings with, and take out college loans with corporations and corporate banks. We are entertained, informed, and bombarded with advertisements by corporations. Many of us work for corporations. There are few aspects of life left that have not been taken over by corporations, from mail delivery to public utilities to our for-profit health-care system. These corporations have no loyalty to the country or workers. Our impoverishment feeds their profits. And profits, for corporations, are all that count.

The corporation is designed to make money without regard to human life, the social good, or the impact of the corporation's activities on the environment. Corporation bylaws impose a legal duty on corporate executives to make the largest profits possible for shareholders. In the 2003 documentary film *The Corporation* by Mark Achbar, Jennifer Abbott, and Joel Bakan, management guru Peter Drucker tells Bakan: "If you find an executive who wants to take on social responsibilities, fire him. Fast." And William Niskanen, chair of the libertarian Cato Institute, says that he would not invest in a company that promoted corporate responsibility.

A corporation that attempts to engage in social responsibility, that tries to pay workers a decent wage with benefit, that protects workers' rights, that invests its profits to limit pollution, that gives consumers better deals, can actually be sued by shareholders. Robert Monks, an investment manager, says in the film: "The corporation is an externalizing machine, in the same way that a shark is a killing machine. There isn't any question of malevolence or of will. The enterprise has within it, and the shark has within it, those characteristics that enable it to do that for which it was designed."

Ray Anderson, the CEO of Interface Corporation, the world's largest commercial carpet manufacturer, calls the corporation a "present-day instrument of destruction" because of its compulsion to "externalize any cost that an unwary or uncaring public will allow it to externalize."

"The notion that we can take and take and take and take, waste and waste, without consequences, is driving the biosphere to destruction," Anderson says.

The film, based on Bakan's book *The Corporation: The Pathological Pursuit of Profit and Power,* asserts that the corporation exhibits many of the traits found in people clinically defined as psychopaths. Psychologist Robert Hare recites in the film a checklist of psychopathic traits and ties them to the behavior of corporations:

- Callous unconcern for the feelings for others;
- Incapacity to maintain enduring relationships;
- Reckless disregard for the safety of others;
- Deceitfulness: repeated lying and conning of others for profit;
- Incapacity to experience guilt:
- Failure to conform to social norms with respect to lawful behavior.

And yet, under the American legal system, corporations have the same legal rights as individuals. They make contributions to candidates. They fund 35,000 lobbyists in Washington and thousands more in state capitals to write corporate-friendly legislation and defang regulatory agencies. They saturate the airwaves, the Internet, newspapers, and magazines with advertisements promoting their brands as the friendly face of the corporation. They have huge legal teams, tens of thousands of employees, and scores of elected officials who ward off public intrusions into their affairs or lawsuits. They hold a near monopoly on all electronic and printed sources of information. A few media giants, such as AOL Time Warner, General Electric, Viacom, Disney, and Rupert Murdoch's NewsGroup, control nearly everything we read, see, and hear.

"Private capital tends to become concentrated in [a] few hands, partly because of competition among the capitalists, and partly because technological development and the increasing division of labor encourage the formation of larger units of production at the expense of the smaller ones," Albert Einstein wrote in 1949 in the *Monthly Review* in explaining why he was a socialist:

> The result of these developments is an oligarchy of private capital the enormous power of which cannot be effectively checked even by a democratically organized political society. This is true since the members of legislative bodies are selected by political parties, largely financed or otherwise influenced by private capitalists who, for all practical purposes, separate the electorate from the legislature. The consequence is that the representatives of the people do not in fact sufficiently protect the interests of the underprivileged sections of the population. Moreover, under existing conditions, private capitalists inevitably control, directly or indirectly, the main sources of information (press, radio, education). It is thus extremely difficult, and indeed in most cases quite impossible, for the individual citizen to come to objective conclusions and to make intelligent use of his political rights.[4]

The growing desperation across the United States is unleashing not simply a recession—we have been in a recession for some time now— but rather a depression unlike anything we have seen since the 1930s. It has provided a pool of broken people willing to work for low wages without unions or benefits. This is excellent news if you are a corporation. It is very bad news if you are a worker. For the bottom 90 percent of Americans, annual income has been on a slow, steady decline for three decades. The majority of that sector's workers had an average annual income that peaked at $33,000 in 1973. By 2005, according to David Cay Johnston in his book *Free Lunch*, it had fallen to a bit more than $29,000 in adjusted dollars, despite three decades of economic expansion. And where did that money go? Ask Exxon Mobil, the biggest U.S. oil and gas company, which made a $10.9 billion profit in the first quarter of 2007. Or better yet, ask Exxon Mobil Corporation Chairman and Chief Executive Officer Rex Tillerson, whose compensation rose nearly 18 percent to $21.7 million in 2007, when the oil company pulled in the largest profit ever for a U.S. company. His take-home pay package included $1.75 million in salary, a $3.36 million bonus, and $16.1 million in stock and option awards, according to a company filing with the U.S. Securities and Exchange Commission. He also received nearly $430,000 in other compensation, including $229,331 for personal security and $41,122 for use of the company aircraft. In addition to his pay package, Tillerson received more than $7.6 million from exercising options and stock awards during the year. Exxon Mobil earned $40.61 billion in 2007, up 3 percent from the previous year. But Tillerson's 2007 pay was not even the highest mark for the U.S. oil and gas industry. Occidental Petroleum Corporation Chairman and CEO Ray Irani made $33.6 million, and Anadarko Petroleum Corporation chief James Hackett took in $26.7 million over the same period.

For each dollar earned in 2005, the top 10 percent received 48.5 cents. That was the top tenth's greatest share of the income pie, Johnston writes, since 1929, just before the Roaring '20s collapsed in the Great Depression. And within the top 10 percent, those who made more than $100,000, nearly all the gains went to the top tenth of 1 percent, people like Tillerson, Irani, or Hackett, who made at least $1.7 million that year. And until we have real election reform, until we make it possible to run for national office without candidates kissing the rings of Tillersons, Iranis, and Hacketts to get hundreds of millions of dollars, this cannibalization of America will continue.

Our elites manipulate statistics and data to foster illusions of growth and prosperity. They refuse to admit they have lost control since to lose control is to concede failure. They contribute, instead, to the collective denial of reality by insisting that another multibillion-dollar bailout or government loan will prop up the dying edifice. The well-paid television pundits and news celebrities, the economists and the banking and financial sector leaders, see the world from inside the comfort of the corporate box. They are loyal to the corporate state. They cling to the corporation and the corporate structure. It is known. It is safe. It is paternal. It is the system.

Our government is being wrecked by corporations, which now get 40 percent of federal discretionary spending. More than 800,000 jobs once handled by government employees have been outsourced to corporations, a move that has not only further empowered our shadow corporate government but also helped destroy federal workforce unions. Management of federal prisons, the management of regulatory and scientific reviews, the processing or denial of Freedom of Information requests, interrogating prisoners, and running the world's largest mercenary army in Iraq—all this has become corporate. And these corporations, in a perverse arrangement, make their money directly off of the American citizen. This devil's deal is an expansion of the corporate welfare enjoyed by the defense industry.

Halliburton in 2003 was given a no-bid and non-compete $7 billion contract to repair Iraq's oil fields, as well as the power to oversee and control Iraq's entire oil production. This has now become $130 billion in contract awards to Halliburton. And flush with taxpayer dollars, what has Halliburton done? It has made sure only thirty-six of its 143 subsidiaries are incorporated in the United States and 107 subsidiaries (or 75 percent) are incorporated in thirty different countries. This arrangement allows Halliburton to lower its tax liability on foreign income by establishing a "controlled foreign corporation" and subsidiaries inside low-tax, or no-tax, countries used as tax havens. Thus the corporations take our money. They squander it. They cleverly evade taxation. And our corporate government not only funds them but protects them.

The financial and political disparities between our oligarchy and the working class have created a new global serfdom. Credit Suisse analysts estimate that the number of subprime foreclosures in the United States by the end of 2012 will total 1,390,000. If that estimate is correct, 12.7 percent of all residential borrowers in the United States will be forced out of their homes.

The bailout for banks and financial firms, who feel no compunction to account for taxpayer funds, pulled the plug on the New Deal. The Great Society is now gasping for air, mortally wounded, coughing up blood. Power no longer lies with the citizens of the United States, who, with ratios of 100 to 1, pleaded with their representatives in Washington not to loot the national treasury to bail out Wall Street investment firms. Power lies with the corporations. These corporations, not we, pick who runs for president, Congress, judgeships, and most state legislatures. You cannot, in most instances, be a viable candidate without their blessing and money. These corporations, including the Commission on Presidential Debates (a private organization), determine who gets to speak and what issues candidates can or cannot challenge, from universal, not-for-profit, single-payer health care to Wall Street bailouts to NAFTA. If you do not follow the corporate script, you become as marginal and invisible as Dennis Kucinich, Ralph Nader, or Cynthia McKinney.

This is why most Democrats opposed Pennsylvania Democratic House Representative John Murtha's call for immediate withdrawal from Iraq—something that would dry up profits for companies like Halliburton—and supported continued funding for the war. It is why most voted to reauthorize the Patriot Act. It is why the party opposed an amendment that was part of a bankruptcy bill that would have capped credit card interest rates at 30 percent. It is why corporatist politicians opposed a bill that would have reformed the notorious Mining Law of 1872, which allows mineral companies to plunder federal land for profit. It is why they did not back the single-payer health-care bill House Resolution 676, sponsored by Representatives Kucinich and John Conyers. It is why so many politicians advocate nuclear power. It is why many backed the class-action "reform" bill—the Class Action Fairness Act (CAFA)—that was part of a large lobbying effort by financial firms. CAFA would effectively shut down state courts as a venue to hear most class-action lawsuits. Workers, under CAFA, would no longer have redress in many of the courts where these cases have a chance of defying powerful corporations. CAFA moves these cases into corporate-friendly federal courts dominated by Republican judges.

The assault on the American working class—an assault that has devastated members of my own family—is nearly complete. In the past three years, nearly one in five U.S. workers was laid off. Among workers laid off from full-time work, roughly one-fourth were earning less than $40,000 annually. There are whole sections of the United States that now resemble the developing world. There has been a Weimarization of the American working class. And the assault on the middle class is now under way. Anything that can be put on software—from finance to architecture to engineering—can and is being outsourced to workers in countries such as India or China, who accept pay that is a fraction of their Western counterparts, and without benefits. And both the Republican and Democratic parties, beholden to corporations for money and power, have allowed this to happen.

Over the past few decades, we have watched the rise of a powerful web of interlocking corporate entities, a network of arrangements within subsectors, industries, or other partial jurisdictions to diminish and often abolish outside control and oversight. These corporations have neutralized national, state, and judicial authority. The corporate state, begun under Ronald Reagan and pushed forward by every president since, has destroyed the public and private institutions that protected workers and safeguarded citizens. Only 7.8 percent of workers in the private sector are unionized. This is about the same percentage as in the early 1900s. There are 50 million Americans in real poverty and tens of millions of Americans in a category called "near poverty."

We hear little about these stories of pain and dislocation. We are diverted by spectacle and pseudo-events. We are fed illusions. We are given comforting myths—the core of popular culture—that exalt our nation and ourselves, even though ours is a time of collapse, and moral and political squalor. We are bombarded with useless trivia and celebrity gossip despite the valiant efforts of a few remaining newspapers such as the *New York Times* and the *Washington Post,* along with Democracy Now, National Public Radio, Pacifica, and Jim Lehrer of the Public Broadcasting Service. These organizations still practice journalism as an ethical pursuit on behalf of the common good, but they are a beleaguered minority. The Federal Communications Commission, in an example of how far our standards have fallen, defines television shows such as Fox's celebrity gossip program *TMZ* and the Christian Broadcast Network's *700 Club* as "bona fide newscasts." The economist Charlotte Twight calls this vast corporate system of spectacle and diversion, in which we get to vote on *American Idol* or be elevated to celebrity status through reality television programs, "participatory fascism."

Washington has become our Versailles. We are ruled, entertained, and informed by courtiers—and the media has evolved into a class of courtiers. The Democrats, like the Republicans, are mostly courtiers. Our pundits and experts, at least those with prominent public platforms, are courtiers. We are captivated by the hollow stagecraft of political theater as we are ruthlessly stripped of power. It is smoke and mirrors, tricks and con games, and the purpose behind it is deception.

Television journalism is largely a farce. Celebrity reporters, masquerading as journalists, make millions a year and give a platform to the powerful and the famous so they can spin, equivocate, and lie. Sitting in a studio, putting on makeup, and chatting with Joe Biden, Hillary Clinton, or Lawrence Summers has little to do with journalism. If you are a true journalist, you should start to worry if you make $5 million a year. No journalist has a comfortable, cozy relationship with the powerful. No journalist believes that serving the powerful is a primary part of his or her calling. Those in power fear and dislike journalists—and they should. Ask Amy Goodman, Seymour Hersh, Walter Pincus, Robert Scheer, or David Cay Johnston.

The comedian Jon Stewart, who hosts the popular *Daily Show with Jon Stewart* on Comedy Central, has become one of the most visible and influential media figures in America. In an interview with Jim Cramer, who hosts a show called *Mad Money* on CNBC, Stewart asked his guest why, during all the years he advised viewers about investments, he never questioned the mendacious claims from CEOs and banks that unleashed the financial meltdown—or warned viewers about the shady tactics of short-term selling and massive debt leveraging used to make fortunes for CEOs out of the retirement and savings accounts of ordinary Americans.[5]

> STEWART: This thing was ten years in the making. . . . The idea that you could have on the guys from Bear Stearns and Merrill Lynch and guys that had leveraged 35 to 1 and then blame mortgage holders, that's insane. . . .

CRAMER: I always wish that people would come in and swear themselves in before they come on the show. I had a lot of CEOs lie to me on the show. It's very painful. I don't have subpoena power. . . .

STEWART: You knew what the banks were doing and were touting it for months and months. The entire network was.

CRAMER: But Dick Fuld, who ran Lehman Brothers, called me in—he called me in when the stock was at forty—because he was saying: "Look, I thought the stock was wrong, thought it was in the wrong place"—he brings me in and lies to me, lies to me, lies to me.

STEWART [feigning shock]: The CEO of a company lied to you?

CRAMER: Shocking.

STEWART: But isn't that financial reporting? What do you think is the role of CNBC? . . .

CRAMER: I didn't think that Bear Stearns would evaporate overnight. I knew the people who ran it. I thought they were honest. That was my mistake. I really did. I thought they were honest. Did I get taken in because I knew them before? Maybe, to some degree. . . . It's difficult to have a reporter say, "I just came from an interview with Hank Paulson, and he lied his darn-fool head off." It's difficult. I think it challenges the boundaries.

STEWART: But what is the responsibility of the people who cover Wall Street? . . . I'm under the assumption, and maybe this is purely ridiculous, but I'm under the assumption that you don't just take their word at face value. That you actually then go around and try to figure it out. *[Applause.]*

Cramer, like most television and many print reporters, gives an uncritical forum to the powerful. At the same time, they pretend they have vetted and investigated the claims made by those in power. They play the role on television of journalists. It is a dirty quid pro quo. The media get access to the elite as long as the media faithfully report what the elite wants reported. The moment that quid pro quo breaks down, reporters—real reporters—are cast into the wilderness and denied access.

The behavior of a Jim Cramer, as Glenn Greenwald pointed out in an article on Salon.com, mirrors that of the reporters who covered the lead-up to the war in Iraq. Day after day, news organizations as diverse as the *New York Times*, CNN, and the three major television networks amplified lies fed to them by the elite as if they were facts. They served the power elite, as Cramer and most of those on television do, rather than the public.

In Bill Moyer's 2007 PBS documentary *Buying the War*, Moyers asked *Meet the Press* host Tim Russert why he had passed on these lies without vetting them—and even more damaging, he contrasted Russert's work with that of Bob Simon of CBS, who had made a few phone calls and had quickly learned that the administration's pro-war leaks, so crucial in fanning public and political support for going to war, were bogus. Moyers focused on a story, given to the *New York Times* by Vice President Dick Cheney's office, that appeared on the front page of the paper the Sunday morning the vice president was also a guest on *Meet the Press*.[6] Moyers began by setting up a video clip of Cheney's performance:

> **BILL MOYERS:** Quoting anonymous administration officials, the *Times* reported that Saddam Hussein had launched a worldwide hunt for materials to make an atomic bomb using specially designed aluminum tubes.

Moyers then ran the clip of Cheney on *Meet the Press* the same morning the *Times* story appeared:

> **CHENEY:** . . . Tubes. There's a story in the *New York Times* this morning, this is—and I want to attribute this to the *Times*. I don't want to talk about obviously specific intelligence sources, but—

Jonathan Landay, a reporter who had written news stories at the time questioning Cheney's prior assertions that Saddam Hussein had been seeking to acquire nuclear weapons, gave us the sneaky reason the White House had leaked the information—*specifically so Cheney could discuss previously top-secret information on national TV*. Even though there was no corroboration of that information (and never would be, since it was inaccurate), Cheney could now speak of it publically as if it were fact. "Now," said Landay, "ordinarily, information like the aluminum tubes wouldn't appear. It was top-secret intelligence, and the Vice President and the National Security Advisor would not be allowed to talk about this on the Sunday talk shows. But, it appeared that morning in the *New York Times* and, therefore, they were able to talk about it."

Moyers went back to the clip of the Cheney performance:

CHENEY: It's now public that, in fact, he has been seeking to acquire, and we have been able to intercept to prevent him from acquiring through this particular channel, the kinds of tubes that are necessary to build a centrifuge, and the centrifuge is required to take low-grade uranium and enhance it into highly enriched uranium, which is what you have to have in order to build a bomb.

Moyers, in the studio, asked Bob Simon of CBS what he thought of Cheney's actions:

MOYERS: Did you see that performance?
BOB SIMON: I did.
MOYERS: What did you think?
SIMON: I thought it was remarkable.
MOYERS: Why?
SIMON: Remarkable. You leak a story, and then you quote the story. I mean, that's a remarkable thing to do. . . .

Moyers continued the video clip, with *Meet the Press* host Russert asking a question that appears to accept, credulously and uncritically, the very statement Cheney had just made.

TIM RUSSERT [To CHENEY]: What specifically has [Saddam] obtained that you believe will enhance his nuclear development program?

Moyers, back in the studio, asked Russert, who was with him, why he had not been more incisive and skeptical with his questions, especially with material that was so unprecedented and potentially explosive:

> **MOYERS:** Was it just a coincidence in your mind that Cheney came on your show and others went on the other Sunday shows, the very morning that that story appeared?
>
> **TIM RUSSERT:** I don't know. The *New York Times* is a better judge of that than I am.
>
> **MOYERS:** No one tipped you that it was going to happen?
>
> **RUSSERT:** No, no. I mean—
>
> **MOYERS:** The Cheney office didn't leak to you that "there's gonna be a big story"?
>
> **RUSSERT:** No. No. I mean, I don't have the—this is, you know—on *Meet the Press*, people come on and there are no ground rules. We can ask any question we want. I did not know about the aluminum tubes story until I read it in the *New York Times*.
>
> **MOYERS:** Critics point to September 8, 2002, and to your show in particular, as the classic case of how the press and the government became inseparable. Someone in the administration plants a dramatic story in the *New York Times*. And then the Vice President comes on your show and points to the *New York Times*. It's a circular, self-confirming leak.
>
> **RUSSERT:** I don't know how Judith Miller and Michael Gordon reported that story, who their sources were. It was a front-page story of the *New York Times*. When Secretary [Condoleezza] Rice and Vice President Cheney and others came up that Sunday morning on all the Sunday shows, they did exactly that. My concern was, is that there were concerns expressed by other government officials. And to this day, I wish my phone had rung, or I had access to them.

Moyers then told the audience, "Bob Simon didn't wait for the phone to ring," and returned to his conversation with Simon of CBS.

MOYERS [to Bob Simon]: You said a moment ago when we started talking to people who knew about aluminum tubes. What people—who were you talking to?

SIMON: We were talking to people—to scientists—to scientists and to researchers, and to people who had been investigating Iraq from the start.

MOYERS: Would these people have been available to any reporter who called, or were they exclusive sources for *60 Minutes*?

SIMON: No, I think that many of them would have been available to any reporter who called.

MOYERS: And you just picked up the phone?

SIMON: Just picked up the phone.

MOYERS: Talked to them?

SIMON: Talked to them and then went down with the cameras. . . .

Walter Pincus of the *Washington Post* suggested that Russert's failure indicated a larger failure of many media figures: "More and more, in the media, become, I think, common carriers of administration statements, and critics of the administration. And we've sort of given up being independent on our own."[7]

⁓

Russert, like Cramer, when exposed as complicit in the dissemination of misinformation, attempted to portray himself as an innocent victim, as did *New York Times* reporter Judy Miller, who, along with her colleague Michael Gordon, worked largely as stenographers for the Bush White House during the propaganda campaign to invade Iraq. Once the administration claims justifying the war had been exposed as falsehoods, Miller quipped that she was "only as good as my sources." This logic upends the traditional role of reporting, which should always begin with the assumption that those in power have an agenda and are rarely bound to the truth. All governments lie, as I. F. Stone pointed out, and it is the job of the journalist to do the hard, tedious reporting to expose these lies. It is the job of courtiers to feed off the scraps tossed to them by the powerful and serve the interests of the power elite.

Cramer continues to serve his elite masters by lashing out at government attempts to make the financial system accountable. He has repeatedly characterized President Obama and Democrats in Congress as Russian communists intent on "rampant wealth destruction." He has referred to Obama as a "Bolshevik" who is "taking cues from Lenin." He has also used terms such as "Marx," "comrades," "Soviet," "Winter Palace," and "Politburo" in reference to Democrats and asked whether House Speaker Nancy Pelosi is the "general secretary of the Communist Party." On the March 3, 2009, edition of NBC's *Today*, Cramer attacked Obama's purported "radical agenda" and claimed that "this is the most, greatest wealth destruction I've seen by a president." Statements like these from courtiers like Cramer will grow in intensity as the economic morass deepens and the government is forced to be increasingly interventionist, including the possible nationalization of many banks.

The most egregious lie is the pretense that these people function as reporters, that they actually report on our behalf. It is not one or two reporters or television hosts who are corrupt. The media institutions are corrupt. Many media workers, especially those based in Washington, work shamelessly for our elites. In the weeks before the occupation of Iraq, media workers were too busy posturing as red-blooded American patriots to report. They rarely challenged the steady assault by the Bush White House against our civil liberties and the trashing of our Constitution. The role of courtiers is to parrot official propaganda. Courtiers do not defy the elite or question the structure of the corporate state. The corporations, in return, employ them and promote them as celebrities. The elite allow the courtiers into their inner circle. As Saul points out, no class of courtiers, from the eunuchs behind the Manchus in the nineteenth century to the Baghdad caliphs of the Abbasid caliphate, has ever transformed itself into a responsible and socially productive class. Courtiers are hedonists of power.

The rise of courtiers extends beyond the press. Elected officials govern under the pretense that they serve the public, while, with a few exceptions, actually working on behalf of corporations. In 2008, a Congress with a majority of Democrats passed the FISA bill, which provides immunity for the telecommunications companies that cooperated with the National Security Agency's illegal surveillance over the previous six years. Such a bill endangers the work of journalists, human rights workers, crusading lawyers, and whistle-blowers who attempt to expose abuses the government seeks to hide. This bill means we will never know the extent of the Bush White House's violation of our civil liberties. Worst of all, since the bill gives the U.S. government a license to eavesdrop on our phone calls and e-mails, it effectively demolishes our right to privacy. These private communications can be stored indefinitely and disseminated, not just to the U.S. government but to other governments as well. The bill will make it possible for those in power to identify and silence anyone who dares to make information public that defies the official narrative or exposes fraud or abuse of power. But the telecommunications corporations, which spent some $15 million in lobbying fees, wanted the bill passed, so it was passed.

Being a courtier requires agility and eloquence. The most talented of them should be credited as persuasive actors. They entertain us. They make us feel good. They persuade us; they are our friends. They are the smiley faces of a corporate state that has hijacked the government. When the corporations make their iron demands, these courtiers drop to their knees. They placate the telecommunications companies that want to be protected from lawsuits. They permit oil and gas companies to rake in obscene profits and keep in place the vast subsidies of corporate welfare doled out by the state. They allow our profit-driven health-care system to leave the uninsured and underinsured to suffer and die without proper care.

We trust courtiers wearing face powder who deceive us in the name of journalism. We trust courtiers in our political parties who promise to fight for our interests and then pass bill after bill to further corporate fraud and abuse. We confuse how we are made to feel about courtiers with real information, facts, and knowledge. This is the danger of a culture awash in pseudo-events. The Democratic Party refused to impeach Bush and Cheney. It allows the government to spy on us without warrants or cause. It funnels billions in taxpayer dollars to investment firms that committed fraud. And it tells us it cares about the protection of our civil rights and democracy. It is a form of collective abuse. And, as so often happens in the weird pathology of victim and victimizer, we keep coming back for more.

Our political and economic decline took place because of a corporate drive for massive deregulation, the repeal of antitrust laws, and the country's radical transformation from a manufacturing economy to an economy of consumption. Franklin Delano Roosevelt recognized this danger. He sent a message to Congress on April 29, 1938, titled "Recommendations to the Congress to Curb Monopolies and the Concentration of Economic Power." In it he wrote:

> the first truth is that the liberty of democracy is not safe if the people tolerate the growth of power to a point where it becomes stronger than the democratic state itself. That, in its essence, is Fascism— ownership of Government by an individual, by a group, or by any other controlling private power. The second truth is that the liberty of a democracy is not safe if its business system does not provide employment and produce and distribute goods in such a way to sustain an acceptable standard of living.[8]

The rise of the corporate state has grave political consequences, as we saw in Italy and Germany in the early part of the twentieth century. Antitrust laws not only regulate and control the marketplace. They also serve as bulwarks to protect democracy. And now that they are gone, now that we have a state run by and on behalf of corporations, we must expect inevitable and terrifying consequences.

As the pressure mounts, as this despair and impoverishment reach into larger and larger segments of the populace, the mechanisms of corporate and government control are being bolstered to prevent civil unrest and instability. The emergence of the corporate state always means the emergence of the security state. This is why the Bush White House pushed through the Patriot Act (and its renewal), the suspension of habeas corpus, the practice of "extraordinary rendition," the practice of warrantless wiretapping on American citizens, and the refusal to ensure free and fair elections with verifiable ballot-counting. It is all part of a package. It comes together. The motive behind these measures is not to fight terrorism or to bolster national security. It is to seize and maintain internal control.

Hints of our brave new world seeped out when the director of national intelligence, retired admiral Dennis Blair, testified in February and March 2009 before the Senate Intelligence Committee. He warned that the deepening economic crisis posed perhaps our gravest threat to stability and national security. It could trigger, he said, a return to the "violent extremism" of the 1920s and '30s. "The primary near-term security concern of the United States is the global economic crisis and its geopolitical implications," Blair told the Senate:

> The crisis has been ongoing for over a year, and economists are divided over whether and when we could hit bottom. Some even fear that the recession could further deepen and reach the level of the Great Depression. Of course, all of us recall the dramatic political consequences wrought by the economic turmoil of the 1920s and 1930s in Europe, the instability, and high levels of violent extremism.[9]

The road ahead is grim. The United Nations' International Labor Organization estimates that some 50 million workers will lose their jobs worldwide in 2009. The collapse had already seen close to 4 million lost jobs in the United States by mid-2009. The International Monetary Fund's prediction for global economic growth in 2009 is 0.5 percent—the worst since the Second World War. There were 2.3 million properties in the United States that received a default notice or were repossessed in 2008. And this number is set to rise, especially as vacant commercial real estate begins to be foreclosed. About 20,000 major global banks collapsed, were sold, or were nationalized in 2008. An estimated 62,000 U.S. companies are expected to shut down in 2009.

We have few tools left to dig our way out. The manufacturing sector in the United States has been dismantled by globalization. Consumers, thanks to credit card companies and easy lines of credit, are $14 trillion in debt. The government has spent, lent, or guaranteed $12.8 trillion toward the crisis, most of it borrowed or printed in the form of new money. It is borrowing to fund our wars in Afghanistan and Iraq. And no one states the obvious: We will never be able to pay these loans back. We are supposed to spend our way out of the crisis and maintain our part of the grand imperial project on credit. We are supposed to bring back the illusion of wealth created by the bubble economy. There is no coherent and realistic plan, one built around our severe limitations, to stanch the bleeding or ameliorate the mounting deprivations we will suffer as citizens. Contrast this with the national security state's preparations to crush potential civil unrest, and you get a glimpse of the future.

Senator Frank Church, as chairman of the Select Committee on Intelligence in 1975, investigated the government's massive and highly secretive National Security Agency. He was alarmed at the ability of the state to intrude into private lives. He wrote when he finished his investigation:

> That capability at any time could be turned around on the American people and no American would have any privacy left, such is the capability to monitor everything: telephone conversations, telegrams, it doesn't matter. There would be no place to hide. If this government ever became a tyranny, if a dictator ever took charge in this country, the technological capacity that the intelligence community has given the government could enable it to impose total tyranny, and there would be no way to fight back, because the most careful effort to combine together in resistance to the government, no matter how privately it was done, is within the reach of the government to know. Such is the capability of this technology. . . . I don't want to see this country ever go across the bridge. I know the capability that is there to make tyranny total in America, and we must see to it that this agency and all agencies that possess this technology operate within the law and under proper supervision, so that we never cross over that abyss. That is the abyss from which there is no return. . . . [10]

At the time Senator Church made this statement, the NSA was not authorized to spy on American citizens. Today it is.

The military can be ordered by the president into any neighborhood, any town or suburb, capture a citizen and hold him or her in prison without charge. The executive branch can do this under the Authorization for Use of Military Force, passed by Congress after 9/11, that gives the president the power to "use all necessary and appropriate force" against anyone involved in planning, aiding, or carrying out terror attacks. And if the president can declare American citizens living inside the United States to be enemy combatants and order them stripped of constitutional rights, which he effectively can under this authorization, what does this mean for us? How long can we be held without charge? Without lawyers? Without access to the outside world?

The specter of social unrest was raised at the Strategic Studies Institute of the U.S. Army War College in November 2008, in a monograph by Nathan Freier titled *Known Unknowns: Unconventional "Strategic Shocks" in Defense Strategy Development*. The military must be prepared, Freier warned, for a "violent, strategic dislocation inside the United States" that could be provoked by "unforeseen economic collapse," "purposeful domestic resistance," "pervasive public health emergencies," or "loss of functioning political and legal order." The resulting "widespread civil violence," the document said, "would force the defense establishment to reorient priorities in extremis to defend basic domestic order and human security."[11]

"An American government and defense establishment lulled into complacency by a long-secure domestic order would be forced to rapidly divest some or most external security commitments in order to address rapidly expanding human insecurity at home," it went on.

"Under the most extreme circumstances, this might include use of military force against hostile groups inside the United States. Further, [the Department of Defense] would be, by necessity, an essential enabling hub for the continuity of political authority in a multistate or nationwide civil conflict or disturbance," the document read.

In plain English, this translates into the imposition of martial law and a de facto government run and administered by the Department of Defense. They are considering it. So should we.

Blair warned the Senate that "roughly a quarter of the countries in the world have already experienced low-level instability such as government changes because of the current slowdown." He noted that the "bulk of anti-state demonstrations" internationally have been seen in Europe and the former Soviet Union, but this did not mean they could not spread to the United States. He told the senators that the collapse of the global financial system is "likely to produce a wave of economic crises in emerging market nations over the next year." He added that "much of Latin America, former Soviet Union states, and sub-Saharan Africa lack sufficient cash reserves, access to international aid or credit, or other coping mechanism."

"When those growth rates go down, my gut tells me that there are going to be problems coming out of that, and we're looking for that," he said. He referred to "statistical modeling" showing that "economic crises increase the risk of regime-threatening instability if they persist over a one- to two-year period."

Blair articulated the newest narrative of fear. As the economic unraveling accelerates, we will be told it is not the bearded Islamic extremists who threaten us most, although those in power will drag them out of the Halloween closet whenever they need to give us an exotic shock, but instead the domestic riffraff, environmentalists, anarchists, unions, right-wing militias, and enraged members of our dispossessed working class. Crime, as it always does in times of poverty and turmoil, will grow. Those who oppose the iron fist of the state security apparatus will be lumped together in slick, corporate news reports with the growing criminal underclass.

The destruction the corporate state has wrought has been masked by lies. The consumer price index (CPI), for example, used by the government to measure inflation, is meaningless. To keep the official inflation figures low, the government has been substituting basic products they once tracked to check for inflation with ones that do not rise very much in price. This trick has kept the cost-of-living increases tied to the CPI artificially low. The disconnect between what we are told and what is actually true is worthy of the deceit practiced in the old East Germany. The *New York Times*' consumer reporter, W. P. Dunleavy, wrote that her groceries now cost $587 a month, up from $400 one year earlier. This is a 40 percent increase. California economist John Williams, who runs an organization called Shadow Statistics, contends that if Washington still used the CPI measurements applied back in the 1970s, inflation would be about 10 percent.

The advantage of false statistics to the corporations is huge. An artificial inflation rate, one far lower than the real rate, keeps down equitable interest payments on bank accounts and certificates of deposit. It masks the deterioration of the American economy. The fabricated statistics allow corporations and the corporate state to walk away from obligations tied to real adjustments for inflation. These statistics mean that less is paid out in Social Security and pensions. These statistics reduce the interest on the multitrillion-dollar debt. Corporations never have to pay real cost-of-living increases to their employees.

The lies employed to camouflage the economic decline have been in place for several decades. President Ronald Reagan included 1.5 million U.S. Army, Navy, Air Force, and Marine service personnel with the civilian work force to magically reduce the nation's unemployment rate by 2 percent. President Clinton decided that those who had given up looking for work, or those who wanted full-time jobs but could find only part-time employment, were no longer to be counted as unemployed. His trick disappeared some 5 million unemployed from the official unemployment rolls. If you work more than twenty-one hours a week—most low-wage workers at places like Wal-Mart average twenty-eight hours a week—you are counted as employed, although your real wages put you below the poverty line. Our actual unemployment rate, when you include those who have stopped looking for work and those who can find only poorly paid part-time jobs, is not 8.5 percent but 15 percent. A sixth of the country was effectively unemployed in May of 2009. And we were shedding jobs at a faster rate than in the months after the 1929 crash.

Individualism is touted as the core value of American culture, and yet most of us meekly submit, as we are supposed to, to the tyranny of the corporate state. We define ourselves as a democracy, and meanwhile voting rates in national elections are tepid, and voting on local issues is often in the single digits. Our elected officials base their decisions not on the public good but on the possibility of campaign contributions and lucrative employment on leaving office. Our corporate elite tell us government is part of the problem and the markets should regulate themselves—and then that same elite plunders the U.S. Treasury when they trash the economy. We insist we are a market economy, one based on the principles of capitalism and free trade, and yet the single largest sectors of international trade are armaments and weapons systems. There is a vast and growing disconnect between what we say we believe and what we do. We are blinded, enchanted, and finally enslaved by illusion.

It was the economic meltdown of Yugoslavia that gave us Slobodan Milosevic. It was the collapse of the Weimar Republic that vomited up Adolf Hitler. And it was the breakdown in czarist Russia that opened the door for Vladimir Lenin and the Bolsheviks. Financial collapses lead to political extremism. The rage bubbling up from our impoverished and disenfranchised working class presages a looming and dangerous right-wing backlash. I spent two years traveling the country to write a book on the Christian Right called *American Fascists: The Christian Right and the War on America.* I visited former manufacturing towns where for many the end of the world is no longer an abstraction. They have lost hope. Fear and instability have plunged the working classes into profound personal and economic despair, and, not surprisingly, into the arms of the demagogues and charlatans of the radical Christian Right who offer a belief in magic, miracles, and the fiction of a utopian Christian nation. And unless we rapidly re-enfranchise our dispossessed workers into the economy, unless we give them hope, our democracy is doomed.

In his book *Collapse,* economist Jared Diamond lists five factors that can lead to social decay, including a failure to understand and to prevent causes of environmental damage; climate change; depredations by hostile neighbors; the inability of friendly neighbors to continue trade; and finally, how the society itself deals with the problems raised by the first four factors. A common failing involved in the last item is the dislocation between the short-term interests of elites and the longer-term interests of the societies the elites dominate and exploit.

His last point is crucial. Corruption, mismanagement, and political inertia by an elite, which is beyond the reach of the law, almost always result in widespread cynicism, disengagement, apathy, and finally rage. Those who suffer the consequences of this mismanagement lose any loyalty to the nation and increasingly nurse fantasies of violent revenge. The concept of the common good, mocked by the behavior of the privileged classes, disappears. Nothing matters. It is only about "Me."

As the public begins to grasp the depth of the betrayal and abuse by our ruling class; as the Democratic and Republican parties expose themselves as craven tools of our corporate state; as savings accounts, college funds, and retirement plans become worthless; as unemployment skyrockets and home values go up in smoke, we must prepare for the political resurgence of reinvigorated right-wing radicals including those within the Christian Right. The engine of the Christian Right—

as is true for all radical movements—is personal and economic despair. And despair, in an age of increasing shortages, poverty and hopelessness, will be one of our few surplus commodities.

But our collapse is more than an economic and political collapse. It is a crisis of faith. The capitalist ideology of unlimited growth has failed. It did not take into account the massive depletion of the world's resources, from fossil fuels to clean water to fish stocks to soil erosion, as well as overpopulation, global warming, and climate change. It failed to understand that the huge, unregulated international flows of capital and assault on manufacturing would wreck the global financial system. An overvalued dollar (which could soon deflate); wild tech; stock and housing financial bubbles; unchecked greed; the decimation of our manufacturing sector; the empowerment of an oligarchic class; the corruption of our political elite; the impoverishment of workers; a bloated military and defense budget; and unrestrained credit binges are consequences of a failed ideology and conspire to bring us down. The financial crisis may soon become a currency crisis. This second shock will threaten our financial viability. We let the market rule. Now we are paying for it.

In his book *The Great Transformation*, written in 1944, Karl Polanyi laid out the devastating consequences—the depressions, wars, and totalitarianism—that grow out of a so-called self-regulated free market. He grasped that "fascism, like socialism, was rooted in a market society that refused to function." He warned that a financial system always devolved, without heavy government control, into a Mafia capitalism—and a Mafia political system—which is a good description of our power elite.

Polanyi, who fled fascist Europe in 1933 and eventually taught at Columbia University, wrote that a self-regulating market turned human beings and the natural environment into commodities, a situation that ensures the destruction of both society and the natural environment. He decried the free market's assumption that nature and human beings are objects whose worth is determined by the market. He reminded us that a society that no longer recognizes that nature and human life have a sacred dimension, an intrinsic worth beyond monetary value, ultimately commits collective suicide. Such societies cannibalize themselves until they die. Speculative excesses and growing inequality, he wrote, always destroy the foundation for a continued prosperity.

We face an environmental meltdown as well as an economic meltdown. This would not have surprised Polanyi. Polar ice caps are melting. Sea levels are rising. The planet is warming at an alarming rate. Droughts are destroying croplands. Russia's northern coastline has begun producing huge quantities of toxic methane gas. Scientists with the International Siberian Shelf Study describe what they saw along the coastline recently as "methane chimneys" reaching from the sea floor to the ocean's surface. Methane, locked in the permafrost of Arctic landmasses, is being released at an alarming rate as average Arctic temperatures rise. Methane is a greenhouse gas twenty-five times more powerful than carbon dioxide. The release of millions of tons of it will only accelerate the rate of global warming.

Those who run our corporate state have fought environmental regulation as tenaciously as they have fought financial regulation. They are responsible, as Polanyi predicted, for our personal impoverishment and the impoverishment of our ecosystem. We remain addicted, courtesy of the oil, gas, and automobile industries and a corporate-controlled government, to fossil fuels. Species are vanishing. The great human migration from coastlines and deserts has begun. And as temperatures continue to rise, huge parts of the globe will become uninhabitable. The continued release of large quantities of methane, some scientists have warned, could asphyxiate the human species. NASA climate scientist James Hansen has demonstrated that any concentration of carbon dioxide greater than 350 parts per million in the atmosphere is not compatible with maintenance of the biosphere on the "planet on which civilization developed and to which life on earth is adapted." To halt this self-immolation, he has determined, the world must stop burning coal by 2030—and the industrialized world well before that—if we are to have any hope of ever getting the planet back down below that 350 number. And in the United States coal supplies half of our electricity.

Democracy is not an outgrowth of free markets. Democracy and capitalism are antagonistic entities. Democracy, like individualism, is based not on personal gain but on self-sacrifice. A functioning democracy must often defy the economic interests of elites on behalf of citizens, but this is not happening. The corporate managers and government officials trying to fix the economic meltdown are pouring money and resources into the financial sector because they are trained only to manage and sustain the established system, not change it.

Saul writes that the first three aims of the corporatist movement in Germany, Italy, and France during the 1920s, those that went on to become part of the fascist experience, were "to shift power directly to economic and social interest groups, to push entrepreneurial initiative in areas normally reserved for public bodies," and to "obliterate the boundaries between public and private interest—that is, challenge the idea of the public interest." It sounds depressingly familiar.

The working class, which has desperately borrowed money to stay afloat as real wages have dropped, now face years, maybe decades, of stagnant or declining incomes without access to new credit. The national treasury, meanwhile, is being drained on behalf of speculative commercial interests. The government—the only institution citizens have that is big enough and powerful enough to protect their rights—is becoming weaker, more anemic, and increasingly unable to help the mass of Americans who are embarking on a period of deprivation and suffering unseen in this country since the 1930s. Creative destruction, Joseph Schumpeter understood, is the essential fact about unfettered capitalism.

"You are going to see the biggest waste, fraud, and abuse in American history," Ralph Nader told me when I asked about the bailouts. "Not only is it wrongly directed, not only does it deal with the perpetrators instead of the people who were victimized, but they don't have a delivery system of any honesty and efficiency. The Justice Department is overwhelmed. It doesn't have a tenth of the prosecutors, the investigators, the auditors, the attorneys needed to deal with the previous corporate crime wave before the bailout started last September. It is especially unable to deal with the rapacious ravaging of this new money by these corporate recipients. You can see it already. The corporations haven't lent it. They have used some of it for acquisitions or to preserve their bonuses or their dividends. As long as they know they are not going to jail, and they don't see many newspaper reports about their colleagues going to jail, they don't care. It is total impunity. If they quit, they quit with a golden parachute. Even [General Motors CEO Rick] Wagoner is taking away $21 million."

There are a handful of former executives who have conceded that the bailouts are a waste. The former chairman of American International Group Inc. (AIG), Maurice R. Greenberg, told the House Oversight and Government Reform Committee that the effort to prop up the firm with $170 billion has "failed." He said the company should be restructured. AIG, he said, would have been better off filing for Chapter 11 bankruptcy protection instead of seeking government help.

"These are signs of hyper-decay," Ralph Nader said from his office in Washington. "You spend this kind of money and do not know if it will work."

"Bankrupt corporate capitalism is on its way to bankrupting the socialism that is trying to save it," he added. "That is the end stage. If they no longer have socialism to save them, then we are into feudalism. We are into private police, gated communities, and serfs with a twenty-first-century nomenclature."

We will not be able to raise another $3 or $4 trillion, especially with our commitments now totaling more than $12 trillion, to fix the mess. It was not long ago that such profligate government spending was unthinkable. There was an $800 billion limit placed on the Federal Reserve. The economic stimulus and the bailouts will not bring back our casino capitalism. And as the meltdown shows no signs of abating, and the bailouts show no sign of working, the recklessness and desperation of our capitalist overlords have increased. The cost to the working and middle class is becoming unsustainable. The Fed reported that households lost $5.1 trillion, or 9 percent, of their wealth in the last three months of 2008, the most ever in a single quarter in the fifty-seven-year history of record-keeping by the central bank. For the full year, household wealth dropped $11.1 trillion, or about 18 percent. These figures did not record the decline of investments in the stock market, which has probably erased trillions more in the country's collective net worth.

The bullet to our head, inevitable if we do not radically alter course, will be sudden. We have been borrowing at the rate of more than $2 billion a day over the last ten years, and at some point it has to stop. The moment China, the oil-rich states, and other international investors stop buying U.S. Treasury Bonds, the dollar will become junk. Inflation will rocket upward. We will become Weimar Germany. A furious and sustained backlash by a betrayed and angry populace, one unprepared intellectually and psychologically for collapse, will sweep aside the Democrats and most of the Republicans. A cabal of proto-fascist misfits, from Christian demagogues to simpletons like Sarah Palin to loudmouth talk-show hosts, whom we naïvely dismiss as buffoons, will find a following with promises of revenge and moral renewal. The elites, the ones with their Harvard Business School degrees and expensive vocabularies, will retreat into their sheltered enclaves of privilege and comfort. We will be left bereft, abandoned outside the gates, and at the mercy of the security state.

Lenin said that the best way to destroy the capitalist system was to debauch its currency. As our financial crisis unravels, and our currency becomes worthless, there will be a loss of confidence in the traditional mechanisms that regulate society. When money becomes worthless, so does government. All traditional standards and beliefs are shattered in a severe economic crisis. The moral order is turned upside down. The honest and industrious are wiped out while the gangsters, profiteers, and speculators walk away with millions. There are signs that this has begun. Look at Lehman Brothers CEO Richard Fuld. Many of his investors lost everything and yet he pocketed $485 million. An economic collapse does not mean *only* the degradation of trade and commerce, food shortages, bankruptcies, and unemployment. It also means the systematic dynamiting of the foundations of a society. I watched this happen in Yugoslavia. I watch it now in the United States.

The free market and globalization, promised as routes to worldwide prosperity, have been exposed as two parts of a con game. But this exposure does not mean our corporate masters will disappear. Totalitarianism, as George Orwell pointed out, is not so much an age of faith as an age of schizophrenia. "A society becomes totalitarian when its structure becomes flagrantly artificial," Orwell wrote. "That is when its ruling class has lost its function but succeeds in clinging to power by force or fraud."[12] They have engaged in massive fraud. Force is all they have left.

There are powerful corporate entities, fearful of losing their influence and wealth, arrayed against us. They are waiting for a moment to strike, a national crisis that will allow them, in the name of national security and moral renewal, to take complete control. The tools are in place. These antidemocratic forces, which will seek to make an alliance with the radical Christian Right and other extremists, will use fear, chaos, the hatred for the ruling elites, and the specter of left-wing dissent and terrorism to impose draconian controls to extinguish our democracy. And while they do it, they will be waving the American flag, chanting patriotic slogans, promising law and order, and clutching the Christian cross. By then, exhausted and broken, we may have lost the power to resist.

In Joseph Roth's book *The Emperor's Tomb*, which chronicles the decay of the Austro-Hungarian Empire, he wrote that at the very end of the empire, even the streetlights longed for morning so that they could be extinguished. The undercurrent of a world like ours, where people are reduced to objects and where there are no higher values, where national myths collapse, triggers a similar longing for annihilation and a moral decline into hedonism and giddy, communal madness. The earth is strewn with the ruins of powerful civilizations that decayed—Egypt, Persia, the Mayan empires, Rome, Byzantium, and the Mughal, Ottoman, and Chinese kingdoms. Not all died for the same reasons. Rome, for example, never faced a depletion of natural resources or environmental catastrophe. But they all, at a certain point, were taken over by a bankrupt and corrupt elite. This elite, squandering resources and pillaging the state, was no longer able to muster internal allegiance and cohesiveness. These empires died morally. The leaders, in the final period of decay, increasingly had to rely on armed mercenaries, as we do in Iraq and Afghanistan, because citizens would no longer serve in the military. They descended into orgies of self-indulgence, surrendered their civic and emotional lives to the glitter, excitement, and spectacle of the arena, became politically apathetic, and collapsed.

The more we sever ourselves from a literate, print-based world, a world of complexity and nuance, a world of ideas, for one informed by comforting, reassuring images, fantasies, slogans, celebrities, and a lust for violence, the more we are destined to implode. As the collapse continues and our suffering mounts, we yearn, like World Wrestling Entertainment fans, or those who confuse pornography with love, for the comfort, reassurance, and beauty of illusion. The illusion makes us feel good. It is its own reality. And the lonely Cassandras who speak the truth about our misguided imperial wars, the economic meltdown, or the imminent danger of multiple pollutions and soaring overpopulation, are drowned out by arenas full of excited fans chanting, "Slut! Slut! Slut!" or television audiences chanting, "JER-RY! JER-RY! JER-RY!"

The worse reality becomes, the less a beleaguered population wants to hear about it, and the more it distracts itself with squalid pseudo-events of celebrity breakdowns, gossip, and trivia. These are the debauched revels of a dying civilization. The most ominous cultural divide lies between those who chase after these manufactured illusions, and those who are able to puncture the illusion and confront reality. More than the divides of race, class, or gender, more than rural or urban, believer or nonbeliever, red state or blue state, our culture has been carved up into radically distinct, unbridgeable, and antagonistic entities that no longer speak the same language and cannot communicate. This is the divide between a literate, marginalized minority and those who have been consumed by an illiterate mass culture.

Mass culture is a Peter Pan culture. It tells us that if we close our eyes, if we visualize what we want, if we have faith in ourselves, if we tell God that we believe in miracles, if we tap into our inner strength, if we grasp that we are truly exceptional, if we focus on happiness, our lives will be harmonious and complete. This cultural retreat into illusion, whether peddled by positive psychologists, Hollywood, or Christian preachers, is a form of magical thinking. It turns worthless mortgages and debt into wealth. It turns the destruction of our manufacturing base into an opportunity for growth. It turns alienation and anxiety into a cheerful conformity. It turns a nation that wages illegal wars and administers off-shore penal colonies where it openly practices torture into the greatest democracy on earth.

The world that awaits us will be painful and difficult. We will be dragged back to realism, to the understanding that we cannot mold and shape reality according to human desires, or we will slide into despotism. We will learn to adjust our lifestyles radically, to cope with diminished resources, environmental damage, and a contracting economy, as well as our decline as a military power, or we will die clinging to our illusions. These are the stark choices before us.

But even if we fail to halt the decline, it will not be the end of hope. The forces we face may be powerful and ruthless. They may have the capacity to plunge us into a terrifying dystopia, one where we will see our freedoms curtailed and widespread economic deprivation. But no tyranny in history has crushed the human capacity for love. And this love—unorganized, irrational, often propelling us to carry out acts of compassion that jeopardize our existence—is deeply subversive to those in power. Love, which appears in small, blind acts of kindness, manifested itself even in the horror of the Nazi death camps, in the killing fields of Cambodia, in the Soviet gulags, and in the genocides in the Balkans and Rwanda.

The Russian novelist Vasily Grossman wrote of the power of these acts in his masterpiece *Life and Fate*:

> I have seen that it is not man who is impotent in the struggle against evil, but the power of evil that is impotent in the struggle against man. The powerlessness of kindness, of senseless kindness, is the secret of its immortality. It can never be conquered. The more stupid, the more senseless, the more helpless it may seem, the vaster it is. Evil is impotent before it. The prophets, religious teachers, reformers, social and political leaders are impotent before it. This dumb, blind love is man's meaning.
>
> Human history is not the battle of good struggling to overcome evil. It is a battle fought by a great evil struggling to crush a small kernel of human kindness. But if what is human in human beings has not been destroyed even now, then evil will never conquer.[13]

What was a scrap of paper to a commander of the Khmer Rouge or Joseph Stalin? What was a scrap of paper to the Russian poet Osip Mandelstam, extinguished in Stalin's reign of terror, or the Hungarian poet Miklós Radnóti, on whose body, found in a mass grave, were poems that condemned his fascist killers and are today taught to schoolchildren in Hungary? "I'm a poet who's fit for the stake's fire," Radnóti had scribbled, "because to the truth he's testified. One, who knows that the snow is white, the blood is red, as is the poppy, and the poppy's furry stalk is green. One, whom they will kill in the end, because he himself has never killed." What were the teachings of Jesus to the Roman consuls or the sayings of Buddha to the feudal warlords? Whose words, decades later, do we heed: the pompous and grandiose rants of the dictator and the politician, or the gentle reminders that call us back to the human?

I am not naïve about violence, tyranny, and war. I have seen enough of human cruelty. But I have also seen in conflict after conflict that we underestimate the power of love, the power of a Salvadorian archbishop, even though he was assassinated, to defy the killing, the power of a mayor in a small Balkan village to halt the attacks on his Muslim neighbors. These champions of the sacred, even long after they are gone, become invisible witnesses to those who follow, condemning through their courage their own executioners. They may be few in number but their voices ripple outward over time. The mediocrities who mask their feelings of worthlessness and emptiness behind the façade of power and illusion, who seek to make us serve their perverse ideologies, fear most those who speak in the language of love. They seek, as others have sought throughout human history, to silence these lonely voices, and yet these voices always rise in magnificent defiance. All ages, all cultures, and all religions produce those who challenge the oppressor and fight for the oppressed. Ours is no exception. The ability to stand as "an ironic point of light" that "flashes out wherever the just exchange their messages," is the ability to sustain a life of meaning. It is to understand, as Cyrano said at the end of his life, "I know, you will leave me with nothing—neither the laurel nor the rose. Take it all then! There is one possession I take with me from this place. Tonight when I stand before God—and bow low to him, so that my forehead brushes his footstool, the firmament—I will stand again and proudly show Him that one pure possession—which I have never ceased to cherish or to share with all—"

Our culture of illusion is, at its core, a culture of death. It will die and leave little of value behind. It was Sparta that celebrated raw militarism, discipline, obedience, and power, but it was Athenian art and philosophy that echoed down the ages to enlighten new worlds, including our own. Hope exists. It will always exist. It will not come through structures or institutions, nor will it come through nation-states, but it will prevail, even if we as distinct individuals and civilizations vanish. The power of love is greater than the power of death. It cannot be controlled. It is about sacrifice for the other—something nearly every parent understands—rather than exploitation. It is about honoring the sacred. And power elites have for millennia tried and failed to crush the force of love. Blind and dumb, indifferent to the siren calls of celebrity, unable to bow before illusions, defying the lust for power, love constantly rises up to remind a wayward society of what is real and what is illusion. Love will endure, even if it appears darkness has swallowed us all, to triumph over the wreckage that remains.

Notes

CHAPTER 1: THE ILLUSION OF LITERACY

1. John Ralston Saul, *Voltaire's Bastards* (New York: Vintage, 1992), 460.

2. The World Wrestling Entertainment phenomenon is immense, both internationally and within the United States. WWE is consistently in the top ten daily searches globally on Yahoo's Buzz Index and other search engines. The official site of World Wrestling Entertainment, http://www .wwe.com, receives within the United States alone a monthly average of 7.7 million unique visitors and a daily average of 517,000 unique visitors, according to a six-month survey done by Omniture SiteCatalyst from October 2006 to March 2007. Within the United States it had a monthly average of 214.4 million page views, a daily average of 7 million page views, a monthly average of 16.2 million video streams, and an average of 524,000 video streams per day. The WWE audience, according to a study conducted in May 2006 by Forrester Consulting, is 86 percent male, with an average age of twenty-four. Thirty-six percent are ages twelve to seventeen, and 40 percent are ages eighteen to thirty-four. Forty-one percent are students. Sixty-two percent of the males eighteen to thirty-four are employed full-time. According to http://www.quantcast.com, 81 percent access wwe.com daily or several times a week. Fifty-seven percent have no college education. Twenty-six percent have an annual income of $30,000 or less, and another 30 percent make between $30,000 and $60,000. Fifty-one percent have children aged six to seventeen. Sixty-four percent are Caucasian, 14 percent African American, and 16 percent Hispanic.

3. Neal Gabler, *Life: The Movie: How Entertainment Conquered Reality* (New York Vintage, 2000), 238.

4. Paul A. Cantor, "Pro Wrestling and the End of History," *The Weekly Standard* 5:3 (4 Oct. 1999): 17–22.

5. Daniel J. Boorstin, *The Image: A Guide to Pseudo-Events in America* (New York: Atheneum, 1961), 240.

6. Ibid., 198.

7. Gabler, *Life: The Movie*, 4.

8. James Bradley, *Flags of Our Fathers* (New York: Bantam Books, 2000), 518–519.

9. Antonino D'Ambrosio, *A Heartbeat and a Guitar: Johnny Cash and the Making of Bitter Tears* (New York: Nation Books, 2009).

10. William Deresiewicz, "The End of Solitude," *The Chronicle of Higher Education* 55:21 (30 Jan. 2009): B6.

11. Walter Benjamin, "The Work of Art in the Age of Mechanical Reproduction." http://www.marxists.org/reference/subject/philosophy/works/ge/benjamin.htm.

12. C. Wright Mills, *The Power Elite* (Oxford: Oxford University Press, 1956), 74.

13. Richard Hoggart, *The Uses of Literacy* (Transactions Publishers, London, 1957), 151.

14. Chris Rojek, *Celebrity* (London: Reaktion Books, 2001), 33–34.

15. Neil Postman, *Amusing Ourselves to Death: Public Discourse in the Age of Show Business* (New York: Penguin, 1985), 80.

16. Emily Eakin, "Greeting Big Brother with Open Arms," *New York Times*, Jan. 17, 2004: B9.

17. Dave Eggers, *A Heartbreaking Work of Staggering Genius* (New York: Vintage, 2001), 200–202.

18. Ibid., 209.

19. Ibid., 214.

20. Ibid., 235–237.

21. Cited in Gordon Burn, "Have I Broken Your Heart?" *The Guardian*, March 7 2009. http://www.guardian.co.uk/books/2009/mar/07/gordon-burn.

22. My account of Jade Goody is informed by Burn, "Have I Broken Your Heart?" http://www.guardian.co.uk/books/2009/mar/07/gordon-burn.

23. Hannah Arendt, "The Crisis in Culture," in *Between Past and Future: Eight Exercises in Political Thought* (New York: Penguin, 1993), 207.

24. ABC News, *Living in the Shadows: Illiteracy in America*, Feb. 25, 2008.

25. Statistics were obtained from the following sources: National Institute for Literacy, National Center for Adult Literacy, The Literacy Company, U.S. Census Bureau.

26. "Canada's Shame," *The National*, Canadian Broadcasting Company, May 24, 2006.

27. Cited in Frank Füredi, *Where Have all the Intellectuals Gone?* (New York: Continuum, 2004), 73.

28. Benjamin DeMott, "Junk Politics: A Voter's Guide to the Post-Literate Election," *Harper's Magazine* (November 2003): 36.

29. Boorstin, *The Image*, 61.

30. Ibid., 255.

31. Gabler, *Life: The Movie*, 205.

32. Boorstin, *The Image*, 36.

33. Walter Lippmann, *Public Opinion* (New York: Free Press, 1997), 59.

34. Cited in Gabler, *Life: The Movie*, 197.

35. Wendell Berry, *The Unsettling of America: Culture & Agriculture* (San Francisco: Sierra Club, 1977), 24.

CHAPTER 2: THE ILLUSION OF LOVE

1. "The Directors," *Adult Video News* (2005), 54.

2. *Gag Factor*. http://www.gagfactor.com/gagfactordotcom.html, accessed, April 5, 2009.

3. Postman, *Amusing Ourselves*, 3–4.

4. Marc Cooper, *The Last Honest Place in America* (New York: Nation Books, 2004), 42.

5. Robert Jensen, *Getting Off: Pornography and the End of Masculinity* (Cambridge, Mass.: South End Press, 2007), 126.

6. Bill Margold, quoted in Robert J. Stoller and I.S. Levin, *Coming Attractions: The Making of an X-Rated Video* (New Haven, Conn.: Yale University Press, 1993), 31.

7. Gail Dines, "The White Man's Burden: Gonzo Pornography and the Construction of Black Masculinity," *Yale Journal of Law and Feminism* 18 (2006), 296–297.

8. Ibid., 297.

9. Scott Simon, host. "Promoting Healthcare for the Porn Industry," *Weekend Edition*. National Public Radio, Dec. 8, 2007. http://www.npr.org/templates/story/story.php?storyId=17044239.

10. Lubben, Shelley, and Jersey Jaxin. "Jersey Jaxin on Why She Quit Porn," *YouTube*. Accessed Aug. 12, 2007. Part 1: http://www.youtube.com/watch?v=ACLK5ccKfM and Part 2: http://www.youtube.com/watch?v=U1NObcJV8ro&feature=related.

CHAPTER 3: THE ILLUSION OF LOVE

1. Theodor Adorno, "Education after Auschwitz" (http://grace.evergreen.edu/~arunc/texts/frankfurt/auschwitz/AdornoEducation.pdf), 10.

2. Ibid., 6.

3. Charles Ting, "The Dormitories at U.C. Berkeley." in Nader, Laura, et al., *Controlling Processes: Selected Essays, 1994–2005*. The Kroeber Anthropological Society Papers 92/93 (2005): 197–229.

4. Charles Schwartz, Home page. http://socrates.berkeley.edu/~schwrtz/.

5. Schwartz, "Good Morning, Regents." UniversityProbe.org. http://universityprobe.org/2009/02/good-morning-regents/.

6. Josh Keller, "For Berkeley's Sports Endowment, a Goal of $1 Billion." *The Chronicle of Higher Education*, Jan. 23, 2009. http://chronicle.com/weekly/v55/i20/20a01301.htm.

7. Saul, *Voltaire's Bastards*, 110.

8. Saul, *The Unconscious Civilization* (New York: The Free Press, 1995), 47.

9. Mills, *The Power Elite*, 321.

10. Joseph A. Soares, *The Power of Privilege: Yale and America's Elite Universities* (Stanford, Calf.: Stanford University Press, 2007), http://insidehighered.com/news/2007/04/11/soares; Daniel Golden, *The Price of Admis-*

sion: How America's Ruling Class Buys Its Way into Colleges—and Who Gets Left Outside the Gates (New York: Random House, 2006), http://insidehigh-ered.com/news/2006/09/05/admit.

11. Ludwig Wittgenstein, *Tractatus Logico-Philosophicus* (London: Rout-ledge & Kegan Paul, 1961). This is the last line of the book. The original publication was in the Annalen der Naturphilosophie, 1921: "*Woven man nicht sprechen kann, darüber muss man schweigen.*"

12. William Deresiewicz, "The Disadvantages of an Elite Education," *The American Scholar* (Summer 2008). http://www.theamericanscholar.org/the-disadvantages of-an-elite-education.

13. Richard Hoggart, *The Uses of Literacy* (London: Transaction Publish-ers, 1957), 229.

14. Ibid., 230.

15. Saul, *Voltaire's Bastards*, 121.

16. Cited in Hoggart, *The Uses of Literacy*, 230.

17. Deresiewicz, "Disadvantages."

18. William Hazlitt, "Memoirs of Thomas Holcroft," in *Collected Works*, Vol. 2 (London: J.M. Dent, 1902), 155.

19. Frank Donoghue, *The Last Professors: The Corporate University and the Fate of the Humanities* (New York: Fordham University Press, 2008), 91.

20. Andrew J. Wall, *Andrew Carnegie* (New York, Oxford University Press, rpt. Pittsburgh: University Of Pittsburgh Press, 1989), 837; Richard Teller Crane, *The Utility of all Kinds of Higher Schooling* (Chicago, H.O. Shep-ard, 1909), 106.

21. Donoghue, *The Last Professors*, 3.

22. David L. Kirp, *Shakespeare, Einstein, and the Bottom Line: The Mar-keting of Higher Education* (Cambridge, Mass.: Harvard University Press, 2003), 243.

23. Donoghue, *The Last Professors*, 56.

24. Quoted in full in Condé Nast Portfolio.com, "Daily Brief: Hedge Fund Manager: Goodbye and F——You," Oct. 17, 2008. http://www.portfolio.com/views/blogs/daily-brief/2008/10/17/hedge-fund-manager-good bye-and-f-you.

25. Adorno, "Education after Auschwitz," 6–7.

CHAPTER 4: THE ILLUSION OF HAPPINESS

1. Aldous Huxley, *Brave New World* (London: Grafton Books, 1977), 99–100.

2. Randall Colvin and Jack Block, "Do Positive Illusions Foster Mental Health? An Examination of the Taylor and Brown Formulation," *Psychological Bulletin* 116:1 (July 1994), 3–20.

3. One group that applies positive psychology to business practices, and touts the worldwide goodness this spreads, posts this laudatory message sent to the group in July 2004 by then-U.N. Secretary-General Kofi Annan: "I would like to commend you for your innovative methodology of 'appreciative inquiry' and to thank you for introducing it to the United Nations. Without this, it would have been very difficult, perhaps even impossible, to constructively engage so many leaders of business, civil society, and government." Business as an Agent of World Benefit (BAWB) Global Forum. http://www.bawbglobalforum.org/content/view/47/115.

4. Anthropologist Laura Nader strongly disagrees with the assertion that positive emotions and health go together.

5. Huxley, *Brave New World*, 99–100.

6. Mihály Csikszentmihály, "Brain Channels Thinker of the Year Award: 2000: Mihály Csikszentmihály, 'Flow Theory.'" *Brain Channels*. Accessed April 5, 2009. http://www.brainchannels.com/thinker/mihaly.html; Jamie Chamberlin, "Reaching 'Flow' to Optimize Work and Play," *American Psychological Association Monitor* 29:7 (July 1998), http://www.apa.org/monitor/ju198/joy.html.

7. Csikszentmihály, "'Flow Theory.'"

8. E. Diener, C. Nickerson, R. E. Lucas, and E. Sandvik, "Dispositional Affect and Job Outcomes," *Social Indicators Research* 59 (2002), 229–259.

9. S. E. Taylor, "Adjustment to Threatening Events: A Theory of Cognitive Adaptation, *American Psychologist* 38 (1983), 1161–1173. Quoted in Colvin and Block, "Do Positive Illusions Foster Mental Health?"

10. C. Peterson, "The Future of Optimism," *American Psychologist* 55:1 (Jan. 2000), 4–55.

11. D. A. Jopling, "'Take away the life-lie . . . ' Positive illusions and creative self deception." *Philosophical Psychology* 9 (1996), 525–544.

12. Chris Cochran. "The Production of Cultural Difference: Paradigm Enforcement in Cultural Psychology," *Psychology at Berkeley* Spring 2008.

13. "In Good We Trust," in *Mother Jones*, January/February 2009. http://www.motherjones.com/media/2009/02/books-good-we-trust.

14. Sura Hart and Victoria Kindle Hodson, "Peaceful Parenting," The Greater Good 4:3 (Winter 2007–2008). http://greatergood.berkeley.edu/greatergood/2007winter/HartHodson.html.

15. Richard S. Lazarus, "Author's Response: The Lazarus Manifesto for Positive Psychology," *Psychological Inquiry* 14:2 (2003), 176.

16. "The New Industrial Relations," *Business Week* 2687 (May 11, 1981): 84–89.

17. David Noble, *America by Design* (Oxford: Oxford University. Press, 1977).

18. Frank M. Gyrna Jr., *Quality Circles: A Team Approach to Problem Solving* (New York: American Management Associations, 1981); Neal Q. Herrick, *Joint Management and Employee Participation: Labor and Management at the Crossroads* (San Francisco: Jossey-Bass, 1990); Paul Bernstein, *Workplace Democratization: Its Internal Dynamics* (New Brunswick: Transaction Books, 1976); Robert S. Ozaki. *Human Capitalism: The Japanese Enterprise System as World Model* (Tokyo: Kodansha International, 1991).

19. Roberto González, "Brave New Workplace: Cooperation, Control, and the New Industrial Relations," *Controlling Processes: Selected Essays, 1994–2005.* Kroeber Anthropological Society Papers 92/93 (2005), 113.

20. Gyrna, *Quality Circles*, 53.

21. Ozaki, *Human Capitalism*, 169.

22. Ibid.

23. Satoshi Kamata, *Japan in the Passing Lane: An Insider's Account of Life in a Japanese Auto Factory*, Tatsuru Akimoto, ed. and trans. (New York: Pantheon Books, 1982), 71.

24. Ibid., 24, 30.

25. Ibid., 109–110.

26. González, "Brave New Workplace," 109.

27. Noble, *America by Design*, 274–278.

28. Ibid., 290.

29. Ibid., 259–260.

30. González, "Brave New Workplace," 111.

31. Ibid., 118.

32. Kamata, *Japan in the Passing Lane*, 124.

33. Eric Schmitt, "Pentagon Managers Find 'Quality Time' on a Brainstorming Retreat," *The New York Times*, Jan. 11, 1994: A7; González, "Brave New Workplace," 107.

34. J. P. Womack, D. T. Jones, and D. Roos. *The Machine That Changed the World* (New York: Harper Collins, 1990), 200–203.

35. Kamata, *Japan in the Passing Lane*, 75.

36. R. Ofshe and Margaret T. Singer, "Attacks on Peripheral versus Central Elements of Self and the Impact of Thought Reforming Techniques," *Cultic Studies Journal* 3:1 (1986): 6.

37. González, "Brave New Workplace," 116.

38. Kamata, *Japan in the Passing Lane*, 48.

39. Alejandro Lugo, "Cultural Production and Reproduction in Ciudad Juárez, Mexico: Tropes at Play among Maquiladora Workers," *Cultural Anthropology*, 5:2. (1990): 178–180.

40. Kamata, *Japan in the Passing Lane*, 156–157.

41. Mike Parker, *Inside the Circle: A Union Guide to QWL* (Boston: South End Press, 1985), 19; González, "Brave New Workplace," 115.

42. Parker, *Inside the Circle*, 20; González, "Brave New Workplace," 116.

43. P. C. Thompson, "U.S. Offered Unusual Class on Diversity," *New York Times*, Apr. 2, 1995: 34.

44. R. E. Lane, *The Loss of Happiness in Market Democracies* (New Haven, Conn.: Yale University Press, 2000). Quoted in Barbara S. Held, "The Negative Side of Positive Psychology," *Journal of Humanistic Psychology* 44:1 (Winter 2004), 9, 24.

CHAPTER 5: THE ILLUSION OF AMERICA

1. Andrew J. Bacevich, *The Limits of Power* (New York: Metropolitan Books, 2008), 172.

2. David Barstow, "One Man's Military-Industrial-Media Complex," *New York Times*, Nov. 29, 2008: 172.

3. Robert Bellah, *Habits of the Heart* (Berkeley and Los Angeles, Calif.: University of California Press, 1985), 285.

4. Albert Einstein, "Why Socialism?" *Monthly Review* (May 1949). Rpt. In http://www.huppi.com/kangaroo/Einstein.htm.

5. Cited in Glenn Greenwald, "There's Nothing Unique About Jim Cramer," Salon 13 (March 2009), www.salon.com/opinion/greenwald/2009/03/13/cramer.

6. Ibid.

7. Ibid.

8. Franklin Delano Roosevelt, "Message to Congress on Curbing Monopolies," April 29, 1938. In John T. Woolley and Gerhard Peters, *The American Presidency Project* (Santa Barbara, Calif.: University of California). http://www.presidency.ucsb.edu/ws/index.php?pid=15637.

9. Dennis C. Blair, "Far-Reaching Impact of Global Economic Crisis," *Annual Threat Assessment*, Senate Armed Services Committee (March 10, 2009), 3. http://www.fas.org/irp/congress/2009_hr/031009blair.pdf.

10. Quoted in James Bamford, "Big Brother Is Listening," *Atlantic* (April 2006), http://www.theatlantic.com/doc/200604/nsa-surveillance/4.

11. Nathan Frier, "Known Unknowns: Unconventional 'Strategic Shocks' in Defense Strategy Development," U.S. Army War College, Strategic Studies Institute, http://www.strategicstudiesinstitute.army.mil/pdffiles/PUB890.pdf.

12. George Orwell, *The Collected Letters, Essays and Journalism of George Orwell. Vol, 4: In Front of Your Nose, 1945–1950*. Eds. Sonia B. Orwell and Ian Angus (Boston: David R. Godine, 2000), 67.

13. Vasily Grossman, *Life and Fate*, trans. Robert Chandler (New York: Harper and Row, 1985), 410.

Acknowledgments

This book could not have been written without Eunice. She watched and transcribed everything from professional wrestling, to reality television shows, to the scenes described in the chapter on pornography. She edited and rewrote passages. She clarified incomplete thoughts, challenged shaky assertions, and added paragraphs that always enhanced the points I was trying to make. She stayed up many nights long after I had gone to bed, reworking sections of the book. Nothing I write is published before it goes through her hands. Our marriage is a rare combination of spiritual and intellectual affinity. "She'is all States, and all Princes, I, Nothing else is," as John Donne wrote in his poem "The Sunne Rising":

> Princes doe play us; compar'd to this,
> All honor's mimique; all wealth alchimie.
> Thou, sunne, art halfe as happy'as wee,
> In that the world's contracted thus.

I am deeply indebted to The Nation Institute and the Lannan Foundation. The support of these organizations permitted me to write this book. I am especially grateful to Hamilton Fish, Ruth Baldwin, Taya Grobow, and Jonathan Schell, as well as Peggy Suttle and Katrina vanden Heuvel at *The Nation* magazine. Carl Bromley at Nation Books is a remarkably talented and brilliant editor, a fine writer and scholar in his own right, who helped shape and guide this book. In an age when editing seems to be a dying art, he upholds the highest standards of the craft. He loves books and ideas, and his insight and enthusiasm are infectious. It was a privilege to work with him. Michele Jacob, whom I have worked with before, handled publicity and book events with her usual efficiency. Patrick Lannan and Jo Chapman at the Lannan Foundation have been constant and steadfast supporters of my work. It was Patrick, who has done more than perhaps anyone in the country to nurture, promote, and protect great writing, who first gave me Sheldon Wolin's *Democracy Incorporated*.

The Reverend Coleman Brown, my professor of religion at Colgate University and mentor, once again guided me through the writing. Coleman generously shared his profound wisdom, at once always humbling and always correct. His voice of compassion and deep insight into the human condition serve to temper the tone of my writing and pull me back from the edge of despair to remind me, and my readers, that good exists and is never as powerless as it appears.

John Timpane, a fellow lover of books, poetry, and theater, again edited the final manuscript. All my final manuscripts end up in his hands at my request. John, the greatest line and content editor in the business, is the Olympian authority who makes the last decisions on what is in or out, what should be changed and what amended. No writer could be in better hands, even if he has a hard time accepting my supremacy at Balderdash.

Chris Hebdon, a student at Berkeley, worked tirelessly on the book. He attended the seminar on positive psychology, did all the interviews and recordings, and wrote up the proceedings. The chapter on positive psychology is largely his work. Chris is a very talented young man whose conscience is as impressive as his intellect, which must make some of his professors very uncomfortable. My son Thomas, whose integrity is matched by a superb intellect, as well as a maturity and sensitivity that extend far beyond his years, worked during his Christmas vacation from Colgate University on the book in the Princeton University library. Robert Scheer and Zuade Kaufmann, who run the Web magazine *Truthdig*, where I write a weekly column, care deeply about maintaining the standards of great writing and reporting. I am fortunate to count them as friends and write for their site. Gerald Stern, Anne Marie Macari, Mae Sakharov, Rick McArthur, Richard Fenn, James Cone, Ralph Nader, Maria-Christina Keller, Pam Diamond, June Ballinger, Michael Goldstein, Irene Brown, Margaret Maurer, Sam Hynes, Tom Artin, Joe Sacco, Steve Kinzer, Charlie and Catherine Williams, Mark Kurlansky, Ann and Walter Pincus, Joe and Heidi Hough, Laila al-Arian, Michael Granzen, Karen Hernandez, Ray Close, Peter Scheer, Kasia Anderson, Robert J. Lifton, Lauren B. Davis, Robert Jensen, Cristina Nehring, Bernard Rapoport, Jean Stein, Larry Joseph, Wanda Liu (our patient and skillful Mandarin tutor), as well as Dorothea von Molke and Cliff Simms, who together run one of the finest bookstores in America, are part all of our cherished circle. Cliff was one of the most prescient critics of the manuscript and greatly improved its sharpness and focus. Thanks as well to Boris Rorer, Michael Levien, who recommended David Foster Wallace's brilliant essay on the porn industry, and the staff at Bon Appetit, where I buy my daily baguette.

Lisa Bankoff of International Creative Management, as she has for all my books, negotiated contracts and eased the maddening minutiae of putting this book together. I am fortunate to be able to work with her.

My children, Thomas, Noëlle, and Konrad, are my greatest joy. After years in which I have witnessed too much violent death and suffering, they are the balms to my soul, the gentle reminders that trauma can be slowly healed through love and that redemption is possible.

Bibliography

ABC News. *Living in the Shadows: Illiteracy in America.* Feb. 25, 2008.

Adorno, Theodor. *The Culture Industry.* London: Routledge, 1991.

Andrejevic, Mark. *Reality TV: The Work of Being Watched.* Toronto: Rowman & Littlefield, 2004.

Arendt, Hannah. *On Revolution.* London: Penguin, 1963.

———. *The Origins of Totalitarianism.* New York: Harcourt, 1966.

Arnold, Matthew. *Culture and Anarchy.* New Haven, Conn.: Yale University Press, 1994.

Bacevich, Andrew J. *The Limits of Power: The End of American Exceptionalism.* New York: Metropolitan, 2008.

Bakan, Joel, writer. *The Corporation: The Pathological Pursuit of Profit and Power.* Canada: Big Picture Media Corporation/Zeitgeist Films, 2003.

Barstow, David. "One Man's Military-Industrial-Media Complex." *New York Times* (Nov. 29, 2008). http://www.nytimes.com/2008/11/30/washington/30general.html.

Benjamin, Walter. "The Work of Art in the Age of Mechanical Reproduction." Marxists.org. http://www.marxists.org/reference/subject/philosophy/works/ge/benjamin.htm.

Bernays, Edward. *Propaganda.* New York: Ig Publishing, 1928.

Bernstein, Paul. *Workplace Democratization: Its Internal Dynamics.* New Brunswick, N.J.: Transaction Books, 1976.

Berry, Wendell. *The Unsettling of America.* San Francisco: Sierra Club, 1977.

———. *The Way of Ignorance.* Washington, D.C.: Shoemaker & Hoard, 2005.

Boorstin, Daniel J. *The Image: A Guide to Pseudo-Events in America.* New York: Atheneum, 1961.

Bradbury, Ray. *Fahrenheit 451.* New York: Del Rey, 1996.

Bradley, James. *Flags of Our Fathers.* New York: Bantam, 2000.

Briggs, Asa, and Peter Burke. *A Social History of the Media: From Gutenberg to the Internet*. Cambridge: Polity, 2005.

"Canada's Shame." *The National*. Canadian Broadcasting Company. May 24, 2006.

Cantor, Paul A. "Pro Wrestling and the End of History." *The Weekly Standard* 5:3 (Oct. 4, 1999): 17–22.

Chamberlin, Jamie. "Reaching 'Flow' to Optimize Work and Play." *American Psychological Association Monitor* 29:7 (July 1998). http://www.apa.org/monitor/ju198/joy.html.

Cochran, Chris. "The Production of Cultural Difference: Paradigm Enforcement in Cultural Psychology." *Psychology at Berkeley* 1 (Spring 2008): 62–73.

Colvin, Randall, and Jack Block. "Do Positive Illusions Foster Mental Health? An Examination of the Taylor and Brown Formulation." *Psychological Bulletin* 116:. 1: 3–20.

Conrad, Joseph. *Heart of Darkness*. London: Penguin, 1902.

Cooper, Marc. *The Last Honest Place in America: Paradise and Perdition in the New Las Vegas*. New York: Nation, 2004.

Crane, Richard Teller. *The Utility of all Kinds of Higher Schooling*. Chicago: H. O. Shepard, 1909.

Csikszentmihály, Mihály. "Brain Channels Thinker of the Year Award: 2000: Mihály Csikszentmihály, 'Flow Theory.'" *Brain Channels*. Accessed April 5, 2009. http://www.brainchannels.com/thinker/mihaly.html

D'Ambrosio, Antonino. *A Heartbeat and a Guitar: Johnny Cash and the Making of Bitter Tears*. New York: Nation Books, 2009.

De Botton, Alain. *Status Anxiety*. New York: Pantheon, 2004.

DeMott, Benjamin. *Junk Politics*. New York: Nation, 2003.

Deresiewicz, William. "The Disadvantages of an Elite Education." *The American Scholar* (Summer 2008). http://www.theamericanscholar.org/the-disadvantages-of-an-elite-education.

———. "The End of Solitude." *The Chronicle of Higher Education* 55:21 (Jan. 30, 2009). http://wwww.chronicle.com/free/v55/i21/21b00601.htm.

Diamond, Jared. *Collapse*. New York: Penguin, 2005.

Dines, Gail. "The White Man's Burden: Gonzo Pornography and the Construction of Black Masculinity." *Yale Journal of Law and Feminism* 18 (2006): 283–297.

"The Directors." *Adult Video News* (August 2005): 54.

Donoghue, Frank. *The Last Professors: The Corporate University and the Fate of the Humanities*. New York: Fordham University Press, 2008.

Dworkin, Andrea. *Pornogrpahy: Men Possessing Women*. New York: Plume, 1979.

Eakin, Emily. "Greeting Big Brother with Open Arms." *New York Times* (Jan . 17, 2004): B9+.

Eco, Umberto. *Travels in Hyperreality*. New York: Harcourt, 1983.

Eggers, Dave. *A Heartbreaking Work of Staggering Genius*. New York: Vintage, 2000.

Ellul, Jacques. *Propaganda: The Formation of Men's Attitudes*. New York: Vintage, 1965.

Fromm, Erich. *Escape From Freedom*. New York: Henry Holt, 1941.

Fulbright, William J. *The Pentagon Propaganda Machine*. New York: Vintage, 1985.

Füredi, Frank. *Where Have All the Intellectuals Gone?: Confronting 21st Century Philistinism*. London: Continuum, 2004.

Gabler, Neal. *Life: The Movie: How Entertainment Conquered Reality*. New York: Vintage, 1998.

Gag Factor. http://www.gagfactor.com/gagfactordotcom.html.

Gates, Jeff. *Democracy At Risk: Rescuing Main Street from Wall Street*. Cambridge: Perseus Publishing, 2000.

Golden, Daniel. *The Price of Admission: How America's Ruling Class Buys Its Way into Elite Colleges—and Who Gets Left Outside the Gates*. New York: Random House, 2006.

González, Roberto. "Brave New Workplace: Cooperation, Control, and the New Industrial Relations." In Nader, Laura, et al., *Controlling Processes: Selected Essays, 1994–2005*. The Kroeber Anthropological Society Papers, 92/93 (2005): 107–127.

Grossman, Vasily. *Life and Fate*. Trans. Robert Chandler. New York: Harper and Row, 1985.

Gyrna, Frank M., Jr. *Quality Circles: A Team Approach to Problem Solving*. New York: American Management Associations, 1981.

Hedges, Chris. *American Fascists: The Christian Right and the War on America*. New York: Free Press, 2006.

Held, Barbara S. *The Loss of Happiness in Market Democracies*. New Haven, Conn: Yale University Press, 2002.

————. "Tyranny of the Positive Attitude in America: Observation and Speculation." *Journal of Clinical Psychology* 58: 965–991.

Herrick, Neal Q. *Joint Management and Employee Participation: Labor and Management at the Crossroads*. San Francisco: Jossey-Bass, 1990.

Hoggart, Richard. *The Uses of Literacy*. New Brunswick: Transaction Publishers, 1998.

Huxley, Aldous. *Brave New World*. London: Triad Grafton, 1932.

Jensen, Robert. *Getting Off: Pornography and the End of Masculinity*. Cambridge, Mass.: South End, 2007.

Johnson, Chalmers. *The Sorrows of Empire: Militarism, Secrecy, and the End of the Republic*. New York: Henry Holt, 2004.

Johnston, David Cay. *Free Lunch: How the Wealthiest Americans Enrich Themselves at Government Expense (And Stick You With the Bill)*. New York: Penguin, 2007.

Kamata, Satoshi. *Japan in the Passing Lane: An Insider's Account of Life in a Japanese Auto Factory*. Tatsuru Akimoto, ed. and trans. New York: Pantheon, 1982.

Keller, Josh. "For Berkeley's Sports Endowment, a Goal of $1 Billion." *The Chronicle of Higher Education*, Jan. 23, 2009. http://chronicle.com/weekly/v55/i20/20a01301.htm.

Kindleberger, Charles P., and Robert Aliber. *Manias, Panics, and Crashes*. Hoboken, N.J.: John Wiley & Sons, 1978.

Kirp, David L. *Shakespeare, Einstein, and the Bottom Line: The Marketing of Higher Education*. Cambridge, Mass.: Harvard University Press, 2003.

Korten, David C. *When Corporations Rule the World*. San Francisco: Berrett-Koehler, 1995.

Lazarus, Richard S. "The Lazarus Manifesto for Positive Psychology and Psychology in General." *Psychological Inquiry*, 14:2 (2003): 173–189.

Lippmann, Walter. *Public Opinion*. New York: Simon & Schuster, 1997.

Lubben, Shelley, and Jersey Jaxin. "Jersey Jaxin on Why She Quit Porn." *YouTube*. Accessed Aug. 12, 2007. Part 1: http://www.youtube.com/watch?v=ACLK5ccKfM.

————. Part 2. http://www.youtube.com/watch?v=U1NObcJV8ro&feature=related.

Lugo, Alejandro. 1990. "Cultural Production and Reproduction in Ciudad Juárez, Mexico: Tropes at Play among Maquiladora Workers." *Cultural Anthropology*. 5:2 (1990): 173–196.

MacArthur, John R. *You Can't Be President: The Outrageous Barriers to Democracy in America*. New York: Melville House, 2008.

MacKay, Charles. *Extraordinary Popular Delusions and the Madness of Crowds*. New York: BN Publishing, 2008.

Mellman, Seymour. *The Permanent War Economy: American Capitalism in Decline*. New York: Simon & Schuster, 1985.

Mills, C. Wright. *The Power Elite*. New York: Oxford University Press, 1956.

Nader, Laura. "Controlling Processes: Tracing the Dynamic Components of Power." Mintz Lecture. *Current Anthropology*, 38:5 (1997): 711–737.

———. "Harmony Coerced is Freedom Denied." *The Chronicle of Higher Education*, July 13, 2001: 613–616

———. *Harmony Ideology*. Palo Alto: Stanford University Press, 1990.

———. Personal communication with Chris Hedges. Feb. 27, 2009.

Nader, Laura, and Ugo Mattei. *Plunder: When the Rule of Law Is Illegal*. Hoboken, N.J.: Blackwell Publishers, 2008.

Newport, Cal. *How to Win at College*. New York: Broadway, 2005.

Nevin, Thomas R. *Simone Weil: Portrait of a Self-Exiled Jew*. Chapel Hill: University of South Carolina Press, 1991.

"The New Industrial Relations." *Business Week* 2687 (May 11, 1981): 84–89.

Noble, David. *America by Design*. Oxford: Oxford University Press, 1977.

Ofshe, R., and Margaret T. Singer. "Attacks on Peripheral versus Central Elements of Self and the Impact of Thought Reforming Techniques." *Cultic Studies. Journal*, 3:1 (1986): 3–24.

Ortega y Gasset, José. *The Revolt of the Masses*. New York: W. W. Norton, 1932.

Orwell, George. *1984*. New York: Signet, 1990.

———. *The Collected Letters, Essays and Journalism of George Orwell. Vol, 4: In Front of Your Nose, 1945–1950*. Eds. Sonia B. Orwell and Ian Angus. Boston: David R. Godine, 2000.

Ozaki, Robert S. *Human Capitalism: The Japanese Enterprise System as World Model*. Tokyo: Kodansha International, 1991.

Parker, Mike. *Inside the Circle: A Union Guide to QWL*. Boston: South End, 1985.

Peterson, C. "The Future of Optimism." *American Psychologist* 55 (January 2000): 44–55.

Plato. *The Republic*. Translated by Robin Waterfield. Oxford: Oxford University Press, 1998. .

Polanyi, Karl. *The Great Transformation: The Political and Economic Origins of Our Time*. Boston: Beacon Press, 1944.

Postman, Neil. *Amusing Ourselves to Death: Public Discourse in the Age of Show Business*. New York: Penguin, 1985.

Riesman, David. *The Lonely Crowd: A Study of the Changing American Character*. New Haven, Conn.: Yale University Press, 1950.

Rojek, Chris. *Celebrity*. London: Reaktion Books, 2001.

Roth, Joseph. *The Emperor's Tomb*. New York: Overlook Press, 2002

Saul, John Ralston. *The Unconscious Civilization*. New York: Free Press, 1995.

———. *Voltaire's Bastards: The Dictatorship of Reason in the West*. New York: Vintage, 1992.

Schmitt, Eric. "Pentagon Managers Find 'Quality Time' on a Brainstorming Retreat." *New York Times* (Jan. 11, 1994): A7.

Schurmann, Reiner, ed. *The Public Realm: Essays on Discursive Types in Political Philosophy*. Albany: State University of New York Press, 1989.

Schwartz, Charles. Home page. *http://socrates.berkeley.edu/~schwrtz*.

Schwartz, Charles. "Good Morning, Regents." UniversityProbe.org. *http://universityprobe.org/2009/02/good-morning-regents*.

Seligman, Martin. *Authentic Happiness: Using the New Positive Psychology to Realize Your Potential for Lasting Fulfillment*. New York: Free Press, 2002.

Simon, Scott, host. "Promoting Healthcare for the Porn Industry." *Weekend Edition*. National Public Radio. Dec. 8, 2007. http://www.npr.org/templates/story/story.php?storyId=17044239.

Snow, C. P. *The Two Cultures*. Cambridge: Cambridge University Press, 1998.

Soares, Joseph A. *The Power of Privilege: Yale and America's Elite Colleges*. Stanford, Calif.: Stanford University Press, 2007.

Stoller, Robert J., and I. S. Levine. *Coming Attractions: The Making of an X-Rated Video.*. New Haven, Conn: Yale University Press, 1993.

Taylor, S. E. "Adjustment to threatening events: A theory of cognitive adaptation." *American Psychologist* 38 (1983): 1161–1173.

Thompson, P. C. "U.S. Offered Unusual Class on Diversity." *New York Times* (April 2, 1995): 34.

Ting, Charles. "The Dormitories at U.C. Berkeley." In Nader, Laura, et al., *Controlling Processes: Selected Essays, 1994–2005*. The Kroeber Anthropological Society Papers 92/93 (2005): 197–229.

Wall, J. *Andrew Carnegie*. Pittsburgh: University Of Pittsburgh Press, 1989.

Wallace, David Foster. *Consider the Lobster*. New York: Back Bay, 2006.

Whyte, William H. *The Organization Man*. Philadelphia: University of Pennsylvania Press, 1956.

Wittgenstein, Ludwig. *Tractatus Logico-Philosophicus. London:* Routledge & Kegan Paul, 1961.

Wolin, Sheldon S. *Democracy Incorporated: Managed Democracy and the Specter of Inverted Totalitarianism.* Princeton: Princeton University Press, 2008.

Index

and appearance and lifestyle, 23,
    25–26
and Christian Right, 22
and commodity culture, 37
Eggers on, 40–41
and emptiness and
    purposelessness in life, 27, 47
and fantasies of fame and
    success, 27, 29, 53
and foibles and scandals, 49
gossip, 15, 50, 146, 168, 190
hunger for, 40–41, 42–43
and implosion, 190
interviews and profiles, 19–20,
    169
and love, 193
Mills on, 34, 38
as mirror, 47, 48
and reality television, 169
reporters, 169
and revenge and triumph, 37
and wealth, 22, 26
and wrestling, 4, 5, 6
See also Celebrity culture;
    Corporations: and celebrities
    as sellers
Celebrity culture, 19
and closeness to celebrities, 17,
    19–20
and commodities, 29, 37–38
as culture of narcissism, 27, 33
and degradation as
    entertainment, 34
Deresiewicz on, 22–23
and escape and fantasy, 16, 27
and exhibitionism, 42
and family, 25
and fictional personas, 4
and frustration and despair, 29
hollowness of, 27, 33
and illusion, 15–16, 27, 29, 47,
    190

and immortality, 17
and inauthenticity, 15
and Internet, 22–23
and isolation, 137
and junk politics, 47
and magical thinking, 38
manipulation and deceit of, 20
moral nihilism and void of, 30,
    32–33
and personal screenplays, 16
and politicians' artificial
    intimacy with public, 46
Roth on, 42
and surveillance, 39–40
and validation, 40, 43
Celebrity Driving School (television
    show), 42
Celebrity (Rojek), 37
Celebrity Stars in Their Eyes
    (television show), 42
Celebrity Weakest Link (television
    show), 42
Celebrity Wife Swap (television
    show), 42
Center for Representative Politics,
    152
Center for the Advancement of
    Women, 86
Central Command, U.S., 152
Central Intelligence Agency (CIA),
    128, 144
Chaplin, Charlie, 17
Cheney, Dick, 171–173, 176
China, 133, 144, 158, 168, 188
Chomsky, Noam, 90, 146
Christian Broadcast Network, 168
Christian Right, 22, 37, 51–52, 91, 148,
    183–184, 188, 189
Church, Frank, 179
Civil liberties, 175–176, 177, 179–180
Claremont Graduate University, 115,
    118, 119, 120, 126

Education. *See* Universities
Education Department, U.S., 144
Eggers, Dave, 40–41
Eggers, Toph, 40
Egypt, 154, 189
Einstein, Albert, 115, 164
Eisenhower, Dwight, 91
El Salvador, 192
The Emperor's Tomb (Roth), 189
Empire, American, 103, 147, 148,
    150–151
Environmental Protection Agency,
    U.S., 144
Environmental regulation, 185
Euripides, 97
Extreme Associates, 62
Exxon Mobil, 165

Facebook, 23
Factor, Max, 18
Fahrenheit 451 (Bradbury), 29
Fairbanks, Douglas, 17
Faludi, Susan, 86
Fannie Mae, 159
Fascism, 146, 169, 177, 184, 186, 188,
    191
Federal Aviation Administration
    (FAA), 135
Federal Communications
    Commission, 168
Federal Deposit Insurance
    Corporation, 159
Federal Reserve, 187
FedEx Kinko's, 135–137
Ferrara, Manuel, 85
50 Cent, 87
Figueroa, Elba, 160
Financial Services Modernization
    Act (1999), 159
Finley, Dave, 11–12
Fire, Jada, 67
FISA bill (2008), 175–176

Fitness trainers and gurus, 15, 23
Flags of Our Fathers (Bradley), 21
Flow, 121–122
*Flow: The Psychology of Optimal
    Experience* (Csíkszentmihályi),
    122
Food Research and Action Center,
    161
Ford, Henry, 130
Forever Network, 18
Fox News, 4, 67
Freddie Mac, 159
Frederickson, Barbara, 119, 126–127
Free Lunch (Johnston), 165
Freier, Nathan, 180
Freud, Sigmund, 33
Frot-Coutaz, Cecile, 25–26
Frye, Northrop, 46
Fulbright, J. William, 155
Fuld, Richard (Dick), 170, 188

Gabler, Neal, 16, 23, 49
Gag Factor (movie), 63
Gagnon, Rene, 20–21
Gaza, 73
Geithner, Timothy, 112
General Electric, 164
General Motors, 58, 130, 134, 135, 187
*Getting Off: Pornography and the
    End of Masculinity* (Jensen), 61
Geyman, John, 155–156, 157
The Girls Next Door (television
    show), 87
Giroux, Henry, 90–91, 92
Glass-Steagall Act (1933), 159
Global warming, 153, 184, 185
Globalization, 93, 98, 129, 144, 150,
    151, 160, 178, 188
Golden, Daniel, 102
Goldman Sachs, 103, 112–113
González, Roberto, 130, 131–133, 134
Goodman, Amy, 169

Homeless, 160–161
Honest, Steve, 58
Hooker, Richard, 147
Hornswoggle (wrestler), 12
The Hot Network, 58
Household wealth, 187
How to Win at College (Newport), 106–107
The Howard Stern Show (television show), 34
Human Capitalism (Ozaki), 130
Human Comedy (Balzac), 97
Humanities Indicators Prototype, 108
Hume, David, 147
Hunger, 161, 162
Hussein, Saddam, 6, 171–172
Hustler Video Group, 66
Huston, John, 17
Huxley, Aldous, 39, 115, 121

Ignatowski, Ralph (Iggy), 21
Illiteracy, 119
    and academic specialists, 96
    and divide with literate minority, 190
    epidemic of, 44
    and images and slogans in media, 45, 48
    and lack of understanding, 47–48
Illusion
    and America, 142, 143, 159, 182, 191
    and Auden, 141
    and celebrity culture, 15, 27, 29, 190
    and Christian Right, 52
    and comfort, 190
    creators of, 15–16, 50
    culture of, 53, 138, 143, 149, 192
    and death of cultures, 143
    and economy, 143, 165, 178

and historical amnesia, 98
and illiteracy and language, 44, 45
and love, 192, 193
and pornography, 60, 63, 74, 81, 87
and positive psychology, 119, 123
and pseudo-events, 50–51, 52, 168
and *Sands of Iwo Jima*, 20, 21–22
and war, 21–22
The Image: A Guide to Pseudo-Events in America (Boorstin), 15, 146
Immigration, 157–158
Imperialism, 147, 148
Income inequality, 165
India, 168
Individualism, 33, 130, 182, 185
Inflation, 181, 188
Infrastructure, 63, 144, 145, 153, 154
Inside Higher Education, 102
Institute of Medicine, 156
Interface Corporation, 163
International Monetary Fund, 178
Internet. See Celebrity culture: and Internet; Pornography: and Internet
Internet Filter Review, 58
Interrogations, 128–129
Irani, Ray, 165
Iraq
    and corporations, 166, 167
    and journalists, 171–174, 175
    and mercenaries, 189
    occupation, 103
    War, 73, 85, 92, 100, 145, 149, 150, 155, 178
    and withdrawal, 167
The Irony of American History (Niebuhr), 146
Israel, 142

J. P. Morgan Chase, 117
Jackson, Randy, 28–29

and validation, 45
and wealth, 26
See also Mass media; Reality
television
Temptation Island (television show),
39
Terrorism, 91, 177, 179, 189
Thinking XXX (television special),
86, 87
Thomas, Dylan, 17
Thrill, Jeff, 66–67
Tiberius, 97
Tillerson, Rex, 165
Tina (*Survivor* contestant), 30–32
TMZ (television show), 168
Tocqueville Between Two Worlds
(Wolin), 147
Today (television show), 175
Totalitarianism, 45, 51, 138, 145, 146,
147, 148–149, 158, 184, 188
Town & Country (magazine), 23
Toyota, 130, 131, 132–133, 134
Transformational Positivity, 115–116
Traylor, Ray (Big Boss Man), 8–10
Treasury, U.S., 182, 188
Trenton, New Jersey, 160–162
Trilling, Lionel, 23
Tweed, Jack, 42
Twight, Charlotte, 168–169
Twitter, 23

Undertaker, the (wrestler), 10–11
Unemployment, 26, 51, 92, 119, 144,
160, 161, 182, 183, 188
See also Job losses
Unilever, 135
United Auto Workers, 135
United Nations, 178
Universities
and America's decline, 146
and assault against humanities,
103, 108–111

and corporations, 89, 90, 91, 92,
93–94, 96, 108–109, 110, 111, 112,
113, 150
and critical thinking, 89–90, 91,
95, 102–103, 105–106, 107,
108–109, 113
and deference to authority,
105–106, 107
and diversity, 101
and donors, alumni, and
fund-raising, 102, 104–105
and entitlement and elitism,
98–100, 113
and evil and crimes against
humanity, 91, 92
for-profit, 110
and *How to Win at College*,
106–107
and intelligence, 104
and military-industrial-academic
complex, 91, 153
and professors, 110
and specialization and jargon,
89, 90, 93, 96–98, 103, 111
and standardized tests, 89,
101–102
and student activism, 92–93, 95
and working class, 101
See also specific universities
*The University in Chains:
Confronting the
Military-Industrial-Academic
Complex* (Giroux), 91
The Unsettling of America (Berry),
53
U.S. News & World Report
(magazine), 109
The Uses of Literacy (Hoggart), 37

Valentino, Rudolph, 17, 19
Vasquez, Anthony, 135–137
VegasGirls, 56